4

PATHWAYS

SECOND
EDITION

Listening, Speaking, and Critical Thinking

PAUL MACINTYRE

**NATIONAL
GEOGRAPHIC**
L E A R N I N G

Australia • Brazil • Mexico • Singapore • United Kingdom • United States

NATIONAL GEOGRAPHIC
LEARNING

Pathways 4: Listening, Speaking, and Critical Thinking, 2nd Edition

Paul MacIntyre

Publisher: Sherrise Roehr

Executive Editor: Laura Le Dréan

Managing Editor: Jennifer Monaghan

Associate Development Editor: Lisl Bove

Director of Global and U.S. Marketing: Ian Martin

Product Marketing Manager: Tracy Bailie

Media Research: Leila Hishmeh

Senior Director, Production: Michael Burggren

Manager, Production: Daisy Sosa

Content Project Manager: Mark Rzeszutek

Senior Digital Product Manager: Scott Rule

Manufacturing Planner: Mary Beth Hennebury

Interior and Cover Design: Brenda Carmichael

Art Director: Brenda Carmichael

Composition: MPS North America LLC

For product information and technology assistance, contact us at
Cengage Learning Customer & Sales Support, cengage.com/contact
For permission to use material from this text or product,
submit all requests online at **cengage.com/permissions**
Further permissions questions can be emailed to
permissionrequest@cengage.com

Student Edition: 978-1-337-40774-8
SE + Online Workbook: 978-1-337-56254-6

National Geographic Learning
20 Channel Center Street
Boston, MA 02210
USA

National Geographic Learning, a Cengage Learning Company, has a mission to bring the world to the classroom and the classroom to life. With our English language programs, students learn about their world by experiencing it. Through our partnerships with National Geographic and TED Talks, they develop the language and skills they need to be successful global citizens and leaders.

Locate your local office at **international.cengage.com/region**

Visit National Geographic Learning online at **NGL.Cengage.com/ELT**
Visit our corporate website at **www.cengage.com**

Printed in China

Print Number: 01   Print Year: 2018

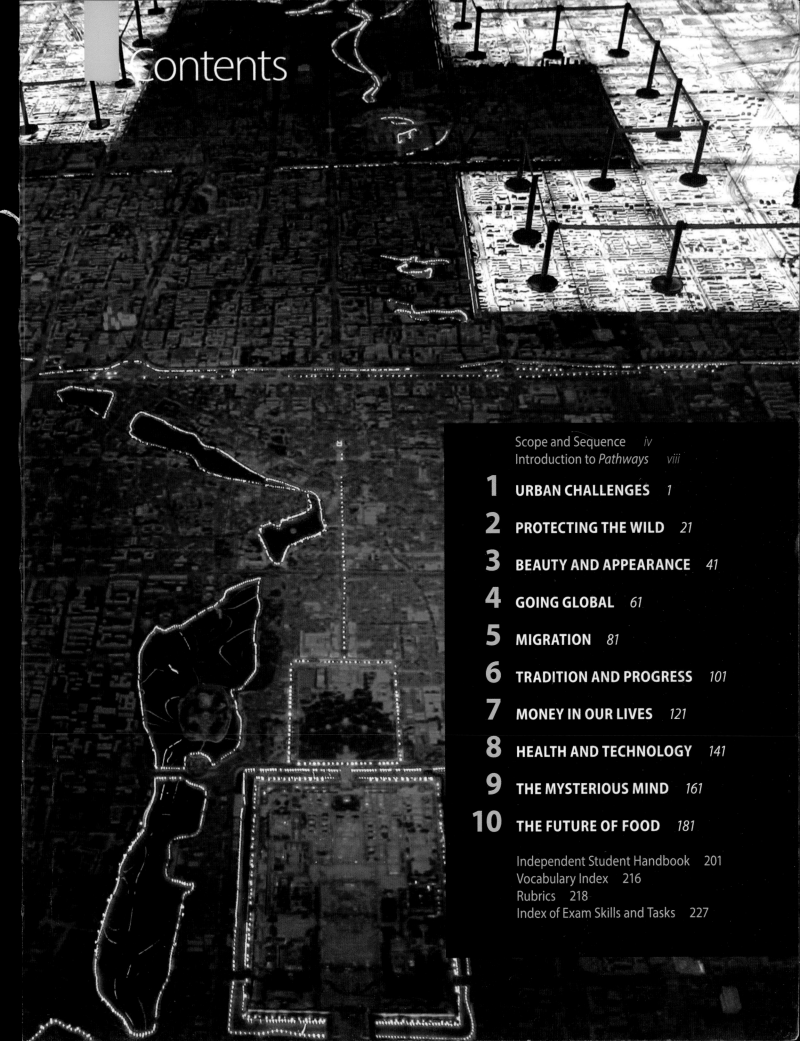

Contents

Scope and Sequence   *iv*
Introduction to *Pathways*   *viii*

1 URBAN CHALLENGES   *1*

2 PROTECTING THE WILD   *21*

3 BEAUTY AND APPEARANCE   *41*

4 GOING GLOBAL   *61*

5 MIGRATION   *81*

6 TRADITION AND PROGRESS   *101*

7 MONEY IN OUR LIVES   *121*

8 HEALTH AND TECHNOLOGY   *141*

9 THE MYSTERIOUS MIND   *161*

10 THE FUTURE OF FOOD   *181*

Independent Student Handbook   201
Vocabulary Index   216
Rubrics   218
Index of Exam Skills and Tasks   227

Scope and Sequence

Unit Title & Theme	Listenings & Video	ACADEMIC SKILLS Listening & Note Taking
1 **URBAN CHALLENGES** *page 1* ACADEMIC TRACK: Urban Studies	**Lesson A** A Lecture about Venice, Italy (with slide show) **VIDEO** Urban Solution: Farming on Rooftops **Lesson B** A Conversation about Singapore	• Understanding the Introduction to a Lecture • Using Abbreviations
2 **PROTECTING THE WILD** *page 21* ACADEMIC TRACK: Life Science	**Lesson A** A Q&A Session about an Extinct Species **VIDEO** Hope for the Mugger Crocodile **Lesson B** A Debate on Legalized Hunting	• Activating Prior Knowledge • Taking Notes during a Q&A
3 **BEAUTY AND APPEARANCE** *page 41* ACADEMIC TRACK: Sociology	**Lesson A** A News Report on Perceptions of Beauty (with slide show) **VIDEO** Skin Mask **Lesson B** A Conversation about Unusual Fashions	• Listening for Specific Information • Using an Outline
4 **GOING GLOBAL** *page 61* ACADEMIC TRACK: Global Studies / Communications	**Lesson A** A Lecture about Succeeding in Business (with slide show) **VIDEO** Sherpa Lives **Lesson B** A Podcast about a Globalizing Technology	• Listening for Advantages • Using Columns
5 **MIGRATION** *page 81* ACADEMIC TRACK: Life Science/History	**Lesson A** A Podcast about Ancient Migration (with slide show) **VIDEO** Wildebeest Migration **Lesson B** A Conversation about the Serengeti	• Listening for Clarification • Using a Time Line

Speaking & Presentation	Vocabulary	Grammar & Pronunciation	Critical Thinking
• Signaling Additional Aspects of a Topic • Presenting in Pairs **Lesson Task** Evaluating the Impact of Tourism **Final Task** Presenting a Problem and Solutions	Word Families: Suffixes	• Passive Voice • Linking with Word-Final *t*	**Focus:** Predicting Analyzing Visuals, Applying, Evaluating, Making Inferences, Organizing Ideas, Reflecting
• Responding to an Argument **Lesson Task** Discussing Environmental Impact **Final Task** A Debate on Wild Animals in Zoos	Two-Part Verbs with *Out*	• Essential Adjective Clauses • Saying and Linking *–s* Endings	**Focus:** Evaluating Arguments in a Debate Analyzing, Analyzing a Chart, Applying, Evaluating, Making Inferences, Predicting, Reflecting
• Paraphrasing • Preparing Visuals for Display **Lesson Task** Conducting a Survey **Final Task** A Presentation about Fashion Trends	Suffix *-ive*	• Tag Questions • Intonation for Clarification	**Focus:** Interpreting a Bar Graph Analyzing, Applying, Evaluating, Interpreting, Organizing Ideas, Predicting, Reflecting
• Defining Terms • Managing Nervousness **Lesson Task** Role-Playing a Job Internview **Final Task** Evaluating a Social Media Platform	Using Collocations	• Gerund Phrases • Saying Parentheticals	**Focus:** Evaluating Analyzing, Applying, Interpreting a Graph, Interpreting a Map, Interpreting Visuals, Organizing Ideas, Ranking, Reflecting
• Approximating • Handling Audience Questions **Lesson Task** Discussing Family Origins **Final Task** A Pair Presentation on Animal Migration	Suffixes *–ant* and *–ist*	• Modals of Past Possibility • Linking with *You* or *Your*	**Focus:** Distinguishing Fact from Theory Applying, Evaluating, Interpreting a Map, Making Inferences, Organizing Ideas, Reflecting, Synthesizing

Scope and Sequence

	Unit Title & Theme	Listenings & Video	**ACADEMIC SKILLS** Listening & Note Taking
6	**TRADITION AND PROGRESS** page 101 ACADEMIC TRACK: Anthropology/Sociology	**Lesson A** A Student Presentation about Bhutan (with slide show) **VIDEO** Preserving Endangered Languages **Lesson B** A Discussion about American Indian Lands	• Listening for a Correction • Using an Idea Map
7	**MONEY IN OUR LIVES** page 121 ACADEMIC TRACK: Economics	**Lesson A** An Interview about Money and Happiness **VIDEO** Bitcoin: The New Way to Pay **Lesson B** A Conversation about Money	• Listening for Shifts in Topic • Summarizing
8	**HEALTH AND TECHNOLOGY** page 141 ACADEMIC TRACK: Health/Technology	**Lesson A** A Lecture about Big Data in Health Care (with slide show) **VIDEO** Biking in the City **Lesson B** A Podcast about Fitness Gadgets	• Listening for Assessments • Using a T-Chart
9	**THE MYSTERIOUS MIND** page 161 ACADEMIC TRACK: Psychology/Brain Science	**Lesson A** A Podcast on the Brain and Intelligence (with slide show) **VIDEO** Memory Man **Lesson B** A Conversation about Memory	• Recognizing Appositives • Highlighting Conclusions
10	**THE FUTURE OF FOOD** page 181 ACADEMIC TRACK: Environmental Studies	**Lesson A** A Lecture about GM Foods (with slide show) **VIDEO** Farming the Open Ocean **Lesson B** A Conversation about Food Prices	• Listening for Suggestions • The Cornell Method

Speaking & Presentation	Vocabulary	Grammar & Pronunciation	Critical Thinking
• Using Rhetorical Questions • Speaking with Confidence **Lesson Task** Conducting an Interview **Final Task** Presenting a Tradition	Collocations: Verb/Adjective + Preposition	• Verb + Object + Infinitive • Stress in Adjective-Noun Combinations	**Focus:** Thinking Outside the Box Analyzing, Applying, Evaluating, Organizing Ideas, Predicting, Synthesizing
• Referencing Research Studies **Lesson Task** Discussing Purchases and Happiness **Final Task** A Role-Play about Financial Advice	Choosing the Right Definition	• Connectors of Concession • Linking Vowel Sounds	**Focus:** Interpreting Visuals Analyzing, Evaluating, Organizing Ideas, Predicting, Ranking, Reflecting, Synthesizing
• Emphasizing Important Information • Engaging Your Audience **Lesson Task** Assessing A City's Health **Final Task** Presenting on a Health Tech Product	Using Synonymns	• Noun Clauses with *That* • Dropped Syllables	**Focus:** Synthesizing Information Evaluating, Interpreting Visuals, Making Inferences, Organizing Ideas, Ranking
• Expressing Causal Relationships • Using Gestures **Lesson Task** Discussing Learning Styles **Final Task** Speaking about a "Life Hack"	Suffixes –*al*, –*tial*, and –*ical*	• Subject-Verb Agreement with Quantifiers • Reduced Function Words	**Focus:** Evaluating Conclusions Analyzing, Concluding, Evaluating, Ranking, Synthesizing
• Referring to Group Opinions **Lesson Task** Role-Playing a Town Hall Meeting **Final Task** Making a Formal Proposal	Investigating Authentic Language	• Subjunctive Verbs in *That* Clauses • Reduced Auxiliary Phrases	**Focus:** Categorizing Analyzing, Applying, Evaluating, Reflecting

Pathways Listening, Speaking, and Critical Thinking, Second Edition

uses compelling National Geographic stories, photos, video, and infographics to bring the world to the classroom. Authentic, relevant content and carefully sequenced lessons engage learners while equipping them with the skills needed for academic success.

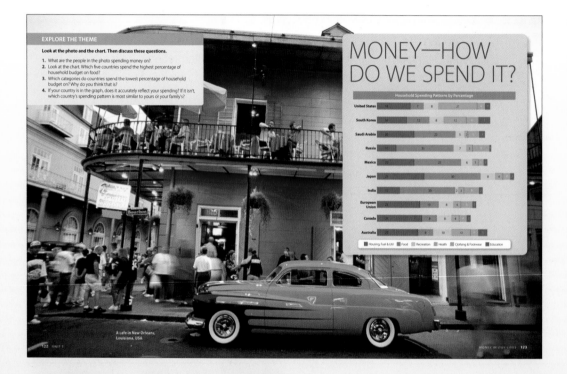

Explore the Theme provides a visual introduction to the unit, engaging learners academically and encouraging them to share ideas about the unit theme.

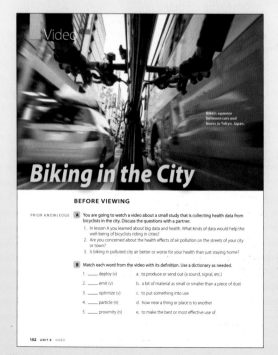

NEW Integrated listening and speaking activities help **prepare students for standardized tests** such as IELTS and TOEFL.

UPDATED *Video* sections use relevant National Geographic **video clips** to give learners another perspective on the unit theme and further practice of listening and critical thinking skills.

Listening Skills

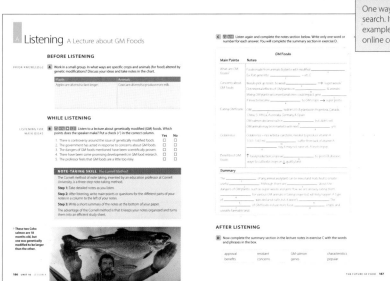

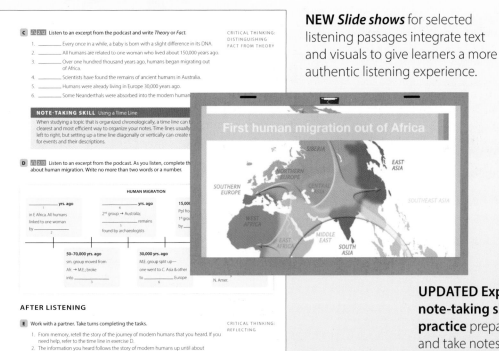

Speaking and Presentation Skills

Speaking lessons guide learners from controlled practice to a final speaking task while reinforcing speaking skills, grammar for speaking, and key pronunciation points.

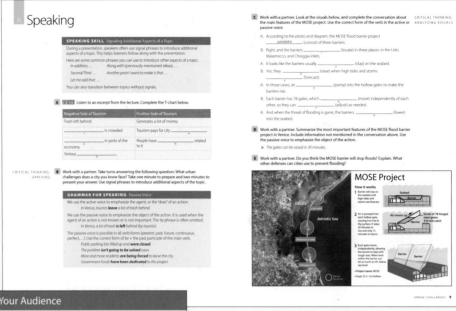

PRESENTATION SKILL Engaging Your Audience

Here are some suggestions to help you engage your audience.

- At the beginning of your presentation, ask some questions that can be answered by a show of hands.
- As appropriate during your presentation, ask for one or more volunteers to assist you or to provide an example for a point.
- Focus on how the points you are making can benefit your audience. When you do, check if they agree.
- Use rhetorical questions to encourage your audience to think about something, to invite them to agree with you, or to ask questions you think your audience would like to ask.

Presentation skills such as starting strong, using specific details, making eye contact, pausing, and summarizing, help learners develop confidence and fluency in communicating ideas.

A **Final Task** allows learners to consolidate their understanding of content, language and skills as they collaborate on an academic presentation.

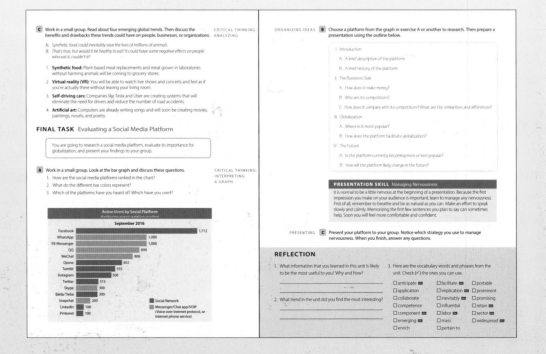

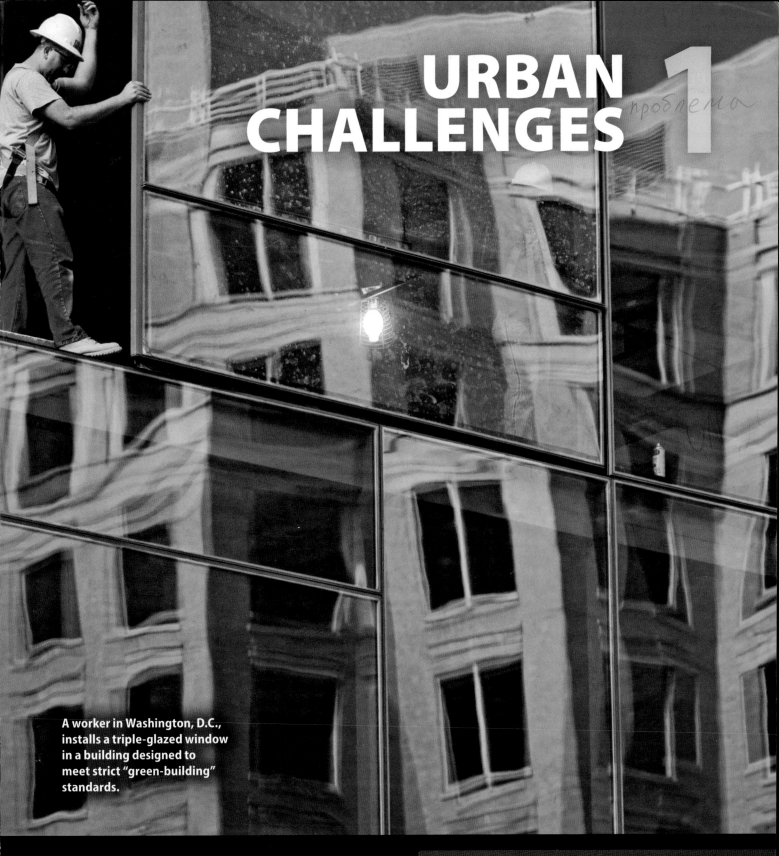

URBAN CHALLENGES

пробле́ма

1

A worker in Washington, D.C.,
installs a triple-glazed window
in a building designed to
meet strict "green-building"
standards.

ACADEMIC SKILLS

LISTENING	Understanding the Introduction to a Lecture
	Using Abbreviations
SPEAKING	Signaling Additional Aspects of a Topic
	Linking with Word-Final *t*
CRITICAL THINKING	Predicting

THINK AND DISCUSS

1 What challenge are green buildings intended to
solve? In addition to windows, in what other ways can
buildings be made "green"?
2 Would you move to a city that is dealing with challenges
such as overcrowding? Explain.

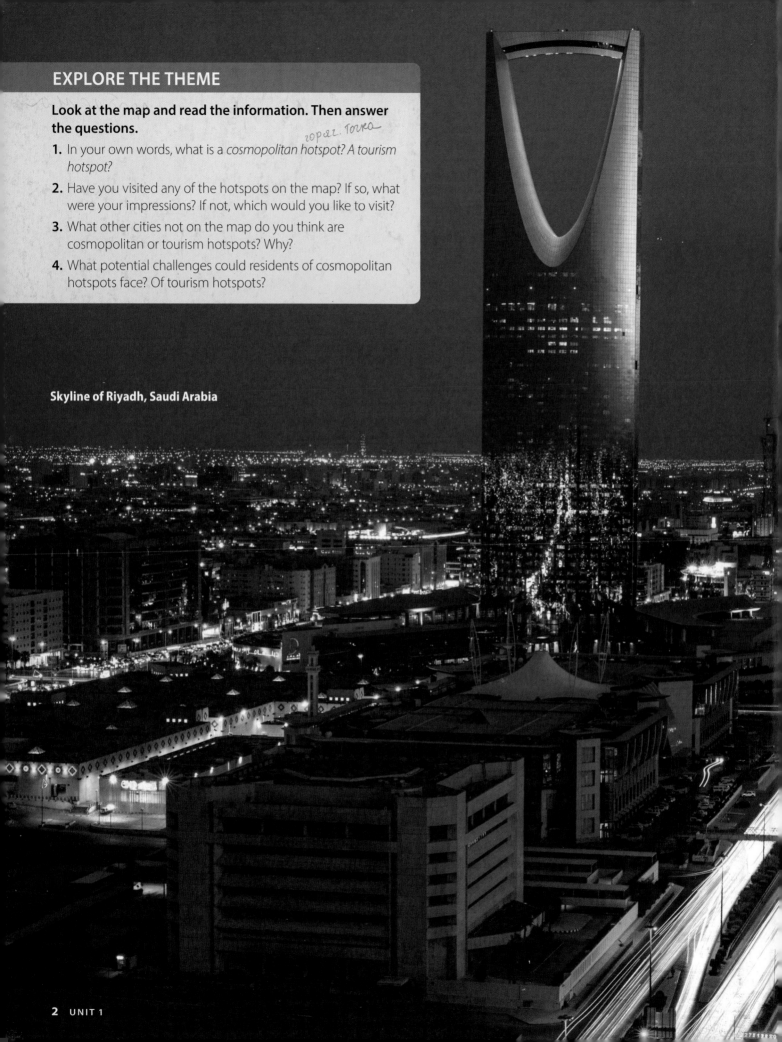

EXPLORE THE THEME

Look at the map and read the information. Then answer the questions.

горяг. точка

1. In your own words, what is a *cosmopolitan hotspot? A tourism hotspot?*

2. Have you visited any of the hotspots on the map? If so, what were your impressions? If not, which would you like to visit?

3. What other cities not on the map do you think are cosmopolitan or tourism hotspots? Why?

4. What potential challenges could residents of cosmopolitan hotspots face? Of tourism hotspots?

Skyline of Riyadh, Saudi Arabia

WORLD CITIES: HOTSPOTS

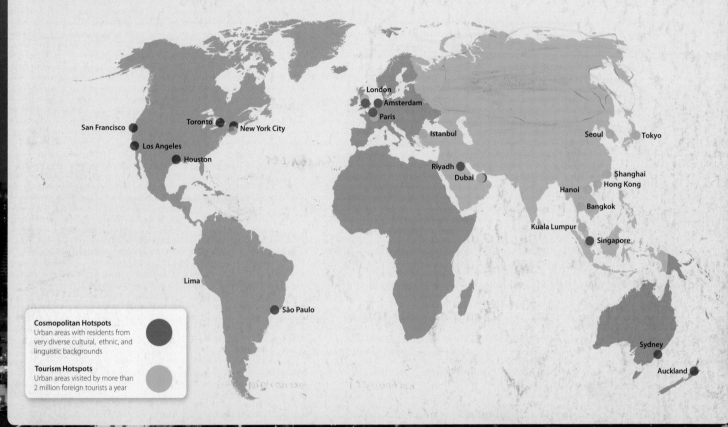

San Francisco

Toronto

New York City

Los Angeles

Houston

London

Amsterdam

Paris

Istanbul

Riyadh

Dubai

Seoul

Tokyo

Shanghai

Hong Kong

Hanoi

Bangkok

Kuala Lumpur

Singapore

Lima

São Paulo

Sydney

Auckland

Cosmopolitan Hotspots
Urban areas with residents from
very diverse cultural, ethnic, and
linguistic backgrounds

Tourism Hotspots
Urban areas visited by more than
2 million foreign tourists a year

A Vocabulary

A 🎧 **1.2** Read and listen to the information. Notice each word in **blue** and think about its meaning.

проблемы

URBAN CHALLENGES

дефи   *безвредные*

Today's urban areas face a variety of challenges. One challenge is a **scarcity** of land for housing. To address this problem, some residents of Tokyo, Japan, have found a unique solution: they are having homes constructed on pieces of land as small as 344 square feet (32 square meters). These "micro-homes" allow residents to live close to central Tokyo and are much more **affordable** than traditional homes in that area. Despite their size, many micro-homes have several floors and big windows that **maximize** sunlight.

Many urban areas also suffer from poor air quality due to pollution and smog.[1] What can these cities do to **regulate** the amount of chemicals from cars and factories? One **innovative** solution has been developed by an Italian company: smog-eating cement. The cement contains a substance that **converts**

превращает

pollution into harmless chemicals that are then washed off roadways when it rains. The smog-eating material has also been effectively used in roof tiles in Los Angeles, California, where air-pollution control is **prioritized**.

Another urban challenge is finding creative ways to build public parks, gardens, and outdoor areas when space is limited. In 2002, the city of New York, for example, **authorized** a project to transform the High Line, an unused railroad line, into an elevated urban park. The **funds** necessary for this **renovation** project were provided through donations, and it was money well spent. The High Line has become one of the most inviting public spaces in the city. Visitors can **stroll** through the gardens, relax on the sundeck, or attend public art exhibits and special events.

экспонаты

---

[1] **smog** (n): a combination of smoke and fog that can damage the health of humans, plants, and animals

---

B Match each sentence beginning to its ending to complete the definitions of the words in **blue** from exercise A.

дефицит

1. When there is a **scarcity** of something, __c__
2. Something that is **affordable** __h__
3. If you **maximize** something, __f__
4. To **regulate** something means __i__
5. An **innovative** idea is __g__
6. If a project is **prioritized**, __d__
7. If a project is **authorized**, __e__   *авторизовать*
8. To provide **funds** to a project means __j__   *фонды*
9. If a building is in need of **renovation**, __a__
10. To **stroll** means __b__   *прогуливаться*

a. it requires repairs or improvements.
b. to walk slowly in a relaxed way.
c. there isn't enough of it.
d. it is given special importance.
e. it is given official approval.
f. you increase it as much as possible.
g. new and creative.
h. can be bought at a reasonable price.
i. to control it.
j. to give it money.

Knowing a word means learning its different forms, or its "family". Keep a log of different word forms. Here are examples of word families.

Noun	Verb	Adjective
creator/creation	create	creative
classification	classify	classified

Often the different forms of a word have different endings, or suffixes. Here are some common suffixes.

Noun	Verb	Adjective
-or/-er, -ity, -tion	-ate, -ify, -ize	-d/-ed, -able, -ing, -ive

C Complete the chart with the correct forms of each word. Use a dictionary to help you.

	Noun	Verb	Adjective
1.	affordability	afford	affordable
2.	authorization	authorise *au*	authorized
3.	innovation	innovate	innovative
4.	maximum	maximize	maximum, maximal
5.	priority	prioritize	prioritized priority
6.	regularity	regulate	regular
7.	renovation	renovate	renovated

D Work with a partner. What other challenges do cities face? What are some solutions? Discuss your ideas. Then list them in a T-chart in your notebook.

прогуливающие

◀ **People strolling through the High Line park in New York City, USA**

Listening A Lecture about Venice, Italy

BEFORE LISTENING

PREDICTING | **A** | Look at the photo. Can you guess how many tourists visit Venice each year? How do you think tourists help the city? How do they hurt it? Discuss your ideas with a partner.

WHILE LISTENING

> **LISTENING SKILL** Understanding the Introduction to a Lecture
>
> Lecture introductions often have two parts:
>
> - In the first part, the speaker provides background information about the topic or reviews what was covered in earlier lectures.
> - In the second part, the speaker announces the specific topic to be discussed and explains how the information will be presented.
>
> Understanding the structure of the introduction can improve your listening comprehension and help you organize your lecture notes.

B | ∩ 1.3 | Listen to the lecture introduction. Then answer the questions.

1. What topic did the lecturer previously speak about?
   a. how tourism has affected waterway repairs
   b. difficulties Venice faces related to flooding
   c. where Venice finds funds for large projects

2. Which *specific* topic is today's lecture going to be about?
   a. the problem of flooding
   b. the effects of the MOSE project
   c. the effects of tourism in Venice

Venice, Italy

Tourists enjoy a gondola ride in Venice.

C 🎧 1.4 ▶ 1.1 Listen to the entire lecture. Check (✓) the three main ideas.

1. ✓ the impact of tourism on city services
2. ____ how tourists could change their behavior
3. ____ the causes of increased tourism in Venice
4. ✓ the effects of tourism on residents of Venice

недостатки

5. ____ the drawbacks of visiting Venice as a tourist
6. ✓ the benefits of tourism for Venice

NOTE-TAKING SKILL Using Abbreviations

There is no right way to abbreviate words. The important thing is to remember what the abbreviation means when you review your notes. Good note takers create their own abbreviations and use them consistently. Here are some examples of abbreviations. *последовательно*

about/around	~	less/more than	</>	number	#	thousand	K
billion	B/bil	million	M/mil	positive	pos/+	with	w/
is/is called/ means	=	negative	neg/-	problem	prob	without	w/o

---

D 🎧 1.5 Listen to an excerpt from the lecture. Complete the notes with abbreviations from the skill box above.

For cent, Ven _____prob_____ of flooding

Acqua alta ____=____ floodwaters
1

MOSE project: > $5 ___B/bill___ on H_2O barriers
2

Serious prob ___w=___ tourism
3

Tourism: ___pos/+___ = profitable
4

___neg/-___ = # of tourists
5

Visitors to Ven in 2014 ___~___ 25 ___M/mill___
6   7

1 holiday wknd, 80 ___K___ tourists
8

E Work with a partner. What other forms of abbreviations do you see in the notes above? What are some examples of abbreviations you use in your notes?

AFTER LISTENING

F Discuss these questions with a partner.

1. Based on the lecture, what is the attitude of Venetian residents toward tourists? Use information from the lecture to support your answer.
2. What is the lecturer's attitude about Venice's future? Explain.

A Speaking

сигнализация дополнительных аспектов темы

переходить между темами с сигналами

отрывок

A 🎧 1.6 Listen to an excerpt from the lecture. Complete the T-chart below.

Negative Side of Tourism	Positive Side of Tourism
Trash left behind	Generates a lot of money *2 bl* *help museum*
public transportation *(переполненный)* is crowded ₁	Tourism pays for city projects ₄
inflation *(инфляция)* in parts of the economy ₂	People have jobs related to it ₅
Serious housing problem ₃	

CRITICAL THINKING: APPLYING

B Work with a partner. Take turns answering the following question: What urban challenges does a city you know face? Take one minute to prepare and two minutes to present your answer. Use signal phrases to introduce additional aspects of the topic.

GRAMMAR FOR SPEAKING Passive Voice

We use the active voice to emphasize the agent, or the "doer," of an action:
> *In Venice, tourists **leave** a lot of trash behind.*

дейст. лицо

We use the passive voice to emphasize the object of the action. It is used when the agent of an action is not known or is not important. The *by* phrase is often omitted. *(пропущ.)*
> *In Venice, a lot of trash **is left** behind (by tourists).*

The passive voice is possible in all verb forms (present, past, future, continuous, perfect, . . .). Use the correct form of *be* + the past participle of the main verb.
> *Public parking lots filled up and **were closed**.*
> *The problem **isn't going to be solved** soon.*
> *More and more residents **are being forced** to leave the city.* *(вынуждены)*
> *Government funds **have been dedicated** to the project.* *(преданы)*

C Work with a partner. Look at the visuals below, and complete the conversation about the main features of the MOSE project. Use the correct form of the verb in the active or passive voice.

CRITICAL THINKING: ANALYZING VISUALS

A: According to the photo and diagram, the MOSE flood barrier project _____consists_____ (consist) of three barriers.

B: Right, and the barriers _are located_ (locate) in three places: in the Lido, Malamocco, and Chioggia inlets.

A: It looks like the barriers usually _____stay_____ (stay) on the seabed.

B: Yes, they _are raised_ (raise) when high tides and storms _are forecasted_ (forecast).

A: In those cases, air _is pumped_ (pump) into the hollow gates to make the barriers rise.

B: Each barrier has 78 gates, which _move_ (move) independently of each other, so they can _be adjusted_ (adjust) as needed.

A: And when the threat of flooding is gone, the barriers _are lowered_ (lower) into the seabed.

D Work with a partner. Summarize the most important features of the MOSE flood barrier project in Venice. Include information not mentioned in the conversation above. Use the passive voice to emphasize the object of the action.

> *The gates can be raised in 30 minutes.*

E Work with a partner. Do you think the MOSE barrier will stop floods? Explain. What other defenses can cities use to prevent flooding?

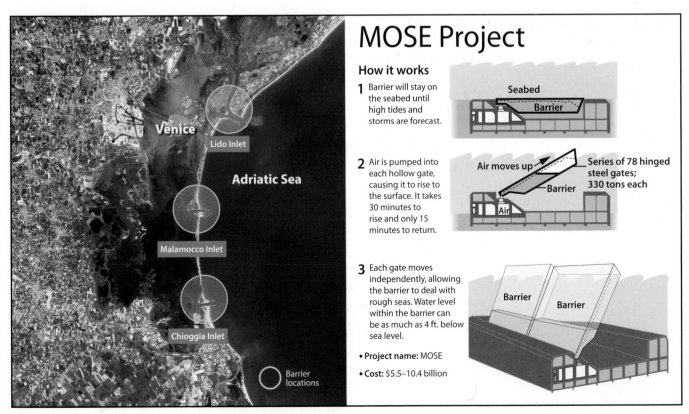

MOSE Project

How it works

1 Barrier will stay on the seabed until high tides and storms are forecast.

2 Air is pumped into each hollow gate, causing it to rise to the surface. It takes 30 minutes to rise and only 15 minutes to return.

3 Each gate moves independently, allowing the barrier to deal with rough seas. Water level within the barrier can be as much as 4 ft. below sea level.

• **Project name:** MOSE
• **Cost:** $5.5–10.4 billion

Seabed
Barrier

Air moves up
Series of 78 hinged steel gates; 330 tons each
Barrier
Air

Barrier
Barrier

Venice
Lido Inlet
Adriatic Sea
Malamocco Inlet
Chioggia Inlet
Barrier locations

F Work in a small group. Imagine that you live by the ocean and your city was hit by a powerful hurricane. Describe the disaster using the verbs below. Use the passive voice when appropriate.

blow off	damage	destroy	flood	hit
injure	lose	rescue	trap	wash away

A: *What a terrible storm! My dog ran off, but luckily he was rescued by some neighbors. My house is OK. It wasn't damaged too much.*

B: *You're lucky! My car was hit by a tree. It's destroyed! Luckily, no one in my family was injured.*

LESSON TASK Evaluating the Impact of Tourism

CRITICAL THINKING: EVALUATING

A Work in a small group. Look at the list of topics. How does tourism impact these aspects of urban life? Discuss your ideas with your group. Add your own topic(s) to the list.

public transportation	job opportunities for residents
culture (arts, restaurants, and museums)	the cost of living
historical sites	the city's reputation
cleanliness	other: _____

Over two million international tourists visit Rio de Janeiro, Brazil, each year.

B Choose a tourist city that you know. What are the pros and cons of tourism there? Write your notes in the chart. *guadalajara*

ORGANIZING IDEAS

City: _*Volgograd*_

Pros	Cons
The city's reputation - popularity	Pollution
job opportunities for residents	crimes
Innovation	scarcity of land
Renovation	
New buildings	

pro·

EVERYDAY LANGUAGE Turn Taking

Why don't I/you start?	*Who wants to go first/next?*
I'll start.	*Does anyone want to go first/next?*
I'll go first/next.	*Does anyone mind if I go first/next/last?*

C Rejoin your group. Use your chart from exercise B to tell your group about the impact of tourism on the city you chose. Explain your ideas and answer questions from the group. Use phrases for turn taking.

CRITICAL THINKING: APPLYING

A: *Who wants to go first?*

B: *I'll start. I chose Muscat. Muscat is the capital of Oman. It is a beautiful city, and tourists from all over the world visit. Tourists bring lots of advantages but also some problems.*

Video

Aerial view of rooftop garden on a parking lot in Chengdu, China

Urban Solution: Farming on Rooftops

BEFORE VIEWING

> **CRITICAL THINKING** Predicting
>
> Before listening to a lecture or watching a video, look at the title and any accompanying visuals, and predict what you will learn about. Thinking about the topic in advance will make you a more active listener and increase your comprehension.

CRITICAL THINKING: PREDICTING

A The video is about Brooklyn Grange, a company working to solve some of the problems of urban life. Look at the title and photo. Then discuss the questions with a partner.

1. What benefits do you think there are to growing vegetables on a rooftop?
2. Farming includes more than just growing vegetables. What other types of farming could be done on a rooftop?

B Match each word from the video with its meaning. Use a dictionary to help you.

импульс -инерция   дв.сила

1. __e__ (n) momentum   a. to do something first
2. __a__ (v) pioneer- *первопроходец*   b. main, central
3. __b__ (adj) core- *ядро, сердцевина*   c. income produced by a business or government
4. __c__ (n) revenue - *доход*   d. separated, disconnected
5. __d__ (adj) alienated   e. increased speed of development or progress
    отчуждать

WHILE VIEWING

C ▶ **1.2** Watch the video. Check (✓) the points that the speakers make.

UNDERSTANDING MAIN IDEAS

огромный
1. ☐ Rooftop farming is having an enormous effect on cities everywhere.
2. ☑ Ben Flanner discovered his passion for farming when he came to New York City.
    рассмотрение   почва
3. ☑ The farmers have given consideration to the soil and water.
    производством
4. ☑ Rooftop farms connect the community with the production of its food.
5. ☐ The farmers' objective is to provide most of New York City's vegetables.

D ▶ **1.2** Read the questions. Then watch the video again. Take notes as you watch. Write no more than three words or a number to answer each question.

UNDERSTANDING DETAILS

масштаб
1. Is rooftop farming practiced on a large scale or a small scale? __small scale__
    существа
2. What type of creatures does their apiary business involve? __New York City's first__ urban apiary
    over a mill. pounds of soil
3. How long did it take to move the soil up onto the roof? __several weeks__
4. How do the stones in the soil compare to a typical rock?
    __the stones in the soil weigh less than a typical rock.__
    ливневая   обходится
5. About how much storm water a year does each farm manage? __about a million gallons__
    __of stormwater per year.__

✳ 6. What influence do the farms have on "urban heat island effect"? *is from the modification of land surfaces.*
    __They clean the air around them__ *due to human activities.* __and decrease the amount of HVAC__
    the upper floors.

E Look back at your predictions in exercise A. Were they correct? Tell a partner.

CHECKING PREDICTIONS

AFTER VIEWING

Since I grew up in a village, I took care of poultry, a cow, lambs, pigs.
I grew vegetables in the garden.

F With your partner, discuss the questions.

PERSONALIZING

1. What experience do you have with growing vegetables or raising animals?
2. Do you feel connected to the production of your food? Explain.
3. If you were given funds to set up a farm to raise crops and animals within your city or town, where would you put it? How could you involve your community?

Vocabulary

A Match each word or phrase with its definition. Use a dictionary to help you.

1. _i_ **affluent** (adj)
2. _d_ **be unique to** (v phr)
3. _j_ **conform** (v)
4. _h_ **debatable** (adj)
5. _e_ **dominant** (adj)
6. _c_ **enforce** (v)
7. _a_ **ethnic** (adj)
8. _f_ **internalize** (v)
9. _b_ **rank** (v)
10. _g_ **restrict** (v)

a. relating to people with the same culture, race, and traditions

b. to occupy a position in a list or in relation to other people or things

c. to make sure that a rule is obeyed

d. to exist only in one place or situation

e. having a strong influence

f. to make a belief part of your way of thinking

g. to limit, often by official rules or laws

h. not certain; questionable

i. wealthy

j. to behave in the same way as other people

B 🎧 1.7 Complete the article with the correct form of a word from exercise A. Then listen and check your answers.

SINGAPORE

Singapore is one of Asia's most interesting countries. Among all the nations of the world, Singapore __ranks__ only 176th in size; nevertheless, it is among the most __affluent__, with an average income of about US$61,000. Many believe that Singapore's economic success is due to the leadership of Lee Kuan Yew, Singapore's first Prime Minister. His ideas have been __dominant__ in Singapore for decades.

Singapore's model of success is unlike that of any other country. The model is a combination of two ideas: the encouragement of business and strict laws that regulate many aspects of life. To follow this model, the people of Singapore have learned to live and work together in an orderly way. There are laws that encourage cooperation between __ethnic__ groups, and like all laws in Singapore, they are strictly __enforced__ by the authorities.

Things such as selling chewing gum, littering, and even spitting are all __restricted__ by law. While these laws, some of which __are unique to__ Singapore, may surprise first-time visitors, most Singaporeans have __internalized__ them, and for the most part, they follow the rules and laws without thinking about them.

Most Singaporeans believe that strict laws are necessary for an orderly and secure society. They are willing to __conform__ to the system if it makes life in Singapore more pleasant. However, for some Singaporeans and people from other countries, the issue is __debatable__. They argue that the laws are too restrictive.

▲ **Skyline of Singapore at night**

C Complete the chart with the correct form of each word. Then complete each sentence below with the correct form of one of the words. Use a dictionary to help you.

	Noun	Verb	Adjective
1.	*debate*	*debate*	debatable
2.	*enforcement*	enforce	*enforced* принудить
3.	*rank*	*rank*	ranked
4.	*restriction*	restrict	*restricted* ограничить

1. Dogs are _restricted_ on public beaches and in many parks.

2. The two candidates for president held a public _debate_.

3. In the United States, a law against chewing gum wouldn't be easy to _enforce_.

4. In the 2016 World Happiness Report, Singaporeans _ranked_ 22nd in happiness.

D Read the statements about Singapore. Guess if they are true or false. Choose T for *True* or F for *False*. Then check your answers at the bottom of the page.

1. The cream-colored giant squirrel is an animal that is unique to Singapore.   skwɜrl   (T)   F   1890

2. The largest ethnic group in Singapore is Malay. — the second   T   (F)

3. In Singapore, where you can eat ice cream is restricted by law.   T   (F)

4. Singapore has a special government agency that enforces anticorruption laws.   (T)   F

E Work in a small group. Discuss the questions.   My family keeps the Sabbath day. We never eat pork and any marine life without scales.   **PERSONALIZING**

1. What is a tradition that is unique to your family? To your culture?

All people of different nationalities are very valuable
2. What is an important value you have internalized? Explain how it impacts you. — A healthy lifestyle is good. I am trying to comply with this rule.

3. Describe a time when you chose to conform to what others were doing. Do you think you made the right choice, or did you regret it later?   never conformed

every person is unique.
each

ANSWERS: 1. T; 2. F (The largest ethnic group in Singapore is Chinese.); 3. F (It is not restricted.); 4. T

Listening   A Conversation about Singapore

BEFORE LISTENING

CRITICAL THINKING:
PREDICTING

A With a partner, predict the answers to these questions about Singapore.

1. What do you think Singapore is famous for?
2. Singapore is a city-state. What do you think *city-state* means? *is an independent city*
3. Look at the photo. Why do you think the Merlion was chosen as the symbol of Singapore? *half lion, half fish*

WHILE LISTENING

LISTENING FOR
MAIN IDEAS

B 🎧 **1.8** Read the statements. Then listen to the conversation about Singapore. Choose T for *True* or F for *False*.   *a small country*

1. The name *Singapura* means "lion city."   (T)   F
2. Singapore is rich in natural resources.   T   (F)
3. Nearly all the people of Singapore belong to one ethnic group.   T   (F)
4. The spirit of *kiasu* is about enjoying life every minute.   T   (F)
5. Nick thinks the laws of Singapore are too strict.   (T)   F
6. Sofia believes strict laws are a positive thing.   (T)   F

has a powerful economy for such a small count

C Compare your answers to exercise B with a partner. Revise the false statements to make them true.

ASIA

Pacific Ocean

Indian Ocean

Singapore

AUSTRALIA

The Merlion, a statue that is half lion, half fish, is the symbol of Singapore.

D 🎧 **1.8** Listen again. Complete the notes with no more than two words or a number.

1. Sing. started off as a _fishing village_
2. Modern Sing. founded in _1819_ .
3. Sing. is ~ _270_ sq. miles.
4. Sing. = _100_ % urbanized.
5. Sing. econ. ranked the _second_ most innovative in the wrld.
6. Lee Kuan Yew's ideas = dominant in _Singapore politics_ for 50 yrs.
7. *Kiasu* = "afraid _to lose_ ."

AFTER LISTENING

E With your partner, discuss these questions.

1. Do you have the spirit of *kiasu*? Explain.
2. Do you think that Singapore's laws are too strict or that they're beneficial? Explain.
3. What annoying behaviors that you see in public would you like to be restricted or made illegal?

F Look at this list of regulations in Singapore and the maximum fines and penalties they carry. Take notes on what you think the purpose of each regulation is.

Regulations and Penalties	Purpose
1. Selling chewing gum ($100,000 or two years in prison)	
2. Spitting in public ($1,000)	
3. Annoying people by playing a musical instrument in public ($1,000)	
4. Connecting to another person's Wi-Fi ($10,000 or three years in prison)	
5. Forgetting to flush a public toilet (around $150)	
6. Allowing mosquitoes to breed in your empty flower pots ($200)	
7. Feeding pigeons ($500)	

G Work in a small group. Discuss whether you think the regulations in exercise F would be a good idea where you live.

> I guess gum can cause problems when people don't throw it away properly. Still, I don't think I'd want it outlawed around here.

B Speaking

PRONUNCIATION Linking with Word-Final *t*

🎧 **1.9** The letter *t* at the end of a word links with the next word in these ways.

1. When *t* is followed by an unstressed word that begins with a vowel, the *t* is pronounced like a quick *d* sound.

   state of sounds like *sta dof*   *what about* sounds like *wha dabout*

2. When *t* is followed by a word that begins with a consonant (other than *t* or *d*), hold your teeth and tongue in a *t* position, but do not release air.

   right now sounds like *right now*   *street can* sounds like *street can*

3. When *t* is followed by *you* or *your*, the *t* becomes soft, like *ch*.

   what you sounds like *wha chyu*   *don't you* sounds like *don chyu*

A Look at the following pairs of words. How is the final *t* of the first word pronounced? Write the phrase in the correct column below.

1. at you	3. hit us	5. thought your	7. eight o'clock
2. upset about	4. what now	6. not you	8. not really

Like a quick *d*	No air	Soft *t*, like *ch*
upset about	what now	at you
hit us	not really	thought your
eight o'clock		Not you

B 🎧 **1.10** Listen and check your answers to exercise A. Then listen again and repeat the phrases.

C 🎧 **1.11** Listen to the conversations. Pay attention to the pronunciation of each word-final -*t*. Then take turns practicing the dialogs with a partner.

1. A: I didn't hear what you said about which plan we'll prioritize.
   B: I'm sorry. I'll say it again.
2. A: Do you want some tips on planning the renovation?
   B: Yes, I would. And how about some help with building regulations?
3. A: About that budget I submitted. Has it been authorized yet?
   B: Not yet.
4. A: What are you going to do to maximize rentals?
   B: See that ad? We're going to put it everywhere online.
5. A: What are you so upset about?
   B: Haven't you heard? There are no funds for that project!

Customers play with a cat at "Café des Chats", the first cat cafe in Paris.

D Work with a partner. Read the statements related to different urban issues. Do you agree or disagree with each? Explain why to your partner.

CRITICAL THINKING: EVALUATING

> *I agree that smoking should be prohibited in all public places. Second-hand smoke is unhealthy.*

1. It's impossible for people from different ethnic groups to live together in peace.
2. It's the government's responsibility to provide housing for homeless people. ✓
3. Billboards beside the road are ugly and distracting. They should be illegal. ✓
4. In crowded cities, the government should limit the number of cars a family can have. ✓
5. Smoking should be prohibited in all public places, both indoors and outdoors. ✓
6. Pets should be allowed in restaurants, shops, and movie theaters.

FINAL TASK Presenting a Problem and Solutions

> You and your partner will present a problem affecting a city and propose solutions to the problem.

A Work with a partner. Discuss problems affecting a city you are both interested in. Make a list. Use your own knowledge and experience. If necessary, research the city.

PRESENTATION SKILL Presenting in Pairs

When dividing up material for a pair presentation, you can try different techniques:

- Simply divide the material to present in half.
- Take a "tag-team" approach where you take turns presenting the various points. This can help keep the audience's attention for longer presentations, but avoid switching back and forth too much.
- Assign different parts of the presentation based on who is best qualified to present each part. It's important to consider the strengths of each presenter. A qualified presenter is more confident and will make a better impression on the audience.

B With your partner, choose one of the problems you discussed in exercise A. Discuss the causes of the problem and possible solutions. Use the spider map to organize your ideas.

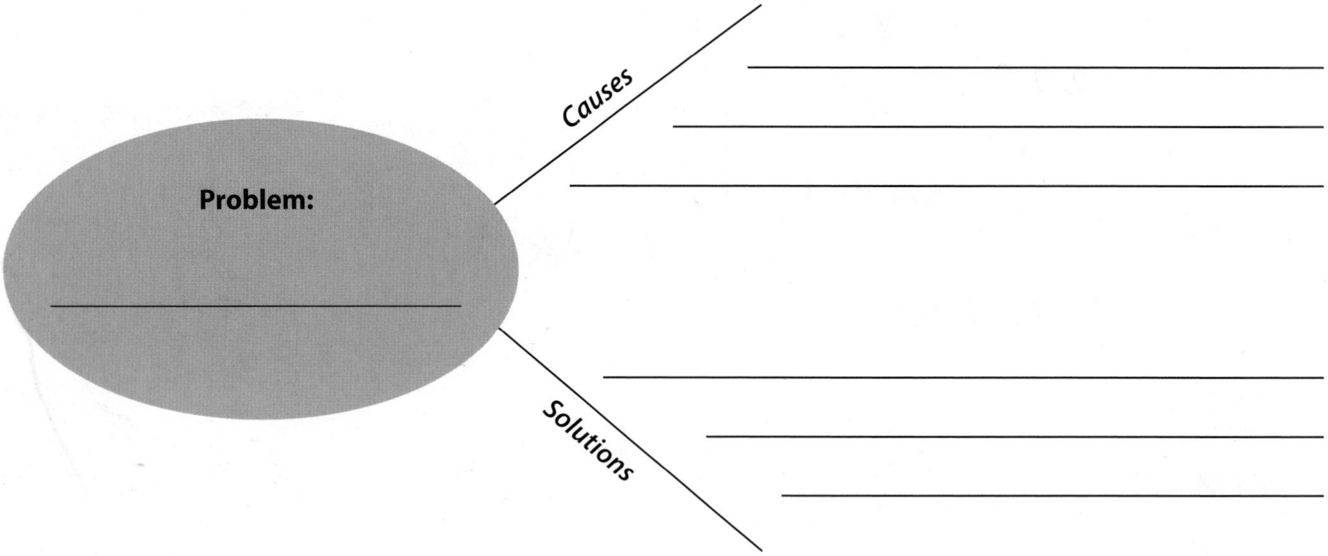

Causes

Problem:

_____

_____

_____

_____

Solutions

_____

_____

_____

C Decide who will present each part of the presentation. Then practice giving the presentation and make any adjustments needed.

регулировка

D With your partner, present your problem and solutions to the class.

A: *We'd like to talk about the problems with the current public transportation system. This issue isn't unique to our city, but . . .*

B: *One place to start is to request that the city modernize the subway stations . . .*

E As a class, decide which pair presented the most innovative solution to an urban challenge.

REFLECTION

1. What are some useful abbreviations you can use to take notes more quickly?

_____

_____

2. What is the most useful or interesting thing you learned in this unit?

_____

_____

3. Here are the vocabulary words and phrases from the unit. Check (✓) the ones you can use.

соблюдение

☐ affluent	☐ enforce AWL	☐ rank
☐ affordable	☐ ethnic AWL	☐ regulate AWL
☐ authorize	☐ funds AWL	☐ renovation
☐ be unique to	☐ innovative AWL	☐ restrict AWL
☐ conform AWL	☐ internalize AWL	☐ scarcity
☐ debatable AWL	☐ maximize AWL	☐ stroll
☐ dominant AWL	☐ prioritize AWL	

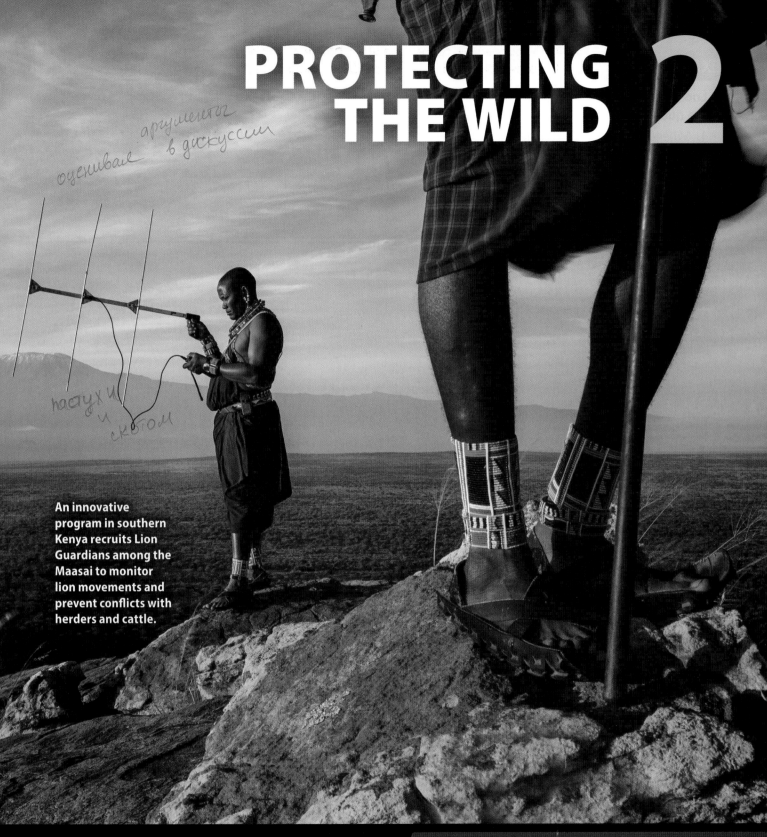

PROTECTING THE WILD 2

An innovative program in southern Kenya recruits Lion Guardians among the Maasai to monitor lion movements and prevent conflicts with herders and cattle.

ACADEMIC SKILLS

LISTENING	Activating Prior Knowledge
	Taking Notes during a Q&A
SPEAKING	Responding to an Argument
	Saying and Linking –s Endings
CRITICAL THINKING	Evaluating Arguments in a Debate

THINK AND DISCUSS

1 Where are these men, and what are they doing?
2 What are some reasons that animals become extinct?
3 Who do you think should be responsible for protecting endangered species? Governments? Companies? Citizens?

A Look at the photo and read the caption. Then discuss the questions.

1. Where are the man and the gorilla? What do you think the man's responsibilities are?

2. How does the photograph make you feel? Explain.

B Read the infographic and discuss the questions.

1. What do the 11 animals have in common?

2. What is the Photo Ark? What is its purpose?

OUR WILD FRIENDS

An orphaned mountain gorilla sits with a warden in the gorilla sanctuary of Virunga National Park in the Democratic Republic of the Congo. The orphans in the sanctuary have been the victims of poachers or animal traffickers.

MEET SOME OF THE SPECIES FACING EXTINCTION IN THE WILD

(OF THE 7,000 SPECIES IN THE PHOTO ARK)

Many species are endangered and could disappear in our lifetimes. The National Geographic Photo Ark, led by photographer Joel Sartore, is a long-term project that aims to:

- photograph every species living in the world's zoos and other protected areas
- teach and inspire the public
- help save wildlife by supporting various projects

SOUTH CHINA TIGER

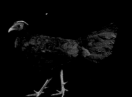

EDWARDS'S PHEASANT

SUMATRAN ORANGUTAN

MITCHELL'S LORIKEET

ARAKAN FOREST TURTLE

ATELOPUS NANAY

NORTHERN WHITE RHINO

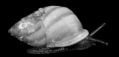

BUTTERFLY SPLITFIN

PARTULA SNAILS

RABBS' FROG (EXTINCT)

COLUMBIA BASIN PYGMY RABBIT (EXTINCT)

A Vocabulary

A 🎧 **1.12** Read and listen to the information. Notice each word or phrase in **blue** and think about its meaning.

SAVE THE WHALES! *китов*

Of the nearly 90 species of whales and dolphins, nearly all have been affected by human activity.

Are all whales endangered?

Not all, but many. The populations of most species of baleen whales[1], such as blue and humpback whales, have been significantly reduced. Their **status** today is the result of commercial whaling from the 18th to the 20th century. For hundreds of years, they've been sold for meat and oil, and some species were nearly **wiped out**. *—уничтожать* Although most whale populations have been coming back, five species of baleen whales are still endangered, and the evidence shows that many toothed whales are in danger of dying out. Hunting, **habitat** destruction, and pollution all **threaten** *угрожать* whale populations. In each case, humans **are to blame**. *спасись*

What kinds of conservation efforts are taking place?

Many **ongoing** *непрерывных* conservation strategies are helping whale populations. For example, the International Whaling Commission (IWC) **imposed** *наложенных* a ban on commercial whaling, and the United States has been leading an effort to phase out[2] whale hunting completely. Nevertheless, a number of countries continue to hunt whales.

Can whale populations recover?

Although it may be too late for some species, there are some signs that conservation efforts are working. For example, the California gray whale, which was nearly **extinct**, has made an amazing recovery and is no longer endangered. *вымирание*

How can you help save the whales?

You can help by learning about whales and their habitats. You can donate your time to conservation organizations. Finally, you can **modify** your behavior so that you create as little waste as possible. If we all participate in these efforts, we can help these magnificent animals **thrive**. *— процветать*

---

[1] **baleen whales** (n): whales that, instead of having teeth, have plates in their mouth that separate food from the water
[2] **phase out** (v): to bring to an end in a gradual manner

North Atlantic right whales were heavily hunted in the 18th and 19th centuries. Their name came from hunters, who said that they were the "right" whale for oil, meat, and other valuable body parts.

B Match each word or phrase with its definition.

1. __a__ are to blame (v phr)
2. __h__ extinct (adj)
3. __d__ habitat (n)
4. __i__ imposed (v) – наложении
5. __j__ modify (v) – видоизм.
6. __b__ ongoing (adj) – непрерыв
7. __c__ status (n)
8. __g__ threaten (v) – угрожать
9. __e__ thrive (v) – процветать
10. __f__ wiped out (v phr)
   уничтожен.

a. are responsible for doing something wrong
b. continuing to happen
c. a state or condition at a particular time
d. the natural environment of an animal or plant
e. to grow or develop very well
f. completely eliminated or destroyed
g. to put at risk or in danger
h. no longer existing; died out
i. forced something on, such as a law or punishment
j. to change slightly

VOCABULARY SKILL Two-Part Verbs with *Out*

Two-part verbs, also called phrasal verbs, are common in speaking. Often the two words together have a new meaning. Learn them to help you speak more naturally. In two-part verbs, *out* has three basic meanings.

1. **Outside, or from inside to outside:** *eat out, take out, let out, lock out, leave out*
   Many verbs of motion can be used with *out*: *go out, run out, fly out, walk out*
2. **To distribute:** *send out, hand out, give out, pass out*
3. **To finish or end completely:** *die out, fade out, phase out, wipe out, back out, sign out, wait out*

C Choose the correct verb or verb phrase to complete the sentences.

1. One country (backed / _backed out_) of the whaling ban agreement at the last minute.
2. The first agreement to regulate whaling was (signed / signed out) in 1946.
3. Whales are good survivors, and very few species have actually (died / _died out_).
4. When the storm began, our ship headed into port to (wait it / _wait it out_).
5. British adventurer Tom McClean plans to (_cross_ / cross out) the Atlantic in a whale-shaped boat.
6. A man was (handing / _handing out_) brochures for a whale-watching tour.
7. This copy of *Moby Dick* is missing pages. Someone (tore them / _tore them out_).
8. We should also protect dolphins. Let's not (leave them / _leave them out_).

D Work in a small group. Discuss these questions.

CRITICAL THINKING: REFLECTING

1. Whale-watching tours are popular around the world. Why are people fascinated by whales? If you have seen a whale, what was the experience like?
2. Should bans on hunting whales be imposed on everyone? Explain.
3. How do humans modify animal habitats in ways that can threaten the animals?
4. What are examples of "modifying behavior to create as little waste as possible"?

Listening A Q&A Session about an Extinct Species

BEFORE LISTENING

PREDICTING

A Work in a small group. Look at the photo and read the caption. Then discuss the questions.

Merritt Island Florida

1. What kind of habitat do you think this bird lived in?
2. The dusky seaside sparrow is now extinct. What do you think are some possible causes for its extinction? *humans are to blame*
3. What types of laws could protect endangered animals?
4. What are some drawbacks *—недостатки* of passing laws to protect endangered species?

palution
hunting

extinct

воробей

The dusky seaside sparrow was a bird species of southern Florida.

PREVIEWING

B 🎧 1.13 Listen to the first part of a question and answer (Q&A) session and look at the student notes. Notice the use of abbreviations and symbols.

basic cause was habitat destruction   *exhibit — экспонат*   *June 16th 1987*

Dusky Seaside Sparrow

Stat.: Extinct *1987 Jun 6*

Former habitat: Merritt Isl., FL   *Marritle Island Florida*

Causes of extinction

  1. Chems used for killing mosqs.   *Chemicals — mosquitas*

  2. Modified wetlands → no longer good habitat for sparrows

CHECKING PREDICTIONS

C Look back at the predictions you made in exercise A. Were they correct?

WHILE LISTENING

NOTE-TAKING SKILL Taking Notes during a Q&A

When taking notes during a talk presented in a question and answer (Q&A) format, it is helpful to organize your notes according to the questions and their responses. Number the questions (Q1, Q2, etc.). Below each question, write notes on the answer, numbering (A1, A2, etc.) and indenting them as needed.

отступ

    Q1: *What caused extinction?*

    A1: *Destruction of habitat*

D 🎧 1.14 Look at the notes for the Q&A session. Notice the format. Then listen and complete the notes *only* for the questions (Q1–Q4).

Dusky Seaside Sparrow (DSS)   *extinction?*

Q1: _What caused them to go extinct?_

A1: Basic cause: _____ *Habitat of destruction*
    ₁

DSS only on Merritt Isl. in FL. Lots of wetlands & mosquitoes

Chems used _Wipe out_ mosqs. Chems killed ↑ DSS
           ₂

Wtlnds modified. No longr _suitable habitat_ for DSS. Died out
                          ₃

Q2: _Are there any lessons we can take away?_

A2: Yes. Must protect animals & their _habitat_

The 1973 Endangered _Species Act_ (ESA) protects both
                     ₅   ₄

Ex: steelhead trout & Columbia Riv. both protected

Q3: _How can we protect large areas like rivers and forests?_

A3: ESA diffclt to fully _enforced_
                         ₆

Ongoing conflict betw. _landowners_ & govt *land owners*
                        ₇

Ex: gray wolf

   Once common in N. Am.; 1930s—nearly wiped out

   1973, wolves protected by ESA → ban on _hunting wolves_
                                                      ₈

   Ranchers want right to shoot wolves that threaten their anmls

Q4: _Is the law working?_

A4: Situation of endangrd animals is _worse_ now vs. 1973
                                     ₉

Now >1,400 in U.S. on endangrd list

39 spec. removed—only 14 recovrd, 9 extinct, others = mistake

Meanwhile, _another 300_ more species to be added to list
           ₁₀

E 🎧 1.14 Listen again and complete the notes for the answers (A1–A4). Write no more than two words or a number for each blank.

AFTER LISTENING

1973 The Endangered Species Act

F Work with a partner. What are some reasons we should care about the extinction of species? *because all life on earth is interconnected. If living connections are broken, then whole eco system are broken, this means humanity could be in jeopardy. The diversity of animal and plant life provide us with many of our life - saving medicines. Everything living has a connection with each other!*

A Speaking

BRAINSTORMING **A** Work in a small group. Look at the list of different habitats. Brainstorm examples of plants and animals that live in each one and the dangers that they may face. Use the expressions in the skill box to suggest ideas. Complete the chart.

Habitat	Plants and Animals	Dangers
polar	polar bear	hunting – climate change
desert	varang	rod buck
rainforest	jaguar .	hunting – black market
ocean	whale	hunting – pollution ocean

пустыня (next to desert)
Тропич. леса – (next to rainforest)

B With your group, have a discussion about the dangers you wrote in exercise A and what the animals might do when faced with such dangers.

A: *Melting ice can threaten animals in a polar habitat—polar bears, for example.*
B: *I agree. I think it forces the bears to swim long distances when they hunt in the open ocean because there's no ice to rest on.*

▼ **A young polar bear leaps between ice floes in the Barents Sea, Svalbard, Norway.**

лунг / *прыгает* / *по глыбам* (handwritten notes)
Швицберг / *заставляет* (handwritten notes)

We use adjective clauses, also called relative clauses, to give more information about a noun. The adjective clause usually comes after the noun it is modifying. An adjective clause is introduced by a relative pronoun. *Who, whom,* and *that* are used for people. *Which* and *that* are used for things. In essential adjective clauses, *that* is preferred. *Whose* is used for possessives.

Essential adjective clauses provide information that is necessary to identify a noun. The information is not optional, and commas are *not* used to separate the clause.

> The birds **that are on the fence** are wrens.
> The scientist **who did the research** is available to answer questions.

When the relative pronoun is the subject of the clause, it is followed by a <u>verb</u>.

> We saw a sparrow **that <u>was eating</u>** crumbs on the sidewalk.

When the relative pronoun is the object of the clause, it is followed by a <u>subject + verb</u>. The relative pronoun is optional in this case.

> The birds **<u>(that)</u> we see** in our yard a lot are finches.

Whose + noun is used to indicate possession.

> The birds **<u>whose habitat</u> was destroyed** are at risk of extinction.

C Work with a partner. Combine the sentences into one, adding an adjective clause after the underlined noun.

1. The police initiated an <u>investigation</u>. It led to several arrests.
2. The <u>woman</u> is an advocate for protecting wildlife. She's speaking tonight.
3. I know a <u>man</u>. He keeps two tigers as pets.
4. I think it was a <u>black bear</u>. It was to blame for all the tree damage.
5. There are many <u>people</u>. They care about endangered species.
6. The dodo was a <u>flightless bird</u>. It was wiped out in the 17th century.
7. Irresponsible <u>actions</u> should be fined. They harm wildlife.
8. Greenpeace is an environmental <u>group</u>. Its mission is to protect animal habitats.
9. The <u>wolves</u> are thriving. The government introduced them to this area.
10. The <u>tree</u> was over 200 years old. The environmentalists saved it.

D Complete these sentences with your own ideas. Use essential adjective clauses. Then share your sentences with a partner and explain your ideas.

PERSONALIZING

1. I'm fascinated by animals that _____.

2. I really admire people who _____.

3. Let me tell you about the time that _____.

4. I saw a video that _____.

5. I know someone whose _____.

6. The teacher _____ made the students laugh.

🎧 1.15 The letter *s* at the end of nouns, verbs, and possessives is pronounced in three ways. If you put your hand on your throat and say *zeeeee*, you should feel a vibration. This is a voiced sound. If you put your hand on your throat and say *ssssss*, there is no vibration. This is a voiceless sound.

• After voiced consonants and all vowels, *s* is pronounced /z/:
    bir**ds**, mosquit**oes**, chemica**ls**

• After voiceless consonants, *s* is pronounced /s/:
    sto**ps**, resul**ts**, photogra**phs**

• After words ending in *ss, sh, ch, ce, se, ge, x,* or *z, s* is pronounced /əz/ or /ɪz/:
    circumstanc**es**, ranch**es**, wish**es**

When a word ending in *s* is followed by a word that starts with a vowel, the two words are linked.

    stop**s** *a*head   Endangered Specie**s** *A*ct   wishe**s** *o*f ranchers

---

E How is the final *s* pronounced in each word? Check (✓) the correct sound.

	/s/	/z/	/əz/			/s/	/z/	/əz/
1. hacks	✓	☐	☐		5. fifths	✓	☐	☐
2. lambs	☐	✓	☐		6. sparrows	☐	✓	☐
3. causes	☐	☐	✓		7. inboxes	☐	☐	✓
4. whales	☐	✓	☐		8. tongues	☐	✓	☐

F 🎧 1.16 Listen and check your answers in exercise E. Then listen again and repeat the words you hear.

G 🎧 1.17 Draw a link between the words with a final *s* and the next word with a vowel. Then, with a partner, practice saying the phrases. Listen and check your pronunciation. Then take turns making statements with the phrases.

> *Tourists in cities like to go shopping and visit museums.*

1. tourists in cities
2. animals in movies
3. causes of extinction
4. parks in cities
5. whales and dolphins

6. kids and pets
7. images in ads
8. ponds and lakes
9. habitats in danger
10. species under protection

LESSON TASK Discussing Environmental Impact

A Read the description of the imaginary *Pristine Island*. Why do you think the land birds are decreasing? Why are the trees endangered? Tell a partner your ideas.

CRITICAL THINKING: MAKING INFERENCES

Herpouyrui

умеренный

Pristine Island is a small, undeveloped island. It has several beautiful beaches that are home to sea turtles. Wandering around the island are groups of deer, and a moderate but decreasing number of land birds live there as well. There is also a species of endangered trees scattered throughout the island.

B Work in a small group. Imagine that you are in charge of developing Pristine Island for residences and businesses, and you want to impact wildlife as little as possible. Discuss how the factors in the chart could impact wildlife. Write notes in the chart.

BRAINSTORMING

Type of Development	Impact on Wildlife
new roads	loss of habitat,
tourists on beaches	pollution, loss of habitat, desease
residential areas	loss of habidat, hunting, paching, pollution,
high-rise hotels	

A: *I'm concerned that animals could be hit by cars on the new roads.*
B: *That's true. The deer would probably be crossing the roads all day.*
C: *Also, when building roads, we might have to cut down some trees.*

C Work with your group. Discuss solutions to the issues you identified above. Choose three that you think could be the most effective, and share them with the class.

CRITICAL THINKING: APPLYING

> *To help minimize the impact of car accidents on deer, we will add deer-crossing signs on all major roads.*

Issue strict laws for environmental pollution.
Toughen laws for poaching.
Control the flow of tourists monthly

Video

Mugger crocodiles are native to India and surrounding countries and can grow up to 16.4 feet (5 meters) in length.

Hope for the Mugger Crocodile

Индийский крокодил.

BEFORE VIEWING

PREDICTING

A Look at the photo and read the caption. What do you think is the biggest problem for mugger crocodiles? Discuss your predictions with your class.

MEANING FROM CONTEXT

B Use the context to choose the correct definition of the **bold** word or phrase in these sentences from the video.

1. Crocs live in wetlands, but most of India's swamps and riversides are now rice fields and farms. So crocs have lost **virtually** all their habitat.
   a. almost   b. not real   c. wholly   d. approximately

2. Man, this place is absolutely **teeming with** crocodiles. I just counted 140 crocodiles. Probably give or take 20 or 30.
   a. working with   b. playing with   c. filled with   d. empty of

3. But when mating season approaches, they're also intensely **territorial**, and any spot with deep water is worth fighting for.
   a. on land   b. global   c. shy   d. protective

4. Contrary to popular legend, muggers are for the most part pretty **laid-back**, sociable animals. In fact, they spend much of their time just basking in the sun.
   a. relaxed   b. happy   c. shy   d. aggressive

WHILE VIEWING

C ▶ **1.3** Watch the beginning of the video. Complete the sentences with words from the box.

habitat	threaten	to blame	captive

1. Human population growth is ___to blame___ for animals' problems.
2. Growing human populations ___threaten___ crocodiles.
3. Crocodiles have lost their ___habitat___ to rice fields and farms.
4. Madras Crocodile Bank has the world's largest ___captive___ population of muggers.

D ▶ **1.4** Watch the next section of the video. Read the statements. Choose T for *True*, F for *False*, or NG for information *Not Given*.

1. The mugger has nearly been wiped out from Iran to Myanmar. (T) F NG
2. Muggers have opportunities for success in the wild outside Sri Lanka. T (F) NG
3. Muggers live in pools once used in agriculture. (T) F NG
4. The muggers seem to be thriving where Whitaker visited. (T) F NG
5. The park asked Whitaker to find out the status of the muggers. T F (NG) *NOT Given*
6. Whitaker thought finding one small crocodile was a bad sign. T (F) NG

E With your partner, discuss your answers to exercise A. Were your predictions correct?

F ▶ **1.5** Watch the rest of the video and take notes. Then work with a partner and answer the questions.

1. What kind of conditions were the animals experiencing at the time of Whitaker's visit?
2. Why do animals coming close to the water to drink need to stay alert?
3. Why is Whitaker observing the muggers at night? What does he do as he observes them?
4. Why do the males fight? Are many of them killed?

AFTER VIEWING

G Work in a small group. Discuss the questions.

1. Large crocodiles can be quite dangerous to humans. Why do you think Rom Whitaker works so hard to save them?
2. What are some of the similarities and differences between the situation of these mugger crocodiles and the endangered species discussed in the Q&A session you heard in Lesson A?
3. After watching this video, do you think mugger crocodiles can look forward to a bright future in Sri Lanka? Why or why not?

B | Vocabulary

A 🎧 1.18 Read and listen to the article. Notice each word or phrase in **blue** and think about its meaning.

THE YELLOWSTONE WOLF PROJECT

Wolves were once common throughout North America, but by the mid-1930s, most had been killed. In 1995, wildlife **authorities** in the United States and Canada **initiated** a program of capturing wolves in Canada and freeing them in Yellowstone National Park. This program, known as the Yellowstone Wolf Project, cost only $267,000 in government funds. It was a huge success. Today, the Yellowstone wolf population has recovered and reached a **sustainable** level.

Contrary to the wishes of many farmers and ranchers, wolf populations have also been recovering in other parts of the western United States. As the number of wolves has grown, they have become the focus of bitter **controversy**. It is **undeniable** that wolves occasionally kill sheep, cattle, and other farm animals, and farmers and ranchers naturally feel authorities are **neglecting** their rights.

On the other hand, these efficient **predators** help control populations of the animals they **prey on**, such as elk, moose, and deer. The presence of wolves also brings financial benefits to Yellowstone Park. Tens of thousands of tourists visit annually to see them. These tourists provide money for the **upkeep** of the park. Tourists also contribute about $35 million a year to the area around the park. There are strong feelings on both sides, and the Yellowstone Wolf Project will no doubt continue to be the focus of public debate for years to come.

Wolves in Yellowstone National Park, USA

B Match each word or phrase with its definition.

1. ___g___ authorities (n)
2. ___j___ contrary to (adj phr)
3. ___i___ controversy (n)
4. ___f___ initiated (v)
5. ___e___ neglecting (v)
6. ___b___ predators (n)
7. ___h___ prey on (v phr)
8. ___d___ sustainable (adj)
9. ___c___ undeniable (adj)
10. ___a___ upkeep (n)

a. maintaining something in good condition

b. animals that kill and eat other animals

c. certain; beyond any doubt or question

d. able to stay at a certain level or in a certain condition

e. not giving something the attention it deserves

f. started a process or action

g. people who have the power to make decisions and to make sure that laws are obeyed

h. to hunt, kill, and eat (as a regular food source)

i. serious and public disagreement

j. different from; opposite

C 🎧 1.19 Read the statements. Then listen to a representative of an environmental organization calling someone to ask for a donation. Write T for *True* or F for *False*.

1. _____ The program to save great whites has been going on for a long time.

2. _____ Great white sharks don't attack humans every year.

3. _____ People think the sharks' natural behavior is to hunt humans.

4. _____ The number of great white sharks is expected to increase over time.

5. _____ Friends of Wildlife assists African officials with policy planning.

6. _____ Friends of Wildlife helps work out conflicts related to animal rights.

7. _____ Friends of Wildlife serves both animals in the wild and in zoos.

8. _____ Friends of Wildlife offers zoos financial support to maintain facilities.

D Work in a small group. Discuss the questions.

CRITICAL THINKING: REFLECTING

1. In many places in the United States, wolves are protected by the Endangered Species Act. If wolf populations have recovered, should they continue to be protected by the law? Explain.

2. If a wolf or another protected predator attacks a farmer's animals, should the farmer have the right to kill the predator? Explain.

3. Do you think the government should pay farmers or ranchers whose animals are killed by wolves or other protected predators? Explain.

4. If an organization like the Friends of Wildlife called you asking for a donation to help great white sharks, how would you react? Explain.

Listening A Debate on Legalized Hunting

BEFORE LISTENING

LISTENING SKILL Activating Prior Knowledge

Studies show that having some prior knowledge about a topic can improve your listening comprehension. In a classroom setting, you can activate your prior knowledge before listening by:

- asking yourself or others *wh-* questions about the topic
- discussing what you already know about the topic
- predicting the kind of information the speaker will talk about
- looking at any accompanying visuals such as photos, charts, or diagrams

PRIOR KNOWLEDGE **A** Work in a small group. Discuss the questions.

1. Why do people hunt? What animals do people typically hunt?
2. Have you ever gone hunting? If so, did you like it? If not, would you try it? Explain.
3. What kinds of information do you think the speakers will discuss in the debate?

WHILE LISTENING

PREVIEWING **B** 🎧 1.20 Listen to the introduction to a student debate about legalized hunting. Are Raoul and Yumi for or against legalized hunting? Complete the sentences.

1. _____Yumi_____ / nobody is arguing in favor of legalized hunting.
2. _____Raoul_____ is arguing against legalized hunting.

Hunters and their dogs at the Elkridge Hartford Hunt Club in Maryland, USA

CRITICAL THINKING   Evaluating Arguments in a Debate

In a debate, speakers take turns presenting their arguments and supporting them. Each speaker also provides information against the opposing arguments or shows that those arguments are incorrect, incomplete, or illogical. This is called _refuting an argument_. To evaluate a debate, think about which speaker presented stronger ideas.

C   🎧 1.21   Listen to the whole debate. Take notes on the speakers' arguments only. (You will listen for the opposing arguments in exercise D.)

NOTE TAKING

1. Yumi's 1st argument: Hunting helps control the populations of animals such as deer.

   Raoul's opposing argument: Deer populations become too large because hunters kill off their natural predators (wolves, mountain lions).

2. Yumi's 2nd argument: hunting supports wildlife conservation through sale of stamps

   Raoul's opposing argument: Money can be raised by having tourists pay to visit an observe animals in natural habitats

3. Raoul's 1st argument: Hunting is cruel. (Hectokui)

   Yumi's opposing argument: Cattle also suffer when killed for meat.

4. Raoul's 2nd argument: There are a lot of illegal/irresponsible hunters.

   Yumi's opposing argument: 90% of hunters follow the laws. (violations are rare) (pegkui)

D   🎧 1.21   Listen again. Now take notes on the speakers' opposing arguments.

NOTE TAKING

AFTER LISTENING

E   With a partner, compare your notes above. Restate the arguments for and against hunting in your own words.

F   Refer back to the debate. Which speaker presented the stronger arguments and made more effective opposing arguments? Explain your opinion to your partner.

CRITICAL THINKING: EVALUATING

Speaking

SPEAKING SKILL Responding to an Argument

There are specific ways to respond to an argument in a debate or conversation. First, you should acknowledge that you have heard the other speaker's argument. Then you should signal that you have a different point of view, followed by your response, or refutation.

Here are some expressions you can use to respond to an argument.

Yes, but . . .	*That's a good argument, but . . .*
That's possible, but . . .	*That may be true, but (on the other hand) . . .*
OK, but . . .	*You're right that . . .; however, . . .*

A 🎧 **1.22** In the debate about hunting, the speakers used a number of expressions for responding to and refuting an argument. Listen and fill in the expressions you hear.

1. **Yumi:** So, for example, without hunting, deer populations would grow too large and no longer be sustainable. They'd eat all the available plants and, as a result, many animals would starve because there wouldn't be enough food for them.

   Raoul: _____ I think you're neglecting an important point.

2. **Raoul:** So, instead of allowing humans to hunt, we should allow populations of meat-eating predators to recover.

   Yumi: _____ don't forget that wolves and mountain lions don't just prey on deer and elk.

3. **Raoul:** There was also this case in Shenandoah National Park in Virginia recently where authorities caught a group of hunters who were shooting black bears and selling their body parts for use in medicines.

   Yumi: _____ those kinds of violations occur; _____ , they are rare.

RESPONDING TO
AN ARGUMENT

B Read the statements below. Tell a partner whether you agree or disagree with each and why. If you disagree with your partner, use an expression from the skill box above to respond to your partner's argument with an opposing idea.

A: *I agree that humans have always been hunters. Hunting and killing animals is natural for us.*
B: *That may be true, but modern humans can satisfy their desire to hunt through sports, business, or games.*

1. Humans have always been hunters. Hunting and killing animals is natural for us.
2. We should impose a ban on fishing for a few years to allow fish populations to recover.
3. Just as humans have rights, animals have rights, too.
4. The government does not have the right to stop people from hunting on their own land.
5. It doesn't matter that the dusky seaside sparrow became extinct. It doesn't make any difference in our lives.
6. Parents should teach their children about animal rights.

C Work with a partner. Look at the chart about revenues for wildlife protection in the United States. Then answer the questions.

1. How much revenue do states bring in? How much does the federal government bring in? Is this what you would expect? Explain.

2. How much revenue is made from hunting and fishing licenses? How is it used? What is one way the money might be used to improve these habitats?

3. What is the source of funds for the Federal Aid in Sport Fish and Wildlife Restoration programs? Give an example of an item that would be taxed with this type of tax.

4. At what age are waterfowl hunters required to purchase duck stamps? Do you agree with this age requirement? Explain.

5. In your own words, summarize the information this chart shows.

REVENUE FOR WILDLIFE PROTECTION

STATES

Hunting and fishing licenses — **$1.22 billion**

Helps state wildlife agencies acquire, maintain, and improve fish and wildlife habitat through the North American Wetlands Conservation Act and other programs.

Excise taxes — **$616 million**

on fishing and hunting equipment and motor-boat fuels

Helps state agencies buy land and improve fish and wildlife habitat through the Federal Aid in Sport Fish and Wildlife Restoration programs.

Licenses and excise taxes make up about **75%** of state wildlife agencies' revenue.

FEDERAL

Duck Stamps — **$24 million**

Required of waterfowl hunters age 16 and older

Purchases wetland habitat for the National Wildlife Refuge System through the Migratory Bird Conservation Fund. Sales since 1934 exceed $700 million, and 5.2 million acres have beed preserved.

SOURCES: U.S. FISH AND WILDLIFE SERVICE, CHARITY NAVIGATOR

An Amur Tiger passes through the Big Cat Crossing at the Philadelphia Zoo, Pennsylvania, USA.

FINAL TASK A Debate on Wild Animals in Zoos

> You will evaluate arguments for and against keeping wild animals in zoos. Then you will organize and prepare for a debate on this issue.

CRITICAL THINKING:
EVALUATING

A Read the statements. Write F if the argument is *for* keeping animals in zoos and A if it is *against* keeping animals in zoos.

1. _____ Animals do not have rights, so it is acceptable to keep them in zoos.

2. _____ Zoos educate people about how to protect endangered species.

3. _____ In many zoos, animals are kept in small cages and cannot move around.

4. _____ It costs a lot of money to keep animals in zoos.

5. _____ It is fun to see interesting and unusual animals in zoos.

6. _____ Zoos protect animals that are hunted illegally, such as rhinos and elephants.

7. _____ People can be educated about animals without keeping them in zoos.

8. _____ The artificial environment is stressful for many animals. They often stop eating.

RESPONDING TO AN
ARGUMENT

B With a partner, take turns responding to the statements in exercise A. Use expressions for responding to an argument from the Speaking Skill box.

A: *Animals do not have rights, so it is acceptable to keep them in zoos.*
B: *Yes, but is it so clear that animals don't have rights? Some people think they do.*

C Your teacher will instruct you to prepare arguments either for or against keeping animals in zoos. Write notes to support your position. Try to predict the arguments the other speaker will make, and think about how you will respond to them.

D Your teacher will pair you with a student who prepared the opposite side of the issue. You will hold a three to five minute debate in front of the class or a small group. The student who speaks in favor of zoos should begin.

REFLECTION

1. What methods of activating prior knowledge work best for you?

_____

_____

2. Did the information you learned in this unit change your mind about protecting the wild? If so, how?

_____

_____

3. Here are the vocabulary words and phrases from the unit. Check (✔) the ones you can use.

☐ authority AWL   ☐ initiate AWL   ☐ sustainable AWL

☐ be to blame   ☐ modify AWL   ☐ threaten

☐ contrary to AWL   ☐ neglect   ☐ thrive

☐ controversy AWL   ☐ ongoing AWL   ☐ undeniable AWL

☐ extinct   ☐ predator   ☐ upkeep

☐ habitat   ☐ prey on   ☐ wipe out

☐ impose AWL   ☐ status AWL

BEAUTY AND APPEARANCE 3

A model on the runway during the Arts University Bournemouth show in London, England.

ACADEMIC SKILLS

LISTENING   Listening for Specific Information
            Using an Outline
SPEAKING   Paraphrasing
            Intonation for Clarification
CRITICAL THINKING   Interpreting a Bar Graph

THINK AND DISCUSS

1 Look at the photo and read the caption. Why do you think people go to fashion shows?
2 How would you describe the items this man is wearing?
3 What surprises or interests you about this photo?

Look at the photo and read the information. Then discuss the questions.

1. Why do you think the man is getting a shave? Is this a common ritual in your country?

2. Do you agree with the top reasons for trying to look good? Do you think the gender differences are accurate?

3. Do you think the reasons for trying to look good change with age? With culture?

4. What other reasons are there for trying to look good?

LOOKING GOOD

How much of a person's beauty is based on physical appearance? On personality? How much depends on what a person wears? Is there a universal standard of beauty, or do these standards vary from country to country? One certainty is that looking good matters, and rituals like the one in the photo can be found everywhere.

Ali Marili gives a man a shave in his barbershop in Kilis, Turkey. Marili's father opened the shop in 1942, and his son uses the same traditional methods today.

Top three reasons for trying to look good*

To feel good about myself

60%

♂ 52% 67% ♀

To make a good impression on people I meet for the first time

44%

♂ 44% 45% ♀

To set a good example for my children

40%

♂ 39% 41% ♀

Weekly time spent on personal grooming*

4.0 h

♂ 3.2 h 4.9 h ♀

*Average across 22 countries

A Vocabulary

A 🎧 **1.23** Read and listen to the article. Notice each word in **blue** and think about its meaning.

HIGH-FASHION MODELING

In the world of high-fashion modeling, you don't see the variations in body type that you find with **random** people on the street. Designers have traditionally shown a **distinct** preference for tall and thin runway models to show off their latest creations. However, images of extremely thin models as seen in fashion shows and magazines can be **alarming** for some people. Some models have a height-to-weight **ratio** that is unhealthy. For example, a model might be around five feet nine inches (175 centimeters) tall but weigh only 110 pounds (50 kilograms).

The modeling business is slowly **evolving**, and the type of model that designers prefer is changing, too. The high-fashion modeling profession is no longer **exclusively** for the thinnest of the thin. The good news is that in recent years, healthy-looking models have also been seen strolling down runways. In some countries—Australia, for example—the government has even asked fashion designers and magazines to stop hiring **excessively** thin models for fashion shows and photo shoots. Now, designers **envision** people with various body types wearing their clothing. This informs their designs and is reflected in the models we are starting to see. As a result, how people **perceive** fashion models and their opinion of what **constitutes** beauty are starting to change.

A model walks down a runway at a fashion show.

B Write each word in **blue** from exercise A next to its definition.

1. _envision_ (v) to have or form a mental picture
2. _evolving_ (v) gradually changing and developing
3. _exclusively_ (adv) in a limited way
4. _ratio_ (n) a proportion, e.g., 2:1
5. _excessively_ (adv) more than is necessary, normal, or desirable
6. _constitutes_ (v) composes or forms
7. _alarming_ (adj) shocking or frightening
8. _random_ (adj) chosen without a method or plan
9. _distinct_ (adj) clear
10. _perceive_ (v) to recognize; be aware of

C Complete the sentences with the correct form (noun, verb, adjective, or adverb) of the word in parentheses. If necessary, use a dictionary.

1. Jia was _alarmed_ when she discovered a gray hair on her head. (alarming)

2. That black hat looks _distinctly_ better on you than the blue one. (distinct)

3. The designer said the dress wasn't as stylish as what she _envisined_. (envision)

4. There has been an _evolution_ of workplace fashion from formal to casual. (evolve)

5. Experts warn that the _excessiveness_ use of makeup can be quite unhealthy. (excessively)

6. Members of our shopping club receive _exclusive_ discounts. (exclusively)

7. There is a general _perception_ that Paris is the world capital of fashion. (perceive)

8. The winners were _randomly_ selected from the audience. (random)

D Work with a partner. Choose the word that forms a collocation with the vocabulary word in **bold** and the underlined words.

1. I never plan what I'm going to wear. I just <u>choose</u> my clothes (<u>at</u> / for) **random**.
2. The **ratio** (for / <u>of</u>) women <u>to</u> men in my class is 2 to 1.
3. Men's shirts <u>are</u> **distinct** (to / <u>from</u>) women's as the buttons are on opposite sides.
4. These beauty products <u>are</u> **exclusively** (<u>for</u> / to) our loyal customers.
5. The increase in extreme dieting is an **alarming** (<u>trend</u> / movement).
6. His small business gradually **evolved** (to / <u>into</u>) a great fashion company.
7. Men who wear neckties <u>are</u> **perceived** (in / <u>as</u>) being professional.
8. Those new fashions <u>are</u> **excessively** (beautiful / <u>expensive</u>).

E Work with a partner. Take turns using the collocations in exercise D to say sentences.

> *I don't think it's a good idea to choose your college major at random.*

F Work in a small group. Discuss the questions.

CRITICAL THINKING: REFLECTING

1. If you asked a random teenager on the street what constitutes beauty, what might he or she say? What celebrities might the teen envision?
2. If you knew someone who was excessively concerned with physical appearance, what could you say to convince him or her that attractiveness is not exclusively physical?
3. Are there any modern trends that you find alarming? Explain.
4. Society's perception of beauty always seems to be evolving, at least in certain ways. What evidence can you give of this?
5. What makes a person look distinctive?

BEAUTY AND APPEARANCE **45**

A Listening A News Report on Perceptions of Beauty

BEFORE LISTENING

CRITICAL THINKING:
EVALUATING

A With a partner, discuss the questions.

1. Look at the two rows of photos. These photos were shown to people who participated in a study on beauty. In each row, select the photo that you think shows the most beautiful face. Do you and your partner agree?

2. Look at the photos again. According to researchers, most people would choose Photo 4 and Photo 9 as the most beautiful faces. Why do you think most people chose these photos?

prg.

Row A

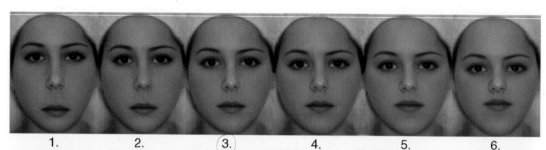

1.   2.   ③.   4.   5.   6.

Row B

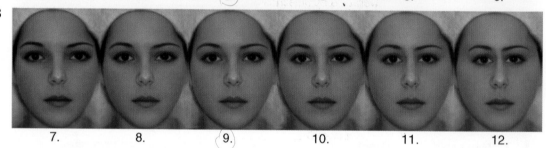

7.   8.   ⑨.   10.   11.   12.

WHILE LISTENING

LISTENING FOR
MAIN IDEAS

B 🎧 1.24 ▶ 1.6 Listen to a news report. Match each scientist or group of scientists to their research result.

Scientists	Research Results
1. _b_ Judith Langlois	a. Men's ideas about beauty and attractiveness evolved over thousands of years.
2. _c_ Pamela M. Pallett/ Stephen Link/Kang Lee	b. Symmetry is a key part of what makes a face beautiful.
3. _d_ Victor Johnston/David Perrett	c. There is a "golden ratio" for the ideal distance between the eyes, the mouth, and the edge of the face.
4. _a_ Don Symons	d. Men prefer large eyes, full lips, and a small nose and chin.

Using an outline as you listen can help you organize main ideas and details. A formal outline looks like the outline in exercise C below. Notice how the outline shows the structure of the talk, with roman numerals for main ideas, capital letters for supporting ideas, and numbers for details.

C 🎧 1.24 Listen again and take notes to complete the outline. Write one word only in each blank.

NOTE TAKING

I. Intro: What is beauty?

   A. Does each person perceive beauty differently?

   B. Does social/cultrl __background__ influence ideas?
                     1

II. Studies on __beauty__
          2

   A. Langlois

      1. ppl think __average__ –looking faces are beautfl
                   3

      2. symmetrical faces are beautfl

         a. far from average & symmetrical = __alarming__ to observers
                                    4

   B. Pallett, Link & Lee—discovered " __golden__ ratio"
                          край 5

      1. ideal dist. btwn eyes, mouth & edge of face

      2. dist. fr eyes to mouth = 36% __lech__ of face
                                6

   C. Johnston & Perrett—men's prefs

      1. lg. eyes, full lips, sm. nose & __chin__
                              7

      2. Symons—lg. eyes/lips = health & hlthy babies

   D. not all anthroplgsts agree about one __standed idea__ of beauty
                                 8

      1. diff cultrs have diff ideas about beauty

      2. crossed eyes, __shin scars__ & tattooed lips —all beaut.
                       9

III. Conclusion: Beauty not exclusively in eye of beholder

   A. some aspects of beauty are __universal__, e.g., "gldn ratio"
                             10

   B. ppl fr. same cultr see beauty in similar ways

Each person has his own idea of beauty.
What one person finds beautiful may not appeal to another.

AFTER LISTENING

beauty is created by observers.

D Work in a small group. Discuss the questions.

PERSONALIZING

1. Do you agree or disagree that "beauty is in the eye of the beholder"? Explain.

2. Scientists believe that a beautiful face is a symmetrical face. What other features make a face beautiful to you? *a smiling face. happy face.*

3. The report said that perceptions of beauty vary from culture to culture. What are some examples of how your perception of beauty might vary from those in other cultures?

background / average / golden / standed idea
beauty / alarming / of the lip / skin scars
chin / universal.

A Speaking

A 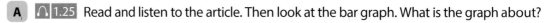 🎧 **1.25** Read and listen to the article. Then look at the bar graph. What is the graph about?

THE GROWING POPULARITY OF COSMETIC SURGERY

If you think the risks of cosmetic surgery are alarming, there's good news! Cosmetic procedures are evolving; many are not excessively dangerous, and some are quite safe. You may be able to get the new look you envision with nonsurgical procedures like tissue fillers and laser treatments, which now constitute 82 percent of cosmetic procedures in the United States. Once exclusively for the rich and famous, cosmetic procedures are being chosen by more people every year.

There is a distinct difference in the way people in different cultures perceive beauty, but cosmetic surgery is a common choice in many parts of the world. The graph Top Markets for Cosmetic Procedures compares 20 countries by procedures per capita[1], total number of procedures, and the ratio of surgical to nonsurgical procedures.

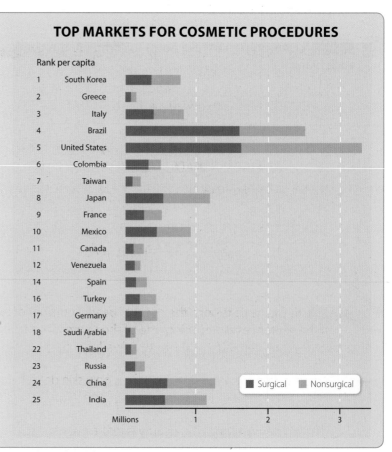

TOP MARKETS FOR COSMETIC PROCEDURES

[1] **per capita** (adj): per person relative to the total population

---

CRITICAL THINKING Interpreting a Bar Graph

To understand a bar graph, it's important to study the following features:

- **the title:** tells you what the graph is about
- **labels:** tell you what the bars or numbers represent
- **the scale:** tells you the unit of measurement
- **color coding/key:** shows you what different colors mean

CRITICAL THINKING:
INTERPRETING A
BAR GRAPH

B Work with a partner. Answer the questions about the bar graph above.

1. What is the title of the graph?
2. Look at the labels. What do the bars represent?
3. How many countries have more than a million cosmetic procedures?
4. Look at the color coding and the key. What do the colors represent?
5. Which country has the highest number of cosmetic procedures per capita? Which has the lowest?
6. What do you find interesting or surprising about the information in the graph?

C Work with a partner. Discuss the questions.

PERSONALIZING

1. Is it a positive trend that cosmetic procedures are now more affordable? Explain.
   споообсТвобало
2. How has technology contributed to the evolution of cosmetic surgery?   *to sing. side effects.*
3. Do you think the risks of cosmetic surgery are alarming? Explain.
4. What are some ways to stay young and healthy looking that avoid the need for cosmetic procedures?   *To eat healthy food and to do exercises.*

SPEAKING SKILL Paraphrasing

When you paraphrase, you express something you said in a different way. Paraphrasing allows you to restate, in a clearer way, information that may be new or difficult for listeners to understand.

> *It's said that beauty lies in the eye of the beholder, yet the opposite seems to be true.* **What I mean by that is people within a culture usually have similar ideas about beauty.**

Here are some expressions you can use to paraphrase information.

I mean . . .	*Let me put it another way.*
In other words, . . .	*To put it another way, . . .*
That is (to say), . . .	*What I mean by that is . . .*

D 🎧 1.26 In the news report, the speaker used a number of expressions to paraphrase. Read the sentences aloud using one of the expressions from the skill box. Then listen and write the expressions that were actually used.

PARAPHRASING

1. An oft-quoted expression is, "Beauty is only skin deep." *In other words*, someone can be beautiful on the outside but be mean or unpleasant on the inside.

2. Another famous saying is, "Beauty is in the eye of the beholder." *That is to say*, each person's idea of beauty is different.

3. In addition, her research shows that a beautiful face is a symmetrical face. *To put it another way*, if both sides of the face are exactly the same, we consider a person beautiful.

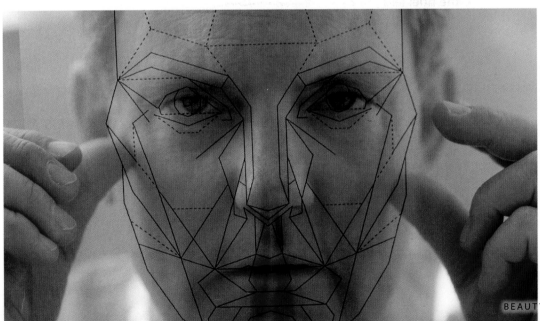

◄ **Cosmetic surgeon Dr. Marquardt uses a grid to ensure facial symmetry for his patients.**

People who smile are often perceived as more attractive.

CRITICAL THINKING: INTERPRETING

E Read these quotations about beauty. In your own words, write what each means.

1. Beauty is not in the face; beauty is a light in the heart. —Kahlil Gibran

   _____

   _____

2. It matters more what's in a woman's face than what's on it. —Claudette Colbert

   _____

   _____

3. I've never seen a smiling face that was not beautiful. —Author Unknown

   _____

   _____

4. Time is a great healer but a poor beautician.[1] —Lucille S. Harper

   _____

   _____

   [1] **beautician (n):** a person who cuts hair and performs other beauty-related tasks for people

PARAPHRASING

F Work with a partner. Take turns reading the quotations in exercise E. Explain each quotation to your partner using a paraphrasing expression from the Speaking Skill box.

LESSON TASK Conducting a Survey

A You are going to conduct a survey about beauty and fashion. Choose four of the
questions below for your survey and write two new questions of your own.

SURVEY QUESTIONS

- Is it better to be beautiful, intelligent, or wealthy? Why do you think so? ✓
- Who do you think is the most beautiful woman alive today? Who is the most
  handsome man alive today?
- What is the minimum age at which people should be allowed to have cosmetic
  surgery?
- What is the most unusual item of clothing you own?
- What do you spend more money on: clothing and beauty supplies, food, or electronics? ✓
- Are there any fashions today that you think are strange? ✓
- *what is ratio of cosmetic operations of men and women?*
- *what consequences of cosmetic operation?*
  negative

EVERYDAY LANGUAGE Conducting a Survey

When you conduct a survey, always be sure to ask politely and to thank your
respondent.

> *Hello! Would you mind answering a few survey questions for me?*
> *Thank you. Now let's move on to the next question.*
> *That's all the questions I have for you today. Thank you for participating in the survey.*
>   *I really appreciate it!*

B Interview three classmates. Ask each classmate your survey questions. Use the
expressions in the Everyday Language box. Take notes on each person's answers.

A: *Is it better to be beautiful, intelligent, or wealthy? Why do you think so?*
B: *Oh, it's definitely better to be intelligent, because beauty is in the eye of the beholder, but
   intelligence isn't based on people's perceptions.* *восприятие*
A: *Interesting. Thank you. Now let's move on to the next question...*

C Work in a small group. Share your survey results. What is interesting or surprising
about the information you heard? How would you answer each question in the survey?
Discuss your thoughts with your group.

CRITICAL THINKING:
APPLYING

> *The people that I surveyed think being intelligent is more important than being beautiful or
  wealthy. I agree with that.*

Video

Skin Mask

A model poses next to a silicone mask of her own face.

BEFORE VIEWING

A Write each word or phrase from the video next to its definition. If necessary, use a dictionary.

| a touch of | conform | master | mold | silicone | special effects |

1. _silicone_ (n) a rubber-like material

2. _mold_ (n) a hollow form into which materials are put to shape objects

3. _conform_ (v) to be similar in form, pattern, or shape

4. _special effect_ (n) sights and sounds that seem real on TV, the radio, and in movies

5. _a touch of_ (n phr) a small amount of something

6. _master_ (adj) main; primary

PREDICTING **B** Look at the photo above and read the caption. This is the skin mask you will see in the video, which was modeled after a real person's face. How do you think the mold was made? Discuss with a partner.

WHILE VIEWING

UNDERSTANDING MAIN IDEAS **C** ▶ 1.7 Watch the video. Check (✓) the two procedures that are shown.

1. ☐ how the material silicone is made
2. ☑ how silicone is used to make a mold
3. ☐ how to choose a model to make a mask
4. ☑ how to make a lifelike mask from a mold
5. ☐ how a lifelike mask is used in special effects

D ▶ 1.7 Watch the video again. Put the steps for making a skin mask in the correct order from 1 to 10.

a. __1__ A cap is placed over the model's hair.

b. __7__ A master mold is prepared.

c. __3__ Artists paint her face in quick-drying silicone.

d. __10__ Makeup, eyebrows, and lashes are added to the skin mask.

e. __8__ Soft silicone is mixed with chemicals, creating a natural color.

f. __6__ The artists create a series of positive and negative masks.

g. __5__ The hardened material comes off, followed by the newly created mold.

h. __9__ The mixture is injected into the master mold.

i. __4__ The model's face is wrapped in plaster bandages. ˈbandijəz y

j. __2__ Vaseline is brushed over her eyebrows and lashes.

AFTER VIEWING

E Work with a partner. Take turns reading the statements from the video. Rephrase them using paraphrasing expressions.

1. "She has to sit motionless for about an hour as the artists brush the icy cold silicone onto her face."
2. "Then the model's face is wrapped in plaster bandages, rather like a living mummy."
3. "A touch of makeup helps bring the skin to life."
4. "The completed mask has all the aspects of real human skin. It has more than just the look. It has the feel."

F Work with a partner. Discuss the questions.

1. Cassandra jokes, "Who said modeling was easy?" What does she mean?
2. Explain how you think special-effects artists choose models to make their skin masks.
3. In Lesson A, you learned that standards of beauty are both universal and cultural. In Lesson B, you will learn about unusual fashions. For fashion to be unusual, it has to differ from standards. What are some fashion standards in your country that are universal? What are some that are cultural?

◀ **The positive cast on the right was made from the negative mold on the left.**

B Vocabulary

A ∩ 1.27 Read and listen to a conversation. Notice each word or phrase in **blue** and think about its meaning.

Customer: Excuse me. What are these shoes made of?

Clerk: They're from an eco-fashion manufacturer that **integrates** natural materials and recycled ones. About half of their materials **are derived from** recycled plastic and metal. As it says on the label, they believe in "the **constructive** use of the waste society produces."

Customer: That's nice. But they're very unusual, aren't they? They look more like a piece of art that you would **exhibit** in a museum than shoes. I mean, they're like something an artist might **daydream** about but that nobody would ever wear in real life.

Clerk: Actually, they're very popular. I bought a pair myself, and they're **unquestionably** the most comfortable pair of shoes I've ever owned.

Customer: Really? Well, comfortable is good, but I do a lot of walking, so I'm not sure they'd be very **practical** for me. I mean, they'd probably fall apart after a week.

Clerk: Not at all. The combination of natural and recycled materials makes them **substantially** stronger than most shoes. Have a seat . . . Now, if you'll just **insert** your right foot in here . . .

Customer: Oh, this is nice! They are comfortable, aren't they? You know, I wasn't going to buy them, but you're very **persuasive**. I think I'll take a pair!

B Write each word or phrase in **blue** from exercise A next to its definition.

1. daydream _____ (v) to lose oneself in pleasant thoughts while awake
2. integrates _____ (v) combines different parts into a united whole
3. substantially _____ (adv) in a large or significant way
4. are derived _____ (v phr) are obtained from a specified source
5. persuasive _____ (adj) able to convince people to do or believe something
6. unquestionably _____ (adv) certainly; beyond doubt
7. insert _____ (v) to put into
8. constructive _____ (adj) promoting improvement
9. practical _____ (adj) useful; capable of being used
10. exhibit _____ (v) to place on public display

C Discuss the questions with a partner.

1. Have you ever received constructive criticism? If yes, what was it?

2. What kinds of exhibitions are you most interested in?

3. What do you sometimes daydream about?

4. What is an example of a piece of clothing that is not practical?

5. What is a situation that requires you to be persuasive?

VOCABULARY SKILL Suffix –ive

The suffix –ive is added to certain verbs to make an adjective. It generally means "doing or tending to do" the action of the verb it is formed from.

> persuasive = persuading, tending to persuade
> attractive = attracting, tending to attract

When adding –ive to a verb, sometimes other changes need to be made.

Example	Rule
affirm → affirm**ative**	ends in m or n: add –ative/-itive
innovat**e** → innovat**ive**	ends in consonant + e: drop e and
defin**e** → defin**itive**	add –ive/–ative/-itive
persua**de** → persua**sive**	irregular form
repe**at** → repe**titive**	irregular form

Check a dictionary if you are not sure of the form.

D Use a verb from the box and the suffix –ive to complete these opinions about fashion. Use a dictionary to help you.

> addict   alternate   construct   decorate   excess   exclude   impress   innovate

1. I think shopping for clothes is _addictive_ —once I start, I can't stop!

2. I think it's more important to look _impressive_ than to feel comfortable.

3. I prefer plain, dark colors and not a lot of _decorative_ designs such as stripes, or flower and animal patterns.

4. I'm always open to criticism about the way I dress, as long as it's _constructive_.

5. I'm into _alternative_ fashion. I think it's boring to look like everyone else.

6. I've seen people wearing a ring on every finger, but I think that's _excessive_.

7. That designer is _innovative_; his clothes are really new and different.

8. Many of the stores in this area are _exclusive_; only the very wealthy shop here.

Listening A Conversation about Unusual Fashions

BEFORE LISTENING

PREDICTING **A** Look at the photos. What do you think these fashion items are? Discuss your ideas with a partner.

1. _antigravity jacket_ _wearable balloon_

2. _Kevlar-_

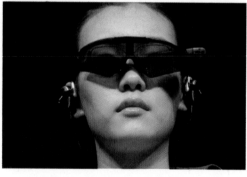

3. _Wearable electronic._

WHILE LISTENING

LISTENING FOR
MAIN IDEAS

B 🎧 1.28 Listen to a conversation between a teenager and her parents. Look back at the photos. Next to each photo, write the name or a brief description of the item.

LISTENING SKILL Listening for Specific Information

Sometimes you need to listen for specific information. When you need to answer a question (during a test, for example), listening to every word can cause you to miss the information you need. Instead, underline and note the key terms related to the information you need. Then listen for those key terms and related words and phrases.

C [🎧 1.28] Read the questions. Notice the underlined key terms in question 1. For questions 2–4, work with a partner to identify and underline the key terms. Then listen again and write your answers, using the underlined terms to guide your listening.

LISTENING FOR SPECIFIC INFORMATION

1. <u>Where</u> was Danish clothing designer <u>Alex Soza</u> when he got the <u>idea</u> for the <u>antigravity jacket</u>? _____

2. When was <u>Kevlar developed</u>? _____

3. <u>How much stronger</u> than <u>steel</u> is <u>spider silk</u>? _____

4. <u>Who provides funds</u> so <u>Ana's friend</u> can <u>develop wearable technology</u>?
   _____

D [🎧 1.28] Listen again and complete the outline. Write one word only in each blank.

NOTE TAKING

I. Antigravity jacket
   A. part ___balloon___ , part jacket today
                1
   B. designer isn't about being ___practical___
                                     2
II. Kevlar: man-made fiber → cloth stronger than steel
   A. used to make ___bullet___-proof vests for police
                       3
   B. used to make ropes for ___ap astronaphts.___
                                4
III. BioSteel: a super-strong fiber
   A. made by inserting spider-silk gene into ___gouts___
                                                5
   B. may be used to pull things up to ___transport___ to space
                                          6
IV. Wearable electronics—integrate ___clothing___ & electrnx
                                      7
   A. Ex.: a jacket w/phone in ___the sleeve___ - рукав
                                 8
   B. Ex: GPS sneakers—to track ___lost___ kids & hikers
                                   9

AFTER LISTENING

E Work with a partner. Discuss the questions.

CRITICAL THINKING: ANALYZING

1. Can you envision any uses for an antigravity jacket, now or in the future? допустимо
2. Goats and spiders are used in the production of BioSteel. Do you think it's acceptable to use animals for the purpose of creating new textiles? Explain.
3. Are there any other uses of GPS sneakers, besides tracking lost people? кроссовки
4. Do you think wearable electronics are a good idea? Why or why not?
5. Which do you think is more profitable: the fashion industry or the electronics industry? Explain.

B Speaking

PRONUNCIATION Intonation for Clarification

🎧 1.29 You can ask for clarification of a term you don't know by simply restating it with a rising intonation. This invites the listener to clarify what he or she meant.

A: *That antigravity jacket was like something out of a science fiction movie.*
B: *Antigravity jacket?*
A: *Yeah. I guess you could say it's . . . it's a wearable balloon.*

A Work with a partner. Take turns making a statement about one of the devices below. Your partner uses intonation to ask for clarification and you respond.

A: *I had no idea that I walked so many miles each week until I got a Fitbit.*
B: *A Fitbit?*
A: *Yeah, a Fitbit. It's a device you wear on your wrist that keeps track of . . .*

Device	Description
Fitbit	a device worn on the wrist that counts the number of steps you take, distance walked, and calories burned
Alexa	a voice-operated personal assistant in an electronic device that can answer questions and do things for you
Ringly	a ring that buzzes when you get a notification on your smartphone from apps like UBER, Slack, Twitter, etc.
Oculus Rift	a helmet that covers your eyes and allows you to "move around" in a virtual world, usually to play 3-D computer games

GRAMMAR FOR SPEAKING Tag Questions

We use tag questions to ask if a statement is correct or if the listener agrees with us. Tag questions are formed by adding a short question (or "tag") to the end of a statement. Affirmative statements have negative tags, and negative statements have affirmative tags.

Tag questions can be confusing to answer. You should respond to the sentence before the tag.

Questions	Responses
That doesn't sound very practical, **does it?**	No, it doesn't. [speaker agrees]
That dog was cute, **wasn't it?**	No, it wasn't. [speaker disagrees]
You haven't worn that before, **have you?**	Yes, I have. [speaker disagrees]
Mom can be pretty persuasive, **can't she?**	Yes, she can. [speaker agrees]

For tag questions, use rising intonation if you aren't sure of the answer and want confirmation or clarification. Use falling intonation if you are sure about the answer and expect the speaker to agree.

B Complete the tag questions. Then ask and answer the questions with a partner, using an appropriate response and intonation.

1. Alex Soza is an imaginative clothing designer, _isn't he?_
2. We've already discussed eco-fashion, _haven't we?_
3. You'd like to learn more about fashion trends, _wouldn't you?_
4. You're not going to wear a wool sweater today, _are you?_
5. It's not possible to make fabric from plastic bottles, _is it?_
6. Ana went to the fashion show with her parents, _didn't she?_
7. You wouldn't wear real animal fur, _would you?_
8. You hadn't heard about Kevlar vests before, _had you?_

FINAL TASK A Presentation about Fashion Trends

> You will give a group presentation about fashion trends in a particular country.

A Work in a small group. First, read the questions in the chart below that will guide your presentation. Then brainstorm fashion trends in a particular city or country, and decide on the location you want to report on. Write it at the top of the chart.

B On your own, research fashion and style trends in your location. Take notes in the chart to help you organize your ideas. Include ideas for visuals.

Location: _____   Ideas for visuals: _____, _____

What types of fabrics are popular?	coton linen paliestra deaim
What clothing fashions are "in"?	jeans fralors t-shirt
How do people wear their hair?	naturally,
What types of shoes do people prefer?	sniekers
What accessories do people like to wear?	silver, gold, rings;
Your own question: _____	

▲ **Young men by Umeda Station in Osaka, Japan**

PRESENTATION SKILL Preparing Visuals for Display

When preparing visuals for a presentation, high-tech options like projectors and slides are nice, but low-tech options like posters and handouts can be just as effective. Remember that the main point of visuals is to add interest and enhance your message. When preparing visuals, ask yourself:

- Is the size of the lettering large enough for everyone to see?
- Is the language clear, correct, brief, and easy to understand?
- Will everyone be able to see the photos and graphics clearly?

ORGANIZING IDEAS **C** In your group, share your notes from exercise B. Prepare a new set of notes in outline form to use during your group's presentation as well as any appropriate visuals. Decide who will present each section and which visuals they will use.

PRESENTING **D** Give your presentation. Afterwards, join with another group. Discuss each group's strengths and give any constructive feedback.

REFLECTION

1. In what situations do you need to paraphrase? What expressions can you use to paraphrase information?

_____

_____

2. What did you learn about beauty, appearance, or clothes that you will apply to your life?

_____

_____

3. Here are the vocabulary words and phrases from the unit. Check (✓) the ones you can use.

- ☐ alarming
- ☐ constitute AWL
- ☐ constructive AWL
- ☐ daydream
- ☐ be derived from AWL
- ☐ distinct AWL

- ☐ envision
- ☐ evolve AWL
- ☐ excessively
- ☐ exclusively AWL
- ☐ exhibit AWL
- ☐ insert AWL
- ☐ integrate AWL

- ☐ perceive AWL
- ☐ persuasive
- ☐ practical
- ☐ random AWL
- ☐ ratio AWL
- ☐ substantially
- ☐ unquestionably

GOING GLOBAL 4

Visual artist Chris Milk hosts the largest collective viewing of virtual reality during his TED Talk in Vancouver, Canada, 2016.

ACADEMIC SKILLS

LISTENING	Listening for Advantages
	Using Columns
SPEAKING	Defining Terms
	Saying Parentheticals
CRITICAL THINKING	Evaluating

THINK AND DISCUSS

1 What do you think these people are seeing or experiencing?

2 How do you think a virtual reality experience is different from usual viewing?

3 What would you like to view with virtual reality glasses?

EXPLORE THE THEME

Look at the photo and read the information. Then discuss the questions.

1. What type of new technology is shown in the photo? How is it useful?
2. What are some other new workplace technologies, and how are they changing the work world?
3. Look at The Future of Work 2020. Rank the drivers from strongest to weakest, in your opinion.
4. Which key skills do you think are most relevant for each driver?

Dmitry Grishin, CEO of Mail.ru, the Russian Internet giant, holding a virtual meeting with his telepresence robots

WORK SKILLS FOR THE FUTURE

The Future of Work 2020

Drivers of Change in the Workplace

данные

| Smart machines and systems | People living longer | Big data | New media | Knowledge sharing | Globally connected world |

ключевые навыки

Key Skills Needed in the Future Workplace

| Creative thinking | Social intelligence | Knowledge of multiple disciplines | Media literacy | Managing mental overload | Computational thinking | Cross-cultural under-standing | Virtual collaboration |

дисциплинс

медиаграмоти. митрси

психит. нагрузк.

вычислительное мышление

межкультурное сотрудничество

A Vocabulary

A 🎧 **2.2** Read and listen to the article. Notice each word or phrase in **blue** and think about its meaning.

GLOBAL EMPLOYMENT TRENDS

Globalization is producing enormous changes in **labor** markets, changes that are creating both winners and losers in the workplace. Here are two areas of change that **pertain to** both employers and employees.

- Advanced technologies, a key **component** of globalization, are more **widespread** than ever before. New developments in technology will continue to **facilitate** tasks in business **sectors** such as architecture and engineering. It is not, however, a **promising** trend for office workers or the administrative sector, where jobs will **inevitably** be lost.

- The globalization of communication means more opportunities to learn via remote sources. Accessing information from global sources can increase a person's career **competence** and earning power. Companies who value their employees and hope to **retain**

Net Employment Forecast by Job Family 2015–2020 / Employees (in thousands)			
−4,759	Office and Administrative	+492	Business and Financial Operations
−1,609	Manufacturing and Production	+416	Management
−497	Construction and Extraction	+405	Computer and Mathematical
−151	Arts, Design, Entertainment, Sports and Media	+339	Architecture and Engineering
−109	Legal	+303	Sales and Related
−40	Installation and Maintenance	+66	Education and Training

them in today's competitive global environment must support and fund learning opportunities for ambitious and motivated workers—or risk losing them!

B Match each word or phrase from exercise A with its definition.

1. ___f___ competence (n)
2. ___j___ component (n)
3. ___h___ facilitate (v)
4. ___g___ inevitably (adv)
5. ___e___ labor (n)
6. ___b___ pertain to (v phr)
7. ___c___ promising (adj)
8. ___d___ retain (v)
9. ___a___ sector (n)
10. ___i___ widespread (adj)

a. area of a society or economy
b. to relate, belong, or apply to
c. showing signs of future success
d. to keep
e. work or employment
f. the ability to do something well
g. certainly, necessarily
h. to make something easier or more efficient
i. existing or happening over a large area
j. a part of a larger whole

C Work in a small group. Look at the information in exercise A. Discuss the questions.

business sectors such as architecture and engineering.   in labor markets

1. For which sectors is the future promising? For which is globalization having a negative effect? Are any of the predictions surprising? Explain.

2. Choose four of the sectors and discuss how globalization might be expanding or shrinking the labor force in each.
сокращение

VOCABULARY SKILL Using Collocations

Словосочетание

Collocations are combinations of words that are frequently used together. Two common patterns are:

Noun + Noun (The first noun acts like an adjective.)

labor markets	*business sector*	*earning power*

Adjective + Noun

private sector	*advanced technologies*	*remote control*

D Complete each global career tip with the correct collocation.

1. Just knowing your ____b____ isn't enough these days. Learn a second one.

   a. natural language   b. native language   c. national language

2. Do your own Internet research to keep up with ____a____ in your chosen field.

   a. major trends   b. upper trends   c. considerable trends

3. Take a trip overseas during ____a____ to explore employment options.

   a. spring break   b. spring pause   c. spring intermission

4. Don't forget that companies often fill their ____b____ with local talent.

   a. superior positions   b. senior positions   c. elder positions

5. If you hope to work in the ____c____, do a leadership training program.

   a. managing sector   b. manager sector   c. management sector

6. If you have an ____a____, look for a position abroad.

   a. adventurous spirit   b. adventurous energy   c. adventurous body

7. Develop the ability to adapt to other cultures, as it's part of a global career *о īзr   карьер* . ____c____.

   a. skill series   b. skill collection   c. skill set *знание и онки.*

8. Join online discussions related to your ____b____ of expertise or interest.

   a. specific region   b. specific field   c. specific environment

---

E Work in a group. Discuss the career tips above. Then use the collocations to make your own career tips.

> *Don't worry if you don't speak English as well as your native language. A lot of successful international businesspeople are still perfecting their English!*

A Listening A Lecture about Succeeding in Business

BEFORE LISTENING

A Work in a small group. Discuss these questions.

1. What does it take to be successful in today's globalized business world?

2. You are going to hear a lecture about four skills, called "competences", needed to succeed in business today. Look at the skills and discuss what you think each means.

- personal competence
- social competence
- business competence
- cultural competence

WHILE LISTENING

LISTENING SKILL Listening for Advantages

When introducing new ideas, speakers often point out the advantages of those ideas. Listen for the following ways speakers express advantages.

- a clear statement of the advantage
  The advantage/benefit (of) . . . is . . .
  . . . is useful/beneficial/important because . . .
  . . . is essential for . . .
- a question before introducing an advantage
  Why is . . . useful/beneficial/important?
- an explanation of what the advantage allows us to do or what it makes possible
  . . . allows/helps us/you (to) . . .
  . . . makes it possible to . . .

▼ **Doing business across different cultures requires a high level of cultural competence.**

To organize two corresponding sets of information, you can use two columns. Write the main ideas in the left-hand column. Then add a column to the right for the supporting ideas or details that pertain to those main ideas. Using arrows or lines between the corresponding information can make it easier to see and remember the connections between the main ideas and the supporting details.

B 🎧 2.3 ▶ 1.8 Listen to the lecture and follow along with the notes in the first column. LISTENING FOR DETAILS

Succeeding in Business

Competences	Advantages
Personal competence	
1. understanding yourself →	helps you use time and __resources__ correctly (1)
2. emotional intelligence →	facilitates __decision making__ (2)
3. be realistic but optimistic →	helps you be positive when things go wrong
Social competence	
1. practical trust →	helps you trust ppl to __get things__ done (3)
2. constructive impatience → конструктивное нетерпение	sends message: do things __get done on time__ (4)
3. connective teaching →	makes poss. for others to teach __and learn from each other__ (5)
Business competence	
1. managing chaos →	allows you to deal w/ __with unexpected changes__ in business. (6)
2. fluency with technology →	makes avail. latest e-bus. __available for you / development__ (7)
3. developing leadership →	helps bus. succeed & __function__ better (8)
Cultural competence	
1. understanding your culture →	allows you to value strengths & __understand weaknesses in certain situations__ (9)
2. international curiosity →	allows you to look beyond yr __own culture__ for opps. opportunities (10)
3. bridge building →	allows creation of connections across cultrs

C 🎧 2.3 Listen again and complete the second column of notes in exercise B. Write no more than two words in each blank. NOTE TAKING

AFTER LISTENING

D Work with a partner. Discuss these questions. PERSONALIZING

1. Which of the competences that the lecturer spoke about is an area of strength for you? If possible, give an example.

2. Which of the competences would you like to develop? Explain.

1 r   get th   unexpected changes   weak
2 d.m   on time   bugen   your own culture
       learn from   function

A Speaking

When giving a presentation, you may sometimes use terms that are related to a specific field. Your listeners may not be familiar with these terms, and their meaning may differ from the dictionary definitions. In these cases, you should define the terms using language that your audience will understand. Here are some expressions you can use:

> The term ... refers to/means ...   By ..., I mean ...
> This means ...   ... is defined as ...

You can also define a term by simply pausing after the term and giving a definition.

A 🎧 2.4 Work with a partner. Take turns reading the sentences aloud using expressions from the skill box. Then listen and fill in the expressions the speaker uses.

1. _____ emotional intelligence, _____ understanding your own emotions and those of others.

2. _____ *social competence* _____ the skills required to engage with and get the best out of other people.

3. The third component of social competence is known as *connective teaching*. _____ being just as eager to learn from others as you are to pass on your knowledge to them.

4. Cultural competence _____ an understanding of cultural differences and how to make use of that knowledge.

B Match each term related to globalization on the left with its definition on the right.

1. _____ coca-colonization   a. the distance food is transported from producer to consumer
2. _____ postnationalism   b. the globalization of American culture through U.S. products
3. _____ food miles   c. inequality in access to computers and the Internet
4. _____ worldlang   d. an active user of social media and the Internet
5. _____ netizen   e. the process by which nations become global entities
6. _____ digital divide   f. a new language created from several modern languages

DEFINING TERMS **C** Work with a partner. Practice saying sentences to introduce and then define the terms in exercise B. Use expressions for defining terms from the Speaking Skill box.

> One aspect of globalization that isn't always welcome is coca-colonization. By coca-colonization, I mean the globalization of American culture through U.S. products.

D Work in a small group. Discuss the advantages and/or disadvantages of the six aspects of globalization. Take notes below. Write an advantage and disadvantage for each.

CRITICAL THINKING: EVALUATING

Aspects of Globalization	Advantages	Disadvantages
1. coca-colonization →	_____	_____
2. postnationalism →	_____	_____
3. food miles →	_____	_____
4. worldlang →	_____	_____
5. netizen →	_____	_____
6. digital divide →	_____	_____

E Work with a partner. Compare the two maps. What conclusion(s) can you make about the relationship between mobile-cellular use and Internet access? Support your ideas with examples from the maps.

CRITICAL THINKING: INTERPRETING A MAP

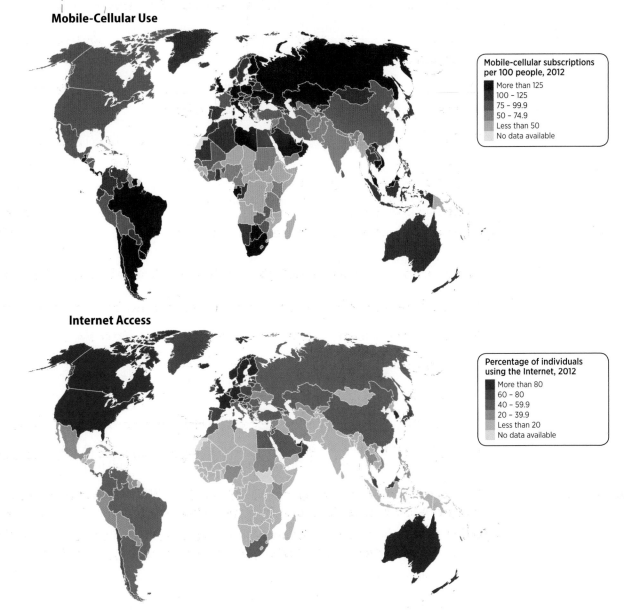

Mobile-Cellular Use

Mobile-cellular subscriptions per 100 people, 2012
- More than 125
- 100 – 125
- 75 – 99.9
- 50 – 74.9
- Less than 50
- No data available

Internet Access

Percentage of individuals using the Internet, 2012
- More than 80
- 60 – 80
- 40 – 59.9
- 20 – 39.9
- Less than 20
- No data available

A gerund phrase is a type of noun phrase. Gerund phrases begin with a gerund (the base form of a verb plus -ing) and include one or more modifiers and additional objects. They are used as the subject or subject complement of a sentence, object of a verb, or object of a preposition.

Being realistic but at the same time optimistic allows us to stay positive—even when things go wrong.

The first component of personal competence is **understanding yourself**.

You should not avoid **making difficult decisions**.

Social competence is essential for **bringing together groups of talented people**.

F Put the words and phrases in the correct order to create sentences with gerund phrases about career skills. More than one answer may be possible.

1. to think critically / is / for problem solving / being able / essential

   _____

2. are vital / accessing current information / Internet search skills / for

   _____

3. huge amounts of data / facilitate / analyzing / Big Data skills

   _____

4. a high level of / working with others successfully / emotional intelligence / requires

   _____

5. decisions / a fundamental skill / of leaders / is / making

   _____

6. many employers / is / solve problems effectively / look for / a skill / being able to

   _____

7. change / is / to welcome / a key skill / being able

   _____

8. a foreign language / toward becoming / a global citizen / is / learning / an important step

   _____

**CRITICAL THINKING:
RANKING**

G Work in a small group. Look at the career skills. Add two more to the list. Then discuss how important they are, and number them from 1 (most useful) to 10 (least useful).

_____ a. analyzing data

_____ b. being able to think critically

_____ c. decision-making

_____ d. researching information online

_____ e. solving problems effectively

_____ f. speaking a foreign language

_____ g. welcoming change

_____ h. working with others

_____ i. _____

_____ j. _____

LESSON TASK Role-Playing a Job Interview

A Work with a partner. You are going to role-play a job interview. Look at the list of interview questions and add one more question about work experience.

> **INTERVIEW QUESTIONS**
> 1. Can you tell me a little about yourself?
> 2. What are your greatest strengths?
> 3. What is your greatest weakness?
> 4. Describe a stressful workplace situation you experienced. How did you handle it?
> 5. What is your approach to working successfully in a team?
> 6. This position requires working with people from different cultural backgrounds. What skills or qualifications do you have to work cross-culturally?
> 7. _____
>   _____

B On your own, study the interview questions and prepare your answers. Make notes to use during the interview. Use any work, school, or life experience you've had, information from this lesson, and your imagination, as necessary.

CRITICAL THINKING: APPLYING

> **EVERYDAY LANGUAGE** Asking about Experiences
>
> *Can you tell me about a time that/when you ... ?*
> *Have you ever had the chance/opportunity to ... ?*
> *Have you ever had any experience with ... ?*

C With your partner, role-play an interview between a hiring manager at an international company and an applicant. Ask the interview questions from exercise A, as well as any follow-up questions as appropriate. Use expressions from the Everyday Language box. Then switch roles and repeat.

▼ **The Hongkong and Shanghai Banking Company (HSBC) is a globally focused company with headquarters in Hong Kong and branches throughout the world.**

A Sherpa replaces rope on Ama Dablam Mountain in the Himalayas.

Video

Sherpa Lives

BEFORE VIEWING

A Work in a small group. Look at the photo and discuss the questions.

1. Where do you think the Sherpa live? What might the climate be like?

2. The Sherpa people are famous for the work they do. What do you think they do?

3. In Lesson A, you learned about some of the ways globalization is affecting job markets and workers. How do you think globalization is affecting the lives and work of the Sherpa people?

WHILE VIEWING

NOTE TAKING **B** ▶ 1.9 Watch the introduction of the video, given by mountain climber and National Geographic Explorer Conrad Anker. Complete the notes. Write no more than two words or a number in each blank.

> ### The Sherpa People
>
> The Sherpa people → One of 70 ethnic groups w/in _Nepal_ 1
>
> Migrated from → _Tibet_ 2
>
> Meaning of "Sherpa" → _easterners_ 3
>
> Activity connected to → _mountain climbing_ 4
>
> Year Sherpa culture changed → _1953_ 5 , the year Tenzing Norgay and Sir Edmund Hillary _climbed mount Everest_ 6

C ▶ 1.10 Watch the entire video. Match each idea with the speaker who expresses it.

1. _e_ Karma Tsering.
2. _c_ Conrad Anker
3. _a_ Max Lowe
4. _b_ Kancha Sherpa
5. _d_ Mahendra Kathet

a. Sherpa education, healthcare, and clothing have all improved. 3
b. Sherpa can earn enough money, although life feels hurried. 4
c. Sherpa society has become much more connected than before. 2
d. Many Sherpa people are ambitious and seek success abroad. 5
e. Sherpas learned a modern skill thanks to a foreigner's gift. 1

D ▶ 1.10 Watch the video again and choose the correct answer.

1. Sir Edmund Hillary rewarded his Sherpa guides with watches as _a bonus_.

    a. payment   b. a bonus   c. a prize

2. In terms of health care, the Sherpa now have _a dentist_ and medical clinics.

    a. an eye doctor   b. a dentist   c. a pharmacy

3. The only issue Kancha Sherpa is concerned about is _global warming_.

    a. making money   b. dealing with tourists   c. global warming

4. Some believe that people are losing the ability to focus on _true happiness_.

    a. true happiness   b. the tourist trade   c. mountain climbing

5. An increase in food _diversity_ has led to healthier diets.

    a. diversity   b. production   c. education

6. You can now use a cell phone _at the base_ _camp of_ Mount Everest.

    a. at the top of   b. from anywhere on   (c.) at the base camp of

AFTER VIEWING

> **CRITICAL THINKING** Evaluating
>
> When you evaluate, you make a judgment based on criteria. To evaluate situations or concepts, make sure you have a good understanding of the criteria you are using. This will allow you to explain your evaluation more clearly to other people. Highlight your evaluation criteria by beginning with one of these expressions:
>
> *In terms of [diet],...*   *With regard to [culture],...*   *As far as [education] goes,...*

E Work in a small group. Use the criteria below to evaluate this statement: *Since 1953, Sherpa life has changed for the better.*

physical well-being   technological level   traditions and culture

Vocabulary

A 🎧 2.5 Listen and check (✓) the words you already know. Use a dictionary to help you with any new words.

обсуждение

всплывающие

переносной

□ anticipate (v) □ emerging (adj) □ influential (adj) □ portable (adj)
□ application (n) □ enrich (v) *обогащать* □ mass (adj) □ prominent (adj)
□ collaborate (v) □ implication (n)

сотрудник

видный - выдающийся

CRITICAL THINKING:
ANALYZING

B Read the definition of *augment*. Then read the "Revealed World" section in the article below. What do you think *augmented reality* means? Discuss your ideas with a partner.

augment (v): to make something larger, stronger, or more effective by adding to it

C 🎧 2.6 Complete the article with words from exercise A. Use the correct form of the words. Then listen and check your answers.

THE WORLD OF AUGMENTED REALITY

раскрытый мир

Revealed World

пузыри плавающие

Imagine bubbles floating before your eyes, filled with cool info about stuff you see on the street. Science fiction? Nope. It's augmented reality. And one day it'll be as routine as browsing the Web.

2009
Smart phone

2012
Eyewear

2020?
Contact lenses

Augmented reality is one of the most promising and _____1_____ global trends of recent years. This much-talked-about _____2_____ technology is most often used to _____3_____ the reality we see through a cell phone or other _____4_____ device with fun or useful information, images, sounds, or videos. Some _____5_____ of augmented reality that are already being widely used include apps that highlight and display information about restaurants, historic sites, museum exhibits, or where you parked your car. A variety of outdoor games use the technology to allow players to _____6_____ as they hunt for digital objects. Among such games, Pokémon Go is the most _____7_____ example; it has introduced augmented reality to a _____8_____ audience. The augmented reality experience is also available through special eyewear or headsets, and soon even contact lenses. As we look toward the future, we _____9_____ many more uses for this promising technology with _____10_____ for nearly every aspect of life in the years to come.

D Complete the chart with the correct form of each word. Use a dictionary to help you.

	Noun	Verb	Adjective
1.	_ion_	collaborate	_ive_
2.	implication		
3.	_ce_	_ce_	influential
4.	_ion_	anticipate	_pant_
5.	_prominence_	X	prominent
6.	_emergence_	emerge	_emergent_

E Work with a partner. Discuss these questions.

1. Look at the photo below and read the caption. What is another way that augmented reality could enrich a museum experience?

2. Would you prefer to access the Internet via glasses or a headset? Explain.

3. Do you think that augmented reality will continue to generate mass interest? What future uses for this emerging technology do you anticipate?

4. Do all uses of augmented reality enrich our lives? Or are there any negative implications of the mass use of this technology? Explain.

CRITICAL THINKING:
EVALUATING

▼ **Augmented reality adds another level of information to museum exhibits. Dinosaur bones get a layer of flesh and the ability to move around at the Royal Ontario Museum, Canada.**

Listening A Podcast about Augmented Reality

BEFORE LISTENING

CRITICAL THINKING:
INTERPRETING
VISUALS

A Work with a partner. Discuss these questions.

1. Where might you see an image like the one below?
2. What kinds of information are available in the image?

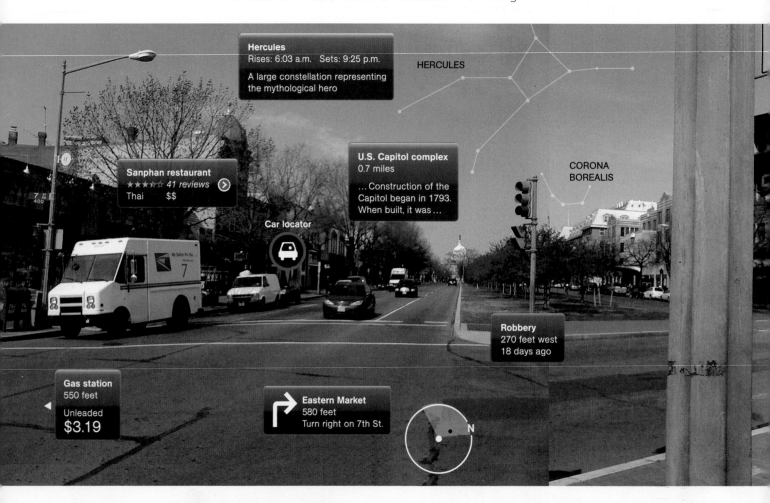

WHILE LISTENING

LISTENING FOR
MAIN IDEAS

B 🎧 **2.7** Listen to a podcast about augmented reality (AR). Check (✓) the two main ideas the speakers discuss.

1. ☑ AR is a useful technology with many different applications.
   способствовала
2. ☐ AR's popularity has contributed to the widespread use of portable devices.
3. ☐ AR is useful when deciding which pieces of furniture to purchase.
4. ☑ AR facilitates the globalization of culture through popular games.
5. ☐ Pokémon Go's popularity has unquestionably benefited local economies.

C 🎧 **2.7** Listen again and complete the outline. Write no more than two words in each blank.

I. Intro to AR—an emerging trend in tech

   A. Combines info/images w/the __real world__
                                         1

   B. Later, AR will integrate sounds

II. AR has importnt implications for globalization of bus.

   A. Potential to enrich _making experiencec_
                                     2

   B. Could imitate facial _expressions_ & glances
                                   3

III. More ppl using AR → more affordable

   A. In industry, machines marked w/ _important instructions_
                                   4

   B. Shopping for furniture—see how looks in room

IV. Pokémon GO

   A. More _daily users_ than Facebook/Twitter in 1 yr
                                   5

   B. How to play

      1. Look for animated _monsters_ (i.e., Pokémon)
                                   6

      2. Goal: capture them in your _Pokémon ball_
                                   7

   C. Reasons for success

      1. Pokémon was already a _well known_ brand
                                   8

      2. Ppl felt better walking around outside

      3. Chances for _interaction with_ other ppl
                                   9

   D. The business side

      1. Has pwr to make areas or _____
                                   10

      2. Hunters may want to buy snacks, drinks, etc.

(handwritten note: businesses busier)

AFTER LISTENING

D Work in a small group. Discuss these questions. Use your notes from exercise C to help you.

1. What is an application of AR that would improve your own life? Explain.

2. Some believe that games that are played worldwide, such as Pokémon GO, have contributed to the globalization of culture. Others see them as global fads that have no significant impact. What is your view?

3. What are some of the benefits of the globalization of culture? What are some of the drawbacks?

Speaking

PRONUNCIATION Saying Parentheticals

🎧 2.8 We sometimes use parenthetical expressions to help clarify our ideas. We separate them with a short pause before and after. The intonation of these expressions begins a bit lower than the phrase before the interruption and rises slightly at the end. This prepares the listener for the continuation of the interrupted sentence.

*Augmented reality, **or AR as it's often called**, has been a prominent trend in recent years …*

*They can join meetings by phone, **which is great**, but it's not the same as being there.*

A 🎧 2.9 Underline the parenthetical expression in each sentence. Then listen and check your work. With a partner, practice saying these sentences, using correct intonation and pauses with the parentheticals.

1. That car service, though convenient and affordable, is taking jobs away from taxi drivers everywhere.

2. Pokémon GO is, at least for now, a wildly popular augmented reality game.

3. Wearable technology, despite all the advertising, hasn't had the mass appeal we'd anticipated.

4. Bollywood-style dance classes, believe it or not, are a growing trend in many places.

5. Digital art that is created for use on the Internet is sometimes, in my opinion, extremely stunning.

6. Robots and other machines, although they are undeniably useful, are causing some people to lose their jobs.

7. People born between 1982 and 2004, sometimes called "millennials," are skilled at using social media to collaborate.

8. The increase in injuries to teens, which few anticipated, is linked to the global extreme sports trend.

B Work with a partner. Make five statements about topics from popular culture (movies, TV, music, sports, fashion, technology, etc.) using the parenthetical expressions in the box below or ones of your own. Use correct intonation and pauses.

A: *Robert Downey, Jr., I think you'll agree, is a really great actor.*
B: *Oh, definitely. He was in the* Iron Man *movies, which I love, and in* Spiderman.

I think you'll agree	though I've never tried it	believe it or not
in my opinion	which I love	as far as I'm concerned

C Work in a small group. Read about four emerging global trends. Then discuss the benefits and drawbacks these trends could have on people, businesses, or organizations.

CRITICAL THINKING: ANALYZING

A: *Synthetic food could inevitably save the lives of millions of animals.*

B: *That's true, but would it be healthy to eat? It could have some negative effects on people who eat it, couldn't it?*

1. **Synthetic food:** Plant-based meat replacements and meat grown in laboratories without harming animals will be coming to grocery stores.

2. **Virtual reality (VR):** You will be able to watch live shows and concerts and feel as if you're actually there without leaving your living room.

3. **Self-driving cars:** Companies like Tesla and Uber are creating systems that will eliminate the need for drivers and reduce the number of road accidents.

4. **Artificial art:** Computers are already writing songs and will soon be creating movies, paintings, novels, and poetry.

FINAL TASK Evaluating a Social Media Platform

> You are going to research a social media platform, evaluate its importance for globalization, and present your findings to your group.

A Work in a small group. Look at the bar graph and discuss these questions.

CRITICAL THINKING: INTERPRETING A GRAPH

1. How are the social media platforms ranked in the chart?
2. What do the different bar colors represent?
3. Which of the platforms have you heard of? Which have you used?

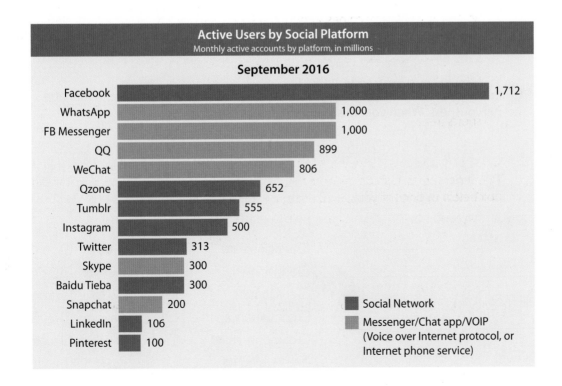

Active Users by Social Platform
Monthly active accounts by platform, in millions

September 2016

Platform	Users (millions)
Facebook	1,712
WhatsApp	1,000
FB Messenger	1,000
QQ	899
WeChat	806
Qzone	652
Tumblr	555
Instagram	500
Twitter	313
Skype	300
Baidu Tieba	300
Snapchat	200
LinkedIn	106
Pinterest	100

■ Social Network
■ Messenger/Chat app/VOIP
(Voice over Internet protocol, or Internet phone service)

B Choose a platform from the graph in exercise A or another to research. Then prepare a presentation using the outline below.

I. Introduction

   A. A brief description of the platform

   B. A brief history of the platform

II. The Business Side

   A. How does it make money?

   B. Who are its competitors? *конкуренты – Kaмлётmuшers*

   C. How does it compare with its competitors? What are the similarities and differences?

III. Globalization

   A. Where is it most popular?

   B. How does the platform facilitate globalization? *облегчает*

IV. The Future

   A. Is the platform currently becoming more or less popular?

   B. How will the platform likely change in the future?

food from your anywhere

dec 4 dec 12

PRESENTATION SKILL Managing Nervousness

It is normal to be a little nervous at the beginning of a presentation. Because the first impression you make on your audience is important, learn to manage any nervousness. First of all, remember to breathe and be as natural as you can. Make an effort to speak slowly and calmly. Memorizing the first few sentences you plan to say can sometimes help. Soon you will feel more comfortable and confident.

C Present your platform to your group. Notice which strategy you use to manage nervousness. When you finish, answer any questions.

REFLECTION

1. What information that you learned in this unit is likely to be the most useful to you? Why and how?

  _____

  _____

2. What trend in the unit did you find the most interesting?

  _____

  _____

3. Here are the vocabulary words and phrases from the unit. Check (✓) the ones you can use.

☐ anticipate AWL

☐ application

☐ collaborate

☐ competence

☐ component AWL

☐ emerging AWL

☐ enrich

☐ facilitate AWL

☐ implication AWL *подразум.*

☐ inevitably AWL

☐ influential

☐ labor AWL

☐ mass – *группа*

☐ pertain to *относится к*

☐ portable *переносной*

☐ prominent *выдающийся*

☐ promising

☐ retain AWL *сохранит*

☐ sector AWL

☐ widespread AWL

add

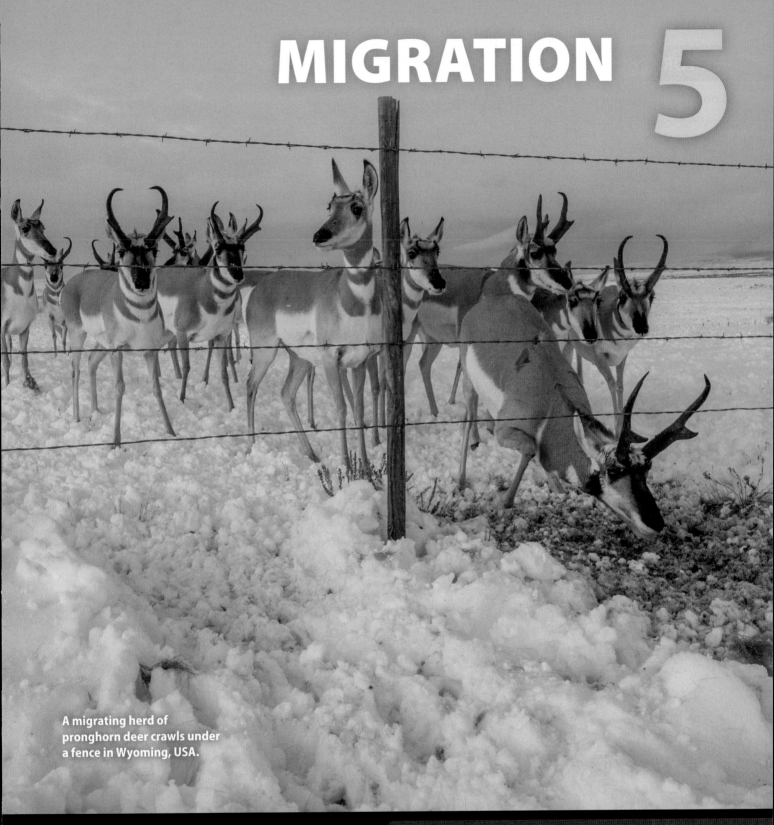

MIGRATION 5

A migrating herd of pronghorn deer crawls under a fence in Wyoming, USA.

ACADEMIC SKILLS

LISTENING   Listening for Clarification
            Using a Time Line
SPEAKING   Approximating
            Linking with *You* or *Your*
CRITICAL THINKING   Distinguishing Fact from Theory

THINK AND DISCUSS

1   Migration is when animals (or people) move from one place to another. Where do you think the deer in the photo are going?

2   What does the photo suggest about the relationship between human development and animal migration?

3   What are reasons people might move from one place to another?

EXPLORE THE THEME

Look at the map and read the information. Then discuss the questions.

1. What route is Paul Salopek taking on his journey, and how is he traveling?
2. What do you think were some reasons that early humans left Africa?
3. Why do you think Salopek is taking this journey?

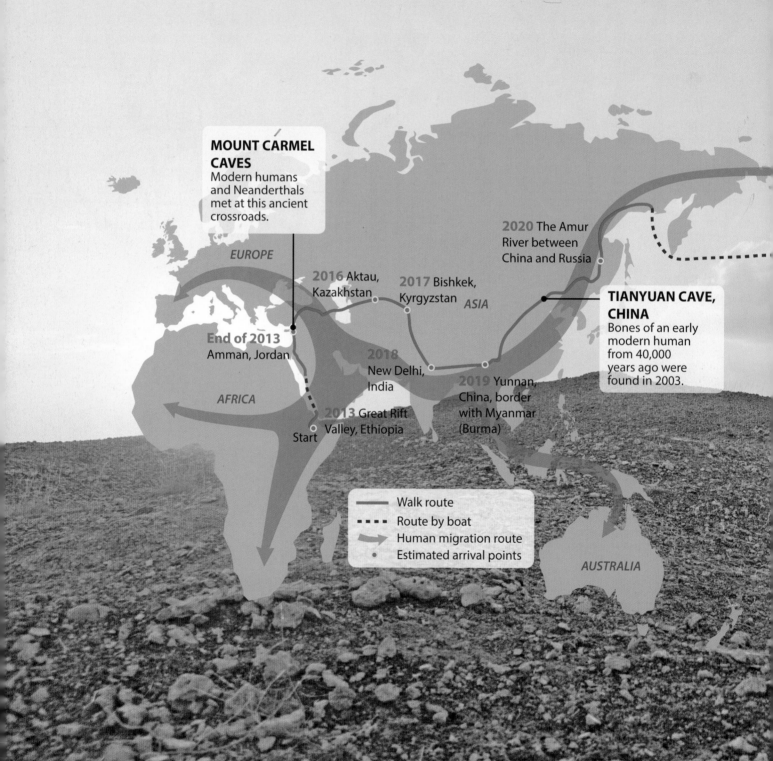

MOUNT CARMEL CAVES
Modern humans and Neanderthals met at this ancient crossroads.

EUROPE

2016 Aktau, Kazakhstan

2017 Bishkek, Kyrgyzstan

ASIA

2020 The Amur River between China and Russia

TIANYUAN CAVE, CHINA
Bones of an early modern human from 40,000 years ago were found in 2003.

End of 2013
Amman, Jordan

2018
New Delhi, India

2019 Yunnan, China, border with Myanmar (Burma)

AFRICA

2013 Great Rift Valley, Ethiopia
Start

Walk route
······ Route by boat
➤ Human migration route
• Estimated arrival points

AUSTRALIA

THE LONGEST WALK

Evidence suggests that *Homo sapiens* set out to discover regions of Earth some 100 to 125,000 years ago, traveling from Ethiopia's Great Rift Valley to the farthest tip of South America. To retrace their steps, writer Paul Salopek has begun his own global journey, a 21,000-mile trek that touches four continents. Calling the project the *Out of Eden Walk*, Salopek is using the latest fossil and genetic findings to plan his route. His reports from the trail are posted regularly at outofedenwalk.org.

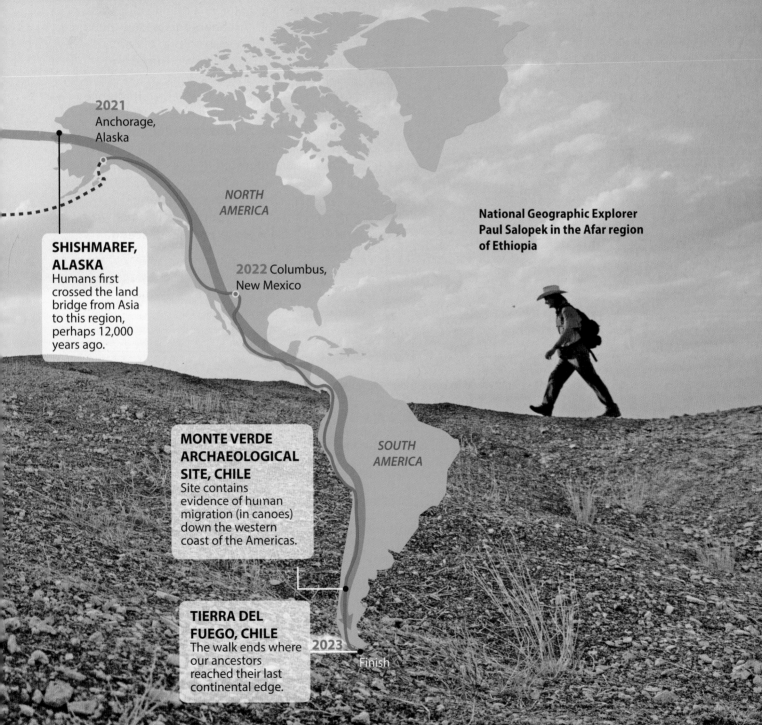

2021
Anchorage, Alaska

NORTH AMERICA

SHISHMAREF, ALASKA
Humans first crossed the land bridge from Asia to this region, perhaps 12,000 years ago.

2022 Columbus, New Mexico

National Geographic Explorer Paul Salopek in the Afar region of Ethiopia

MONTE VERDE ARCHAEOLOGICAL SITE, CHILE
Site contains evidence of human migration (in canoes) down the western coast of the Americas.

SOUTH AMERICA

TIERRA DEL FUEGO, CHILE
The walk ends where our ancestors reached their last continental edge.

2023
Finish

Vocabulary

A ⌒ **2.10** Look at the map. Then read and listen to the information about migration. Notice each word in **blue** and think about its meaning.

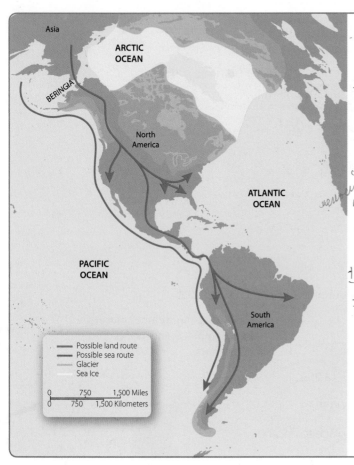

PATHS TO A NEW WORLD

No one is sure how or when the first people got to the Americas. However, recent **notable** discoveries and DNA analyses have changed our **perspective** on the first human migrations into the Americas. **Archaeologists** have found evidence suggesting that a group of perhaps fewer than 5,000 individuals **ventured** from Asia into the Americas over 15,000 years ago. This group, they believe, traveled an **immense** distance along the western coastlines of North and South America. **Subsequently**, after melting glaciers[1] had opened an interior path, a second group **migrated** from Asia following a land route. They aimed to explore and settle the central areas of the Americas. **Genetic** studies have confirmed the **hypothesis** that modern American Indians are indeed the **descendants** of people from Asia.

[1] **glacier** (n): an extremely large mass of ice

B Write each word in **blue** from exercise A next to its definition.

гипотеза — 1. _____hypothesis_____ (n) a possible explanation suggested by evidence h

впоследствии — 2. _____subsequently_____ (adv) later or afterwards s

3. _____perspective_____ (n) point of view p

потомки — 4. _____descendants_____ (n) blood relatives in future generations

рисковать осмелиться — 5. _____ventured_____ (v) went into a place that might be dangerous v

огромный — 6. _____immense_____ (adj) extremely large or great in amount or scale масштаб

7. _____genetic_____ (adj) related to characteristics of the body that are passed from generation to generation d

8. _____archaeologists_____ (n) scientists who study ancient cultures through the tools, buildings, and relics of ancient peoples ar

видающиеся — 9. _____notable_____ (adj) important, interesting, or remarkable n

10. _____migrated_____ (v) moved from one area to another m

C Work in a small group. Discuss the questions and explain your answers. _[handwritten: head transplant, quantum deportation 2018.]_

1. What is a notable discovery of the 21st century? _[handwritten: 8 planet, quantum]_
2. What is a good way to change a person's perspective? _[handwritten: в музии]_
3. Have you ever ventured somewhere unusual or off the beaten track? If you haven't, would you like to?
4. What can you describe as _immense_?
5. Look at the map in exercise A. On which ocean did the 5,000 people who migrated _[handwritten: Atlantic.]_ from Asia travel? About what distance did they travel in the Americas?

VOCABULARY SKILL Suffixes _–ant_ and _–ist_

The suffix _–ant_ is added to some verbs to mean a person who performs the action of the verb. _[handwritten: передаваться по наследству]_

apply → ápplic**ant**   descénd → descénd**ant**

The suffix _–ist_ is added to some verbs or nouns to refer to a person who performs an action, uses an instrument or device, or works in a certain field.

type → typ**ist**   archaeology → archaeolog**ist**

D Write a word ending in _–ant_ or _–ist_ that matches the definition. Use the underlined words and a dictionary to help you.

1. _____ someone who <u>participates</u> in an activity _[handwritten: pant]_
2. _____ someone who works in the field of <u>biology</u> _[handwritten: ist]_
3. _____ a person who studies the <u>future</u> and makes predictions _[handwritten: ist]_
4. _____ a person who <u>migrates</u> from one place to another _[handwritten: rant]_
5. _____ a person who draws <u>cartoons</u> for a living _[handwritten: ist]_
6. _____ a person who <u>defends</u> himself or herself in court _[handwritten: ant]_
7. _____ a scientist who does <u>genetic</u> research _[handwritten: ist]_
8. _____ a person who <u>inhabits</u> a certain region _[handwritten: ANt]_

E Work in a small group. Discuss the questions.

CRITICAL THINKING: REFLECTING

1. Geneticists have discovered that information is written in our DNA. What sort of information has genetic research uncovered? What can it tell us about ourselves and our families?
2. Notable discoveries, such as the discovery of the ancient civilization of the Egyptians that thrived over 5,000 years ago, have changed the way we understand the past. Would you be interested in becoming an archaeologist and doing this kind of research? Explain.
3. A _time capsule_ is a container filled with items that we hope will one day be found by others. If you were going to create a time capsule, what items would you include to best represent your culture today? Explain your choices.

A Listening A Podcast about Ancient Migration

pass from parents to children from generations to generations

BEFORE LISTENING

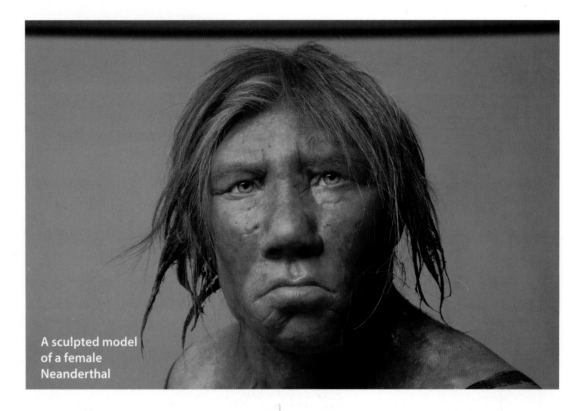

A sculpted model
of a female
Neanderthal

PREDICTING **A** Work with a partner. Look at the photo and caption. Then predict the answers to these questions.

1. Scientists believe that the Neanderthal were a species of ancient humans that became extinct many thousands of years ago. In which regions of the earth do you think Neanderthals lived? *Africa*
2. What do you think happened when modern humans moved into an area that had already been settled by Neanderthals? *they disappeared through interbreeding with humans*
3. Do you think there is any Neanderthal DNA in modern humans?

WHILE LISTENING

CHECKING
PREDICTIONS **B** 🎧 2.11 ▶ 1.11 Listen to the podcast. Were your predictions in exercise A correct?

> **CRITICAL THINKING** Distinguishing Fact from Theory
>
> Distinguishing between fact and theory is an important skill because while facts usually remain true, theories may change. In science, facts are situations that can be observed again and again. Theories provide explanations based on facts. To distinguish between the two, it can be helpful to ask whether the information is an observation (fact) or an explanation (theory).

C 🎧 **2.12** Listen to an excerpt from the podcast and write *Theory* or *Fact*.

1. _Fact_ Every once in a while, a baby is born with a slight difference in its DNA.
2. _Theory_ All humans are related to one woman who lived about 150,000 years ago.
3. _Theory_ Over one hundred thousand years ago, humans began migrating out of Africa.
4. _Fact_ Scientists have found the remains of ancient humans in Australia.
5. _Fact_ Humans were already living in Europe 30,000 years ago.
6. _Theory_ Some Neanderthals were absorbed into the modern human family.

NOTE-TAKING SKILL Using a Time Line

When studying a topic that is organized chronologically, a time line can be the clearest and most efficient way to organize your notes. Time lines usually run from left to right, but setting up a time line diagonally or vertically can create more space for events and their descriptions.

D 🎧 **2.13** Listen to an excerpt from the podcast. As you listen, complete the time line about human migration. Write no more than two words or a number.

NOTE TAKING

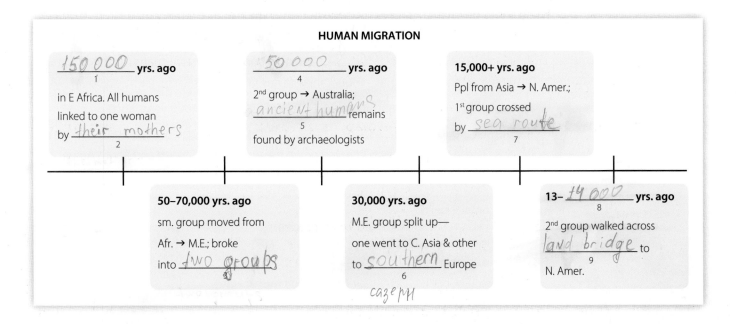

HUMAN MIGRATION

_150 000_ yrs. ago
1
in E Africa. All humans linked to one woman by _their mothers_
2

_50 000_ yrs. ago
4
2nd group → Australia; _ancient humans_ remains
5
found by archaeologists

15,000+ yrs. ago
Ppl from Asia → N. Amer.; 1st group crossed by _sea route_
7

50–70,000 yrs. ago
sm. group moved from Afr. → M.E.; broke into _two groups_
3

30,000 yrs. ago
M.E. group split up— one went to C. Asia & other to _southern_ Europe
6
cazepyi

13– _14 000_ yrs. ago
8
2nd group walked across _land bridge_ to
9
N. Amer.

AFTER LISTENING

E Work with a partner. Take turns completing the tasks.

CRITICAL THINKING: REFLECTING

1. From memory, retell the story of the journey of modern humans that you heard. If you need help, refer to the time line in exercise D.
2. The information you heard follows the story of modern humans up until about 12,000 years ago when they had reached every continent except Antarctica. There have been many other migrations of people since then. Think of an example of a migration of people in the past or present. Explain the circumstances and the reasons for it to your partner. Include any facts you know and theories you have.

1 150 000   4 50 000   7 sea route
2 their mother   5 ancient humans   8 14 000
3 two groups   6 settled   9 land bridge

A Speaking

A 🎧 **2.14** The podcast about migration included a number of expressions for approximating. With a partner, read the sentences aloud, using expressions for approximating. Then listen and write the expressions used.

1. Based on genetic evidence, scientists now think that all humans are related to one woman who lived ___roughly___ 150,000 years ago in East Africa.

2. It was 50,000 years ago ___or so___ that some of these humans reached Australia, where archaeologists have found ancient human remains.

3. One group reached Central Asia ___something like___ 30,000 years ago.

4. The first group crossed ___more than___ 15,000 years ago using a sea route, keeping close to the shore as they continued down the west coast of North and South America.

Early modern humans hunt during the ice age.

B Work with a partner. Ask each other these questions. Answer using expressions for approximating.

1. How much money would you be willing to spend on a car?
2. How much time off do you get in a year?
3. How long have you been studying English?
4. How much money do you spend per month on entertainment?
5. Think of a childhood friend. How long has it been since you last saw him or her?
6. How long has it been since you last used social media?
7. What percentage of Neanderthal DNA do you think you might have?
8. How long do you think you will be studying English?

GRAMMAR FOR SPEAKING Modals of Past Possibility

To make guesses and inferences about the past, use *could have*, *may (not) have*, or *might (not) have* and a past participle.

> Modern humans entering Central Asia **could have run into** Neanderthals.
>
> That group **might not have been** larger than a thousand people.

In short responses that are guesses, do not use the past participle.

> A: *Did they come from the Middle East?*
>
> B: *They* **may have**.

When *be* is the main verb, keep the past participle in the answer.

> A: *Were the Neanderthals absorbed into the modern human family?*
>
> B: *Scientists think some* **might have been**.

If you feel very certain something wasn't true or didn't happen, use *could not have*.

> There **couldn't have been** 10,000 people in the group that left Africa.

C Work with a partner. Read the situations and make guesses about past possibilities for each situation. Use modals of past possibility.

1. Samantha walked halfway to the bus stop this morning, then suddenly turned around and walked back to her house. Why did she turn around? *She might have forgotten to turn off the iron in her house*
2. Yesterday, Ali had to go to the bank after playing basketball. Why did he go there? *He may have wanted to withdraw some cash.*
3. Last week, Gabriela was offered her dream job, but she decided to turn it down. Why didn't she accept the job? *She may not have liked the salary offered for her work.*
4. The lights went out in Dian's home last night. Why did they go off? *I think, there might have been problems with the electrical wires.*
5. In the 20th century, millions of people immigrated to the United States. Why did they do this? *They may have wanted to be free.*
6. Peter got a text and then excused himself from the meeting.
7. Chi failed her math test even though she had studied.
8. The bookstore in our town had to close down recently.

D Work in a small group. Read the scenarios. Then answer the questions by making inferences using modals of past possibility.

1. Archaeologists working at a site in Oklahoma, USA, that is about 10,750 years old found evidence of early humans living there. Arrows with stone heads were found, but the nearest source of this particular stone was in Texas, at least 265 miles (426 km) away. The bones of bison, a large grazing animal of North America, were also found at the site. No metal has ever been found at the site, and none was found in Oklahoma. What do these facts tell us about the early human society there?

2. It is known that Neanderthals lived in Europe and Asia when modern humans first arrived roughly 30,000 years ago. Although researchers have found a small amount of Neanderthal DNA in studies of modern humans, there isn't very much. What happened to the Neanderthals, and why?

E With your group, look at the photo. Use past modals to make inferences about who drew them, how they were drawn, how humans lived at that time, why they made these drawings, and so on.

A: *The pictures of animals may have been drawn by the first modern humans.*

B: *No, they couldn't have been. Modern humans hadn't arrived in Europe yet.*

C: *Neanderthals at that time might have been more skilled at drawing than modern humans.*

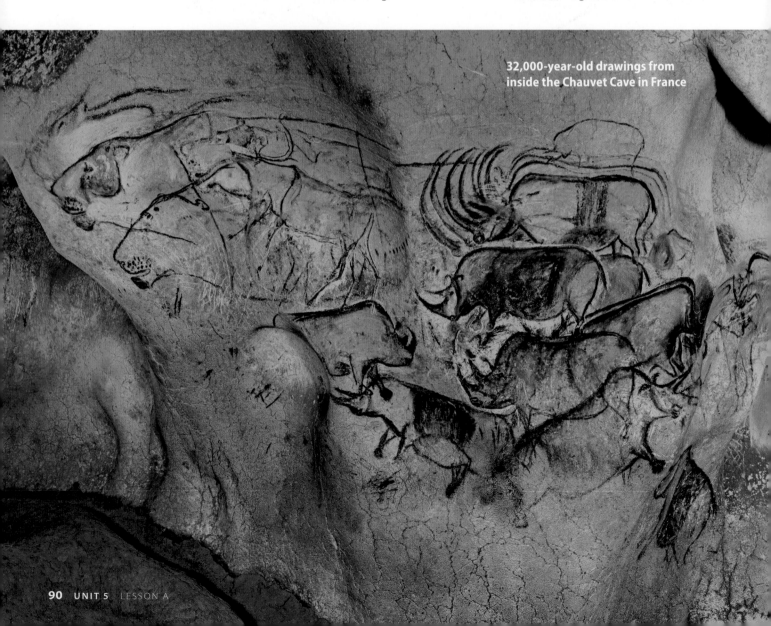

32,000-year-old drawings from inside the Chauvet Cave in France

LESSON TASK Discussing Family Origins

A Where did your family members come from originally? If they left that place, where did they go? Complete the chart with information about your family. If you are not sure about something, write a question mark. *знак*

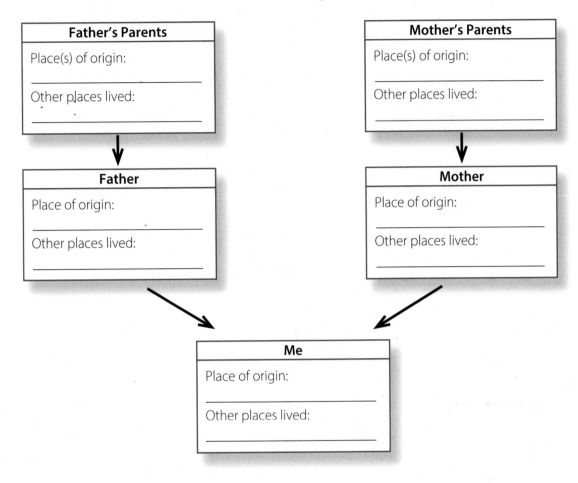

Father's Parents

Place(s) of origin:

_____

Other places lived:

_____

Mother's Parents

Place(s) of origin:

_____

Other places lived:

_____

Father

Place of origin:

_____

Other places lived:

_____

Mother

Place of origin:

_____

Other places lived:

_____

Me

Place of origin:

_____

Other places lived:

_____

EVERYDAY LANGUAGE Showing Surprise

Informal:	*You're kidding (me).*	*That's incredible.*
	Are you serious?	*No way.*
Formal:	*That's really (quite) surprising.*	*That's hard to believe.*
	I never would have guessed.	*I was surprised to learn that... .*

B Work in a small group. Use the information from exercise A to talk about your family. Say where your family members are from and where they have lived. If you are not sure, make a guess. Use expressions of surprise where appropriate. *подходящее*

A: *I was born in Chicago, and my parents were born in Holland. They came to the U.S. in 1967 or so. I'm not sure about my mother's parents. I think they may have migrated from Poland.*

B: *You're kidding. That's where my grandmother is from.*

Wildebeest, zebra, and European storks in Serengeti National Park, Tanzania

Wildebeest Migration

KENYA

TANZANIA

Ikorongo Game Reserve

Grumeti Game Reserve

Loliondo Game Controlled Area

Maswa Game Reserve

NCAA

Ndutu

Serengeti National Park
Migration:
1. Jan-Feb-Mar-April   4. Aug-Sep
2. May   5. Oct
3. June-July   6. Nov-Dec

актиона зиу

BEFORE VIEWING

CRITICAL THINKING: INTERPRETING A MAP

A Look at the map and answer the questions.

1. Which two countries does the wildebeest migration travel through?

_____   _____

2. Use the key to follow the migration of the wildebeest throughout the year. Where are the wildebeest today?

_____

B Match each word in **bold** from the video with its definition.

1. _c_ the **calves** can run   a. ate grass or other growing plants
2. _d_ **carcasses** are left behind   b. large groups of animals of one kind
3. _a_ wildebeest **grazed** these plains   c. young wildebeest
4. _b_ the migrating **herds** arrive   d. the bodies of a dead animals
5. _f_ **sniff** the air   e. causes an event to happen
6. _e_ what **triggers** the migration   f. to smell

WHILE VIEWING

C ▶ **1.12** Watch the video. Does the speaker make these points? Check (✓) the correct answer(s).

	Yes	No
1. The wildebeest make a massive round-trip journey each year.	☑ — 1	☐
2. The migration begins when the herd leader sniffs the air.	☐ 2 —	☑
3. Not all the animals that begin the migration will make it back.	☑ — 3	☐
4. Harsh weather conditions are the main threat to the wildebeest.	☐ 4 —	☑
5. The journey back begins right after the animals have given birth.	☐ 5 —	☑

(handwritten: стадо, нюхает above #2; суровая, условие above #4)

D ▶ **1.12** Watch the video again. Complete the notes. Write no more than three words or a number for each.

Wildebeest Migration

- 2 mil. animals travel almost ___**2000**___[1] miles
- Wildebeest grazed plains more than ___**one million,**___[2] yrs. ago *(handwritten: паслись, равнина)*
- At beg. of yr., all wldbst give ___**birth**___[3] in same mo.
  - Calves can run ___**fastest**___[4] their mothers w/in 2 days *(handwritten: теленок)*
- Nobody knows what ___**triggers the imigration**___[5]
- ~200K of ___**weakest**___[6] wldbst die of starvation, disease, exhaustion
  - Others die from preds.; cat tries to separate calf from ___**its mother**___[7]
- Kenya's Maasai Mara: ___**rains**___[8] create huge area of watered ___**grazing**___[9]
- In Nov., wldbst head south again to the ___**Serengeti**___[10]

AFTER VIEWING

E Work with a partner. Discuss the questions.

1. In the video, you heard that "no one knows what triggers the migration." What are some possible explanations for why the wildebeest start their migration?
2. Recently, the government of Tanzania wanted to build a highway across the Serengeti National Park. The road would have cut across the migration routes of the wildebeest. What arguments could be made against building this highway? What arguments could be made in favor of building it?
3. How do you think human and animal migrations are similar? How are they different?
4. Every year a great animal migration in Tanzania attracts nearly 200,000 tourists to the area. Would you also call this movement of humans a migration? Explain.

B Vocabulary

MEANING FROM CONTEXT **A** 🎧 **2.15** Look at the map and the map key of the Greater Yellowstone Ecosystem. Then read and listen to the description. Notice each word or phrase in **blue** and think about its meaning.

THE GREATER YELLOWSTONE ECOSYSTEM

Yellowstone National Park is a nearly 35,000-square-mile wilderness recreation area in the western United States. Yellowstone features canyons, rivers, forests, hot springs, and geysers. It is home to hundreds of animal species, including bears, wolves, bison, elk, and antelope.

Wildlife within Yellowstone National Park is protected by **legislation**, but the **ecology** of the park—the plants and animals— extends beyond its borders, where the area is divided among federal, state, private, and **tribal** lands. Conflicting interests create nearly **overwhelming** challenges that conservation managers must **confront** as they **monitor** animal movement in and around the park.

On privately owned land, wildlife habitat is **diminishing**. Development often **interferes** with animal migration, and ancient migration routes are being **displaced**. However, some private land is being protected. Billionaire[1] Ted Turner is **dedicated to** helping wildlife; his Flying D Ranch protects some 113,000 acres of wildlife habitat.

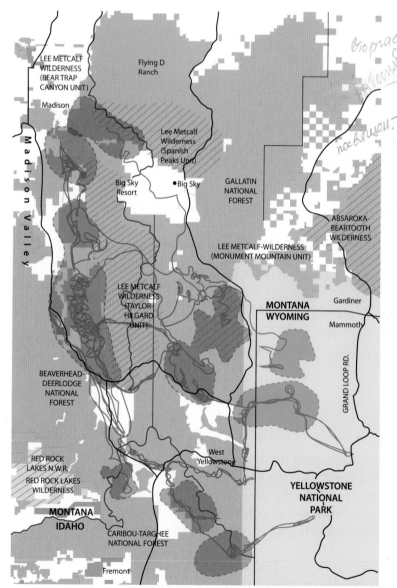

Landownership
- National Park Service
- Wilderness
- U.S. Forest Service
- Private Protected
- Fish and Wildlife Service
- Bureau of Land Management
- Tribal
- State and Local Government
- Private
- Other

Madison Valley Elk Herd
- Summer Range
- Winter Range
- Migration Route

Lines represent seasonal migrations between summer and winter ranges for 11 elk in the Madison Valley herd. GPS collars collected data on their locations every 30 minutes.

[1]**billionaire** (n): a person with more than one billion (1,000,000,000) dollars

B Match each word or phrase with its definition.

1. _b_ confront (v)
2. _j_ dedicated to (adj)
3. _f_ diminish (v)
4. _h_ displace (v)
5. _a_ ecology (n)
6. _d_ interfere (v)
7. _i_ legislation (n)
8. _e_ monitor (v)
9. _c_ overwhelming (adj)
10. _g_ tribal (adj)

a. a habitat, its living things, and their relationships
b. to deal with or face (a problem or challenge)
c. more than can be managed or dealt with
d. to block or get in the way of an activity or goal
e. to follow, check, or observe
f. to get smaller in size, number, importance, etc.
g. belonging or related to a group of native people
h. to force to move from a home or habitat
i. a law or laws
j. very involved in and supportive of

C Work with a partner. Look at the map in exercise A and answer the questions.

CRITICAL THINKING: INTERPRETING A MAP

1. How was information about the movements of elk obtained? приобретено
2. Do the elk spend the winter inside or outside Yellowstone National Park?
3. Do any elk migration routes go through the Flying D Ranch? do not migration
4. Who owns the land between Big Sky and the Big Sky Resort? private
5. Is there any private protected land in Madison Valley? Бам Yes, there is.

D Work in a small group. Read these statements by people living in the Greater Yellowstone Ecosystem. Which landownership group(s) on the map in exercise A might each person belong to?

CRITICAL THINKING: EVALUATING

1. It is of the greatest importance to protect the ecology of the area and live in harmony with nature here as our ancestors did.
2. We need stricter legislation to keep people from interfering with living things in the rivers, streams, and forests.
3. If I don't displace animals from time to time, I won't be able to develop my land. This isn't state land, after all. It's my property.
4. We're dedicated to confronting the problem of diminishing predator populations and believe introducing more bears and wolves into the area is a great solution.
5. A herd of migrating elk can be overwhelming for a town. It's my job to see that they get the resources they need to deal with it.

◀ Herd of elk in summer in Yellowstone, USA

Listening A Conversation about the Serengeti

BEFORE LISTENING

PRIOR KNOWLEDGE **A** Work in a small group. Discuss the questions.

1. What have you learned about the Serengeti National Park in Tanzania and Kenya? Discuss what makes the Serengeti interesting and a popular tourist destination.
2. Think about Yellowstone National Park and the conservation challenges it faces. Could the Serengeti National Park in Tanzania face similar challenges? Explain.

WHILE LISTENING

LISTENING FOR
MAIN IDEAS

B 🎧 2.16 Listen to the conversation. Choose the correct answers.

1. The size of the Serengeti Mara ecosystem has (increased / diminished).
2. The human populations in Kenya and Tanzania have been (increasing / decreasing).
3. Offers of money from tourism companies (have / haven't) persuaded the Robandans to move from their village.
4. Animal populations in the Serengeti Mara ecosystem are (at risk / maintaining their numbers).

LISTENING FOR
DETAILS

C 🎧 2.16 Listen again. Choose T for *True*, F for *False*, or NG for information *Not Given*.

1. In 1950, the authorities probably felt the animals were a higher priority than the Ikoma people.   1 - (T)   F   NG
2. Everyone who eats bush meat in Tanzania is punished for it.   2 - T   (F)   NG
3. An ecotourism group has invested a lot of money to protect the ecology of the Serengeti. *million*   3 - (T.)   F   NG
4. The tourism companies are planning to force the Robandans to move.   4 - T   F   (NG)
5. Brandon suggests that the tourism companies are only concerned with money.   5 - T   (F)   NG
6. Ashley is going to go on a trip soon.   6 - T   F   (NG)

LISTENING SKILL Listening for Clarification

In conversation, speakers often clarify what they have said so that their intended meaning is clear.

Some expressions that signal clarification are:

For the most part yes, although…	*Well, yes/yeah, …, but…*
Yes/Yeah, partly. But…	*Well, you're right that…, but…*
That's true, but…	*Of course, but…*

If you listen for what comes after these expressions, you will better understand the speaker's meaning.

D 🔊 2.17 Read these sentences expressing what Ashley thought before Brandon added a clarification. Then listen to excerpts from their discussion and write the clarification that Brandon provided.

1. Brandon spent his vacation in Tanzania. *once or twice spent in Kenya*

   Kenya twice _____

2. The wildebeest migration takes place in the Serengeti National Park. *ecosystem*

   Partly they migrate around Serengeti and Kenya

3. 16,700 square kilometers is a huge amount of land to set aside for wildlife.

   It has diminished to have its sides

4. Hunting, selling, and eating bush meat must be under control because it's illegal.

   The law It is difficult to enforce.

5. The ecotourism company Brandon mentions is only interested in making money.

   Try to help villagers.

AFTER LISTENING

E Discuss the questions with a partner.

1. In your own words, how would you explain the conflict between the needs of the animals and the needs of people of the Serengeti Mara ecosystem?
2. If you were villagers from Robanda, would you accept the offer of money to move off the land? What would you gain, and what would you lose from your decision?
3. What if, instead of persuading the Ikoma to leave, the tourism companies invited them to be partners in the business? How would the two groups cooperate to give visitors a great experience of the Serengeti? What difficulties might interfere with this collaboration?

Lions in Serengeti National Park, Tanzania

Speaking

PRONUNCIATION Linking with *You* or *Your*

🎧 **2.18** We often link a word that ends in the sound /t/, /d/, or /z/ with *you* or *your*. Those sounds are softened and change as follows:

- /t/ sounds like /tʃ/   *I see what you mean.*
- /d/ sounds like /dʒ/   *I'm glad you had your camera.*
- /z/ sounds like /ʒ/   *How was your trip?*

A Mark the linked words in each sentence and check (✓) the pronunciation.

	/tʃ/	/dʒ/	/ʒ/
1. Would you like me to take your coat?	☐	☑	☐
2. I'm not sure what you said.	☑	☐	☐
3. Are you sure he's your tour guide?	☐	☐	☑
4. Why didn't you call me sooner?	☑	☐	☐
5. I forgot to feed your bird.	☐	☑	☐
6. Why did you leave the door open?	☐	☑	☐

B 🎧 **2.19** Listen and check your answers to exercise A. Then listen again and repeat the sentences.

C Work with a partner. Take turns asking and answering these questions. Be sure that you correctly link *you* and *your*.

1. Would you like to go to Tanzania? Why would you or wouldn't you like to go?
2. Is there another migration, human or animal, that you would like to learn more about? Why did you choose that particular migration?
3. If you had the power, would you give tribal peoples special privileges in national parks? What privileges would you give them?
4. Would you believe me if I told you I'm totally dedicated to learning English? Why would you or wouldn't you believe me?
5. When did you last forget your phone somewhere? What did you do?
6. Think about your life last year. Did you have any notable experiences? Did you have any overwhelming ones?
7. Where would you go to put your English to the test? Why would you choose that place?

D 🎧 2.20 Work with a partner. Listen to a wildlife expert explain some of the ways animals find their way when they migrate. Then discuss with your partner whether each statement below is a theory or a fact. Write *Theory* or *Fact*.

CRITICAL THINKING: DISTINGUISHING FACT FROM THEORY

1. _Fact_ Animals migrate mostly for reasons related to basic needs.
2. _Theory_ Some birds use the sun to find their way as they migrate.
3. _Fact_ Some birds use star patterns to choose the direction to travel.
4. _Fact_ Sea turtles use energy patterns to find their way.
5. _Fact_ Many animals use features of the landscape to find their way.
6. _Theory_ Migration directions may be found in the DNA of some animals.

E Work with a partner. Discuss the questions.

CRITICAL THINKING: APPLYING

1. Think of some migrating animals you know about. Describe their migration and the method(s) you think they use to find their way.
2. What are some of the problems migrating animals encounter along the way? Talk about animals that migrate by land, water, and air.
3. How can humans help to solve the problems animals encounter while migrating and allow them to migrate freely and unharmed?

FINAL TASK A Pair Presentation on Animal Migration

> You are going to research information on a migrating animal. Then you will give a pair presentation to the class with the information you researched.

A Work with a partner. Choose a migrating animal that is not in this unit to research. Then follow the steps on the next page.

Monarch butterflies in the Sierra Chincua Sanctuary, Mexico

1. Research basic facts about the animal you chose, including information such as:
   - physical description
   - how long it lives
   - its habitat and range
   - threats it faces

2. Research information about its migration, such as:
   - the migration path
   - the timing of the migration
   - events related to the migration
   - theories and/or facts that explain the migration and how the animals are able to find their way

3. Find a picture of the animal for your presentation.

4. Create a time line of the migration to use as a visual aid for your presentation.

управление, маневрирование

PRESENTATION SKILL Handling Audience Questions

Questions from the audience can be unpredictable. Here's how to handle them:

- Start by saying "Good question!" to be polite and show interest.
- Repeat the question in your own words. This gives you a little extra time, helps you understand the question, and helps the audience understand it.
- Answer the question as clearly as possible. (If you don't know the answer, say something like "I'm afraid I don't have that information right now. I'll have to get back to you later on that." Then research the question and follow up with the person who asked it.)
- Finish by checking if your answer was understood by asking, "Does that make sense?" or "Is that clear?"

ORGANIZING IDEAS **B** With your partner, organize your presentation (using an outline, numbered notes, index cards, etc.). Decide which parts each of you will present. Then practice giving your presentation, including handling audience questions.

PRESENTING **C** Present the information to the class. Answer any questions from your audience. Use the suggestions in the skill box for handling audience questions.

REFLECTION

1. Which information that you learned in this unit is likely to be the most useful to you? Why and how?

_____

_____

2. Which aspect of human or animal migration in this unit did you find the most interesting? Explain.

_____

_____

3. Here are the vocabulary words and phrases from the unit. Check (✓) the ones you can use.

- ☐ archaeologist
- ☐ confront *противостоять*
- ☐ dedicated to
- ☐ descendant
- ☐ diminish **AWL** *поломки, уменьшать*
- ☐ displace **AWL** *вытеснять*
- ☐ ecology
- ☐ genetic
- ☐ hypothesis **AWL**
- ☐ immense *вмешиваться*
- ☐ interfere
- ☐ legislation **AWL**
- ☐ migrate **AWL**
- ☐ monitor **AWL**
- ☐ notable
- ☐ overwhelming *подавляющий*
- ☐ perspective **AWL**
- ☐ subsequently **AWL** *впоследствии*
- ☐ tribal *родовой, племени*
- ☐ venture *рисковать, осмеливаться*

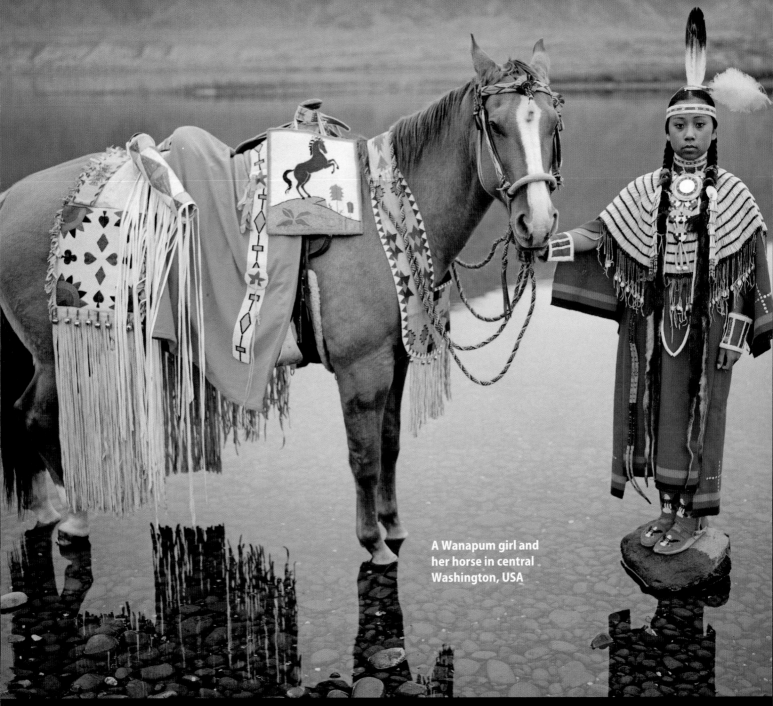

TRADITION AND PROGRESS 6

A Wanapum girl and her horse in central Washington, USA

ACADEMIC SKILLS

LISTENING	Listening for a Correction
	Using an Idea Map
SPEAKING	Using Rhetorical Questions
	Stress in Adjective-Noun Combinations
CRITICAL THINKING	Thinking Outside the Box

THINK AND DISCUSS

1 What cultural values are evident in this photo? Does your culture share any of these values?

2 What does the word *progress* mean to you?

3 What traditions are important to you?

EXPLORE THE THEME

Look at the photos and read the information. Then answer the questions.

1. What traditional peoples and ways of life are represented by each photo?

2. Do you think the Kyrgyz, the Suri, and the Amish people engage in traditional activities by choice or by necessity? Explain.

3. What might these people prefer about their traditional ways of life?

PAST MEETS PRESENT

In Jujuy, a remote province in northwest Argentina, a woman wears a feathered costume to represent the nandu, or sacred bird of the Suris, an indigenous group of this area.

Amish traveling in a horse-drawn buggy in Lancaster County, Pennsylvania, USA

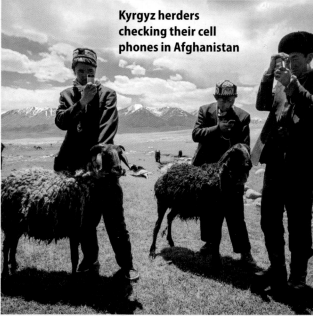

Kyrgyz herders checking their cell phones in Afghanistan

Is modernization universal? Are traditional lifestyles becoming obsolete? Can modern and traditional ways of life coexist? For some cultures, the answers to these questions are critical to their existence. Ultimately, there is no way of stopping progress and its impact on cultures and traditions nearly everywhere.

Vocabulary

A 🎧 **2.21** Read and listen to the article. Notice each word or phrase in **blue** and think about its meaning.

PRESERVING ANCIENT TRADITIONS: THE HADZA

Hunting and gathering food is a survival strategy that scientists believe humans began to **employ** some 1.8 million years ago. Then around 10,000 years ago, a major **transition** occurred: people learned how to grow crops and domesticate[1] animals. However, there is a group of people in an **isolated** region of northern Tanzania that rejects the agricultural way of life. They still **insist on** hunting animals and gathering food. This group, the Hadza people, has lived in the Great Rift Valley for 10,000 years, and the **preservation** of their ancient ways is a priority for them.

The Hadza are nomads[2] who gather food from plants that grow naturally and move according to the travel patterns of the animals they hunt. They are **accustomed to** living in temporary huts made of branches and dried grass that they can quickly and easily **assemble**. It is an interesting **contradiction** that although the Hadza have very little in the way of material possessions, they are happy to share everything they have with others. This **principle**, however, is not followed by local farmers, who have converted 75 percent of the Hadza's traditional homeland to farmland since the 1950s. If the modern world continues to interfere with the Hadza as they try to **pursue** their ancient way of life, that way of life may disappear forever.

[1] **domesticate** (v): to bring wild animals under control and use them to produce food or as pets
[2] **nomad** (n): a person who has no permanent home, but moves constantly in search of water and food

B Match each word or phrase with its definition.

1. _e_ employ (v)
2. _d_ transition (n)
3. _g_ isolated (adj)
4. _j_ insist on (v ph)
5. _a_ preservation (n)
6. _c_ accustomed to (adj ph)
7. _i_ assemble (v)
8. _b_ contradiction (n)
9. _f_ principle (n)
10. _h_ pursue (v)

a. keeping something as it is and protecting it 5
b. a situation containing two opposite truths 8
c. used to; familiar with; in the habit of 6
d. a change from one state to another 2
e. to use 1
f. a guiding rule or idea 9
g. remote and difficult to reach 3
h. to follow or carry out (an activity, plan, policy, etc.) 10
i. to build or put together 7
j. to continue to say or do something despite criticism 4

C Work with a partner. Discuss the questions.

1. What are some methods employed to conserve water?
2. What is a principle that you insist on following?
3. What is something that you had trouble assembling? Explain.
4. When is it acceptable to contradict someone? _under no circumstances._
5. What career are you pursuing?

VOCABULARY SKILL Collocations: Verb/Adjective + Preposition

Some verbs and adjectives are followed by prepositions. When you learn a new adjective or verb, be sure to note which preposition it usually occurs with.

Verb + Preposition
insist on, participate in, approve of, object to, interfere with/in

Adjective + Preposition
accustomed to, responsible for, terrified of, content with, involved with/in

There are no easy rules that specify which preposition to use with verbs and adjectives. If you're not sure, check a dictionary.

D Choose the correct preposition for each collocation. Use a dictionary or ask your teacher if you are not sure.

1. The Hadza are not shy (about / for) giving interviews, and a great deal of information that pertains (on / to) Hadza customs and ways of thinking has been discovered that way.
2. For example, contrary (from / to) popular opinion, the Hadza are not opposed (to / against) development but rather (for / to) land use that is not sustainable.
3. Fewer and fewer cultures are isolated (from / with) the world.
4. Recent studies have shown that Hadza DNA is distinct (from / to) that of their neighbors.
5. Some people in Tanzania interfere (with / to) the ancient traditions of the Hadza.

A Listening A Student Presentation about Bhutan

BEFORE LISTENING

PREVIEWING **A** Look at the images and read the information. Then answer the questions.

1. Where is Bhutan located? What do you know about it?
2. Describe the image on Bhutan's flag. What do you think it means?
3. Bhutan is trying to measure its *Gross National Happiness*. What do you think this phrase means?

The flag of Bhutan

Bhutan Fast Facts

Population: 793,897

Capital: Thimphu

Area: 14,824 square miles (38,394 square kilometers)

WHILE LISTENING

LISTENING FOR
MAIN IDEAS

B 🎧 2.22 ▶ 1.13 Listen and check (✓) the three main topics presented by the speaker.

1. ☐ the circumstances surrounding the decision to open Bhutan up to the world
2. ☐ how Bhutan opened itself up in reaction to external political events
3. ☑ a new approach to development devised by the king of Bhutan ✓
4. ☑ policies to facilitate more rapid and efficient economic development ✓
5. ☐ the rise of a movie industry in Bhutan
6. ☑ social and cultural changes since the Gross National Happiness policy was implemented ✓

LISTENING FOR
DETAILS

C 🎧 2.22 Listen again. Choose T for *True*, F for *False*, or NG for information *Not Given*.

1. The policy of remaining cut off from the world was to blame for problems in public education.   T   (F)   NG
2. The king of Bhutan can take back his absolute power if he decides it is necessary.   T   F   (NG)

3. Bhutan is trying to make its agricultural methods more efficient to maximize exports. （T） F NG

~~ограничение~~

4. The government of Bhutan has placed certain restrictions on what the media is allowed to broadcast. ~~транслировать~~ （T） F NG

5. Movies examining how Bhutanese culture is evolving are very popular in Bhutan. （T） F NG

NOTE-TAKING SKILL Using an Idea Map

An idea map can provide a clear visual overview of a topic and connections between ideas. It is a useful note-taking format for a topic that has a clear structure.

Place the main topic at the top of the idea map. Directly connected to the main topic are sub-topics; details are then connected to the sub-topics.

D 🎧 2.23 Listen to an excerpt from the presentation. Complete the idea map with information from the presentation. Write only one word for each answer.

NOTE TAKING

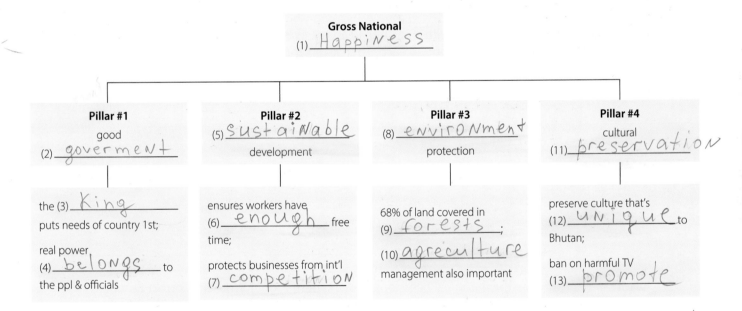

Gross National
(1) _Happiness_

Pillar #1	Pillar #2	Pillar #3	Pillar #4
good	(5) _sustainable_	(8) _environment_	cultural
(2) _goverment_	development	protection	(11) _preservation_
the (3) _King_ puts needs of country 1st;	ensures workers have (6) _enough_ free time;	68% of land covered in (9) _forests_ ;	preserve culture that's (12) _unique_ to Bhutan;
real power (4) _belongs_ to the ppl & officials	protects businesses from int'l (7) _competition_	(10) _agreculture_ management also important	ban on harmful TV (13) _promote_

AFTER LISTENING

E Work in a small group. For each pillar of Gross National Happiness in the idea map, brainstorm additional ideas that Bhutan could try. Write your ideas in your notebook. Then share your best ideas with the class.

CRITICAL THINKING: SYNTHESIZING

> *For good government, I think they could try keeping the taxes low.*

1. happiness   11. preservation
2. goverment   12. unique
3. King   13. promote
4. belongs
5. sustainable
6 enough
7. competition
8. environment
9. forests
10. agreculture

A Speaking

> ### SPEAKING SKILL Using Rhetorical Questions
>
> Rhetorical questions are questions that a speaker asks for dramatic effect or to make a point, not to get an answer. Here are three types of rhetorical questions:
>
> 1. Questions that encourage your audience to think about something:
>
>   *There were no cars or trucks, no phones, and no postal service.* **Can you imagine what life must have been like?**
>
> 2. Questions that invite your audience to agree with you, such as tag questions:
>
>   *Gross domestic product is one way to evaluate a country's success. But it's not really related to the happiness of the people,* **is it?**
>
> 3. Questions you think your audience would like to ask that you then answer:
>
>   **So, what is meant by good government?** *Well, the king puts the needs of the country first.*

A 🎧 2.24 Work with a partner. Read the excerpts from the presentation, adding a rhetorical question to each. Then listen and write the questions the speaker used.

1. Bhutan is known as *Druk Yul,* which in English is . . . land of the thunder dragon. _____ I imagine a brilliantly colored dragon jumping from mountain to mountain and making an incredible noise!

2. _____ Well, part of it is taking into consideration the contributions that families make to the society and to the economy.

3. And I think Gross National Happiness is the right approach. It helps to make sure that we don't lose our beautiful environment and the best parts of our ancient culture. _____

B Are the rhetorical questions above type 1, 2, or 3? Write the correct number.

Question 1: __1__   Question 2: __3__   Question 3: __2__

USING RHETORICAL
QUESTIONS

указаний

C For each item, write a rhetorical question of the type indicated. Then read your questions to a partner.

1. The king of Bhutan had absolute power over his people. That means his power was unlimited, and the people had to do anything he said without question.
    (Type 1) _____

2. Just a short time ago, Bhutan didn't even have electricity. Today, young Bhutanese are addicted to video games, smartphones, social media, and Pokémon Go.
    (Type 2) _____

3. (Type 3) _____
    Well, it's a way of measuring economic growth that also takes happiness into consideration.

1. What kind of images does that bring to mind?   3. We wouldn't want to loss all
2. And what do I mean by sutainable development?   these beautiful things. would we?

PRONUNCIATION Stress in Adjective-Noun Combinations

🎧 2.25 There are two different stress patterns for adjective-noun combinations. When the adjective describes the noun, emphasize the noun. This is the more common pattern.

> I have a <u>light</u> **sche**dule this week.
> He wore a <u>blue</u> **shirt**.

When the two words form a compound that is a fixed expression with a specific meaning, emphasize the adjective. These compounds are sometimes written as one word, as in *mailbox*.

> There were no **light** <u>bulbs</u> in Bhutan.
> People started wearing **blue** <u>jeans</u>.

D **🎧 2.26** Listen to each sentence and check (✓) the correct meaning of the adjective-noun combination it contains.

1. a. ☑ a teacher of the English language
   b. ☐ a teacher who is English

2. a. ☑ juice made from oranges
   b. ☐ orange-colored juice, maybe mango

3. a. ☐ the house painted white
   b. ☑ the White House, Washington, D.C.

4. a. ☑ a difficult drive by car
   b. ☐ a piece of computer equipment

5. a. ☑ bluebirds (a species of bird)
   b. ☐ birds with blue-colored feathers

6. a. ☐ lights positioned up high
   b. ☑ important moments

7. a. ☑ a jacket that is yellow
   b. ☐ a yellow jacket (a species of insect)

8. a. ☐ a right whale (a species of whale)
   b. ☑ the correct whale

E Work with a partner. Use the adjective-noun combinations below to make sentences. Say them to your partner. Your partner will tell you the meaning she hears.

English teacher	orange juice	white house/White House	hard drive
bluebirds/blue birds	yellow jacket	highlights/high lights	right whale

◀ **A traditional dancer at the Paro festival, Paro, Bhutan**

Taktshang, or "Tiger's Nest," monastery in Bhutan

GRAMMAR FOR SPEAKING Verb + Object + Infinitive

Certain verbs can be followed by an object + infinitive.

> Mobile phones **allow people to communicate** more easily than ever before.
> We **invited English teachers to teach** in our schools.

To form the negative of the infinitive, insert *not* before it: *вставить*

> The king **ordered the Bhutanese people not to have connections** with other countries.

These are some of the verbs that can be followed by an object + infinitive.

advise	ask	force	invite	permit	remind	tell
allow	encourage	help	order	persuade	require	warn

F Put the words and phrases in the correct order to create sentences about Bhutan.

1. Bhutan / its citizens / to take / for / encourages / responsibility /the environment

   Bhutan encourages its citizens to take responsibility for the environment.

2. sustainable / asks / The government / to work / companies / in / way / a

   The government asks companies to work in a sustainable way.

3. The government / companies / to cut down / has ordered / not / trees for export

   The government has ordered companies not to cut down trees for export.

4. The king / invites / to implement / other countries / of Bhutan / GNH strategies

   The king invites other countries to implement GNH stratergies of Bhutan. *воплощать в жизнь*

5. Bhutan / to obtain / all visiting tourists / requires / a tourist visa   *получать*

   Bhutan requires all visiting tourists to obtain a tourist visa.

CRITICAL THINKING:
APPLYING

G Work in a small group. Imagine you govern a country. What rules would you create in these areas? Use verbs from the skill box and the object + infinitive pattern. *управляете*

| restaurants | transportation | employment | pet ownership | education |

LESSON TASK Conducting an Interview

A Work with a partner. Take turns completing the interview. Follow these steps.

CRITICAL THINKING: APPLYING

1. Each of you choose a country (or a large city) where you have lived.
2. Take turns interviewing each other to determine the Gross National Happiness of that place. Ask the questions and record your partner's answers in the chart.
3. Ask your partner to explain his or her answers and ask follow-up questions about anything you don't understand.

Gross National Happiness in _____	Yes	No
Pillar 1: Good Government		
1. Is the state of the transportation system satisfactory?		
2. Is the public education system adequate?		
Pillar 2: Sustainable Development		
1. Do most jobs provide enough time off?		
2. Do most jobs pay workers enough to live comfortably?		
Pillar 3: Environmental Protection		
1. Are levels of pollution, noise, and traffic acceptable?		
2. Are there parks or natural areas available to the public?		
Pillar 4: Cultural Preservation		
1. Do people try to maintain traditions along with new practices?		
2. Do young people value and respect the older generations?		

> **EVERYDAY LANGUAGE** Acknowledging an Error
>
> *I made a mistake.* *I'm wrong.*
>
> *I should have checked more carefully.* *My mistake.*
>
> *I wasn't thinking properly.* *You're right.*

B Share the responses to your Gross National Happiness interview with the class. Then discuss these questions as a class.

1. Which countries or cities have the highest level of GNH and which have the lowest, based on the interview results?
2. Are any of the answers surprising to you?
3. What was the most challenging aspect of conducting an interview? What would you do differently if you interviewed another person?

Video

Greg Anderson and David Harrison, National Geographic Explorers and linguists on the Enduring Voices Project, interview two men in Thungri village, Arunachal Pradesh.

Preserving Endangered Languages

BEFORE VIEWING

PREDICTING **A** Read the information about the Enduring Voices Project. Then discuss the questions.

1. How many of the world's 7,000 languages do you think are in danger of extinction?
2. What do you think is the main cause of language extinction?

> **THE ENDURING VOICES PROJECT** The Enduring Voices Project documents and works to preserve endangered languages. They have created online Talking Dictionaries using recordings of native speakers from small language communities.

MEANING FROM CONTEXT **B** Read the sentences with words from the video. Guess the meaning of the underlined words. Then write each word next to its definition.

- A <u>savvy</u> shopper takes advantage of sales, coupons, and other promotions.
- When a city wants to <u>revitalize</u> a neighborhood, it often adds a public green space.
- Adjusting to a new career includes learning the specific <u>lexicon</u> of the job.
- Scientific researchers gain <u>insight</u> into cures for diseases by doing experiments.
- American Indians are the <u>indigenous</u> people of North America.

1. _lexicon_ (n) the vocabulary of a particular field or sector
2. _insight_ (n) the ability to see or know the truth about something
3. _indigenous_ (adj) born in or native to a place
4. _savvy_ (adj) smart, knowledgeable
5. _revitalize_ (v) to give new life or energy to something

WHILE VIEWING

C ▶ 1.14 Watch the video. Check (✓) the statement that is the main message of the video.

UNDERSTANDING
MAIN IDEAS

☐ Talking Dictionaries are rapidly modernizing small languages around the world.

☐ The best way to preserve a language is by insisting that its young people speak it.

☑ The Enduring Voices program helps preserve languages with Talking Dictionaries.

☐ Siletz Dee-ni, Matukar Panau, and Tuvan are isolated, small language communities.

☐ The Enduring Voices Project and the AAAS are concerned about language extinction.

D ▶ 1.14 Watch the video again. Complete this summary with words from the video. Write only one word for each answer.

UNDERSTANDING
DETAILS

There are 7,000 languages in the world, and __half__ (1) of them may __disappear__ (2) in this century. Languages go extinct mostly because of __the social__ (3) pressure and __attitude__ (4) that devalue small languages. The goal of Talking Dictionaries is to give some small languages a first-ever __presents__ (5) on the Internet. The Talking Dictionaries for three languages are highlighted: Siletz Dee-ni language, Matukar Panau, and Tuvan. The Siletz Nation is using the dictionary as a __tool__ (6) to revitalize their language. The speakers of Matukar Panau wanted to see their language on the __Internet__ (7), which shows that their language is just as good as any other. The Tuvan Talking Dictionary was also launched as an iPhone __application__ (8). Since linguistic diversity is such an important part of our __human__ (9) heritage, indigenous communities, along with scientists, are responding to the crisis of language __extinction__ (10).

E Look back at your answers to exercise A. Were your predictions correct? Tell a partner.

CHECKING
PREDICTIONS

AFTER VIEWING

F Work with a partner. Discuss the questions.

CRITICAL THINKING:
EVALUATING

1. The risk of language extinction is higher in isolated communities. Does isolation benefit languages in any way? Why or why not?
2. Can small languages with Talking Dictionaries avoid extinction? Why or why not?
3. When a culture transitions from traditional to modern life, what else is at risk of extinction besides its language?
4. If you were going to create a Talking Dictionary for your language, which words would you start with? Explain.

1. half
2. disappear
3. the social
4. attitude
5. presents
6. tool
7. Internet
8. Application
9. human 10 extinction

Vocabulary

A 🎧 3.2 Read and listen to the article. Notice each word in blue.

REVITALIZING A SWEET TRADITION

While traveling through eastern Turkey in 2008, National Geographic Explorer Catherine de Medici Jaffee was fascinated by the people, culture, and beauty of the area, and especially by the ancient tradition of beekeeping. The great **diversity** of the flowers that grow there gives honey many different flavors. But she also noticed that the local women who relied on honey for their **livelihood** were having trouble earning enough money despite the obvious **merits** of their product. The **hardship** they were experiencing inspired Jaffee to **undertake** a project that would **ultimately** become Balyolu (which means "honey path" in Turkish), "the world's very first honey-tasting **heritage** trail."

Jaffee recalls, "For the next four years, I began planning how I would make it back to the region to work with local communities to bring something like this to life." She obtained the **consent** of local beekeepers to guide tourists to their villages to taste their honey, traveling along ancient footpaths once used by nomads. To further **replicate** the lifestyle of nomads, Balyolu invited visitors to sleep in yurts, traditional round portable tents. Thus, Balyolu was able to provide a better business model to help the community **flourish**. Asked about her favorite experience, Jaffee replied, "My favorite experiences are watching different beekeepers over the years grow and change with their bees. Visiting the same families over and over, I get to become closer to their lives and their hives[1] like a member of a special tribe."

[1] **hive** (or **beehive**) (n): a natural or man-made structure that bees live in

B Write each word in blue from exercise A next to its definition.

1. _undertake_ (v) to start doing a task and take responsibility for it
2. _flourish_ (v) to have success and develop quickly and strongly
3. _diversity_ (n) a wide range of different things
4. _ultimately_ (adv) finally; after a long and often complicated series of events
5. _replicate_ (v) to create a copy of an object or experience
6. _livelihood_ (n) a way of making money or obtaining the necessities of life
7. _consent_ (n) permission from another person to do something
8. _hardship_ (n) a difficult life situation usually due to lack of money
9. _merits_ (n) advantages, benefits, or other good points
10. _heritage_ (n) tradition, passed from generation to generation

C Complete the chart with the correct form of each word. Use a dictionary to help you.

	Noun	Verb	Adjective
1.	consent	consent	consensual – consented
2.	diversity	diversify	diverse
3.	flourish	flourish	flourished
4.	merit		merited
5.	replication	replicate	replicated
6.	undertaker	undertake	undertaking

D Match the words with their synonyms. Use a dictionary to help you if needed.

1. _g_ consent
2. _f_ diversity
3. _a_ flourish
4. _h_ hardship
5. _b_ heritage
6. _i_ livelihood
7. _j_ merit
8. _c_ replicate
9. _e_ ultimately
10. _d_ undertake

a. to thrive 3
b. tradition 5
c. to reproduce 8
d. to start 10
e. in the end 9
f. variety 2
g. approval 1
h. challenge 4
i. occupation 6
j. positive quality 7

E Complete the sentences with your own ideas and discuss with a partner.

PERSONALIZING

1. People flourish when _____

2. The part of my heritage I appreciate most is _____

3. One benefit of hardship is _____

4. A respected livelihood in my country is _____
   источник средств

5. Diversity is important because _we can learn from one another_

6. One merit of studying alone is _that there are no distractions._
   заслуга

7. My parents would never give their consent for me to _do things that do not benefit me for my advancement_

8. Ultimately, my goal _is to be successfull._

B Listening A Discussion about American Indian Lands

BEFORE LISTENING

PREDICTING **A** You will hear a discussion about American Indian lands. Choose the answers you think are correct.

1. How many American Indian reservations are there in the United States?
   a. nearly 100   b. over 300   c. over 500

2. How many American Indian tribes are there in the United States?
   a. nearly 100   b. over 300   c. over 500

3. What percentage of the land area of the United States do reservations occupy?
   a. about 0.5 percent   b. around 2 percent   c. close to 5 percent

WHILE LISTENING

CHECKING PREDICTIONS **B** 🎧 3.3 Listen to the students' discussion. Take notes on the numbers mentioned at the beginning of the discussion. Were your answers in exercise A correct?

> **LISTENING SKILL** Listening for a Correction
>
> Speakers will sometimes say something, realize that what they've said was incorrect, and then correct themselves. Before a correction, you may hear "Sorry" or an admission of the error such as "You're right." Then the speaker will go on to correct the mistake with expressions such as:
>
> What I mean/meant (to say) is/was …   I mean/meant …
> What I'm trying to say is …   Let me rephrase that.
> What I want/wanted to say is/was …   Let me try again.

▶ **Valerie Stanley, a Pomo Indian, in Intertribal Park, an Indian-run wilderness area in California, USA**

C 🎧 **3.4** Read these statements from the discussion. Then listen to the excerpts and correct each statement so it reflects what the speakers meant to say.

1. Oh, you mean the one about Native American tribes? ~~Indian~~ *Indian*

2. For example, I was surprised to learn that there are over ~~500~~ *300* American Indian reservations in the United States.

3. And the land is important to them.

4. The first one was in Mexico, wasn't it? *New Mexico area.*

5. I think it was the InterTribal Sinkyone Wilderness ~~State Park~~.

D 🎧 **3.5** Listen to an excerpt from the discussion and complete the idea map. Write no more than one word or number in each blank. Take your own notes on the Big Cypress Swamp.

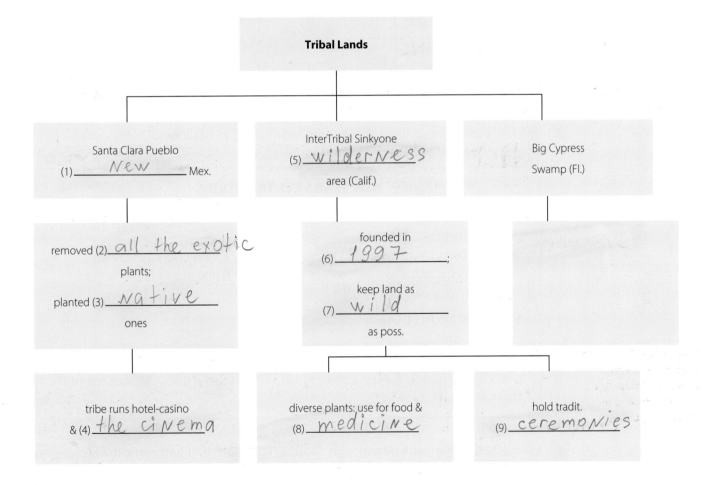

Tribal Lands

- Santa Clara Pueblo
  (1) _New_ Mex.
  - removed (2) _all the exotic_ plants;
  - planted (3) _Native_ ones
    - tribe runs hotel-casino & (4) _the cinema_

- InterTribal Sinkyone
  (5) _wilderness_
  area (Calif.)
  - founded in (6) _1997_;
  - keep land as (7) _wild_ as poss.
    - diverse plants: use for food & (8) _medicine_

- Big Cypress
  Swamp (Fl.)
    - hold tradit. (9) _ceremonies_

AFTER LISTENING

E Work with a partner. Discuss the questions.

1. How does your attitude toward nature compare to the American Indian attitude?

2. Today fewer than half of American Indians live on reservations. Why do you think that is?

1. New
2. all the exotic
3. native
4. the cinema
5. wilderness
6. 1997   [agriculture,
7. wild
8. medicine
9. ceremonies.

Speaking

► Lanterns decorate a door for Chinese New Year Spring Festival, Beijing, China.

A Work in a small group. Read about some New Year's Eve traditions. Discuss which ones you have heard of and any others you know.

NEW YEAR'S EVE TRADITIONS

LUCKY FOOD

Food traditions often represent good luck and happiness in the new year. In the Netherlands, people bring in the new year by eating ring-shaped treats; in Spain, it's custom to eat twelve grapes at midnight, and in Switzerland, it's a tradition to drop ice cream on the floor.

SYMBOLIC FRONT DOORS

Doors also hold special significance for the new year. In China, a red front door signifies happiness and good luck. In Greece, an onion hanging on the front door symbolizes rebirth. In Turkey, sprinkling salt in front of your door brings peace and abundance.

B Complete the chart with information about a New Year's tradition you know.

New Year's Eve Tradition in _____	
Location	
Decorations	
Food and Drink	
Activity/Ritual	

C Work with a partner. Discuss how your celebrations are similar and different.

> **CRITICAL THINKING** Thinking Outside the Box
>
> Thinking outside the box means to look beyond the normal or traditional way of doing things. It is a good way to come up with alternative approaches to situations. When thinking outside the box, don't be afraid to express your ideas–even ones that are out of the ordinary and unconventional. By not judging your ideas as they occur to you, you keep your thoughts flowing, which can lead to some innovative thinking.

D Work in a small group. Suggest new traditions for New Year's Eve celebrations that are interesting, fun, or symbolic. Note your best ideas.

CRITICAL THINKING: THINKING OUTSIDE THE BOX

Suggestions for New Year's Celebration	
Location	
Decorations	
Food and Drink	
Activity/Ritual	

FINAL TASK Presenting a Tradition

> You are going to work with a partner to give a presentation on a current tradition other than a New Year's tradition. You may choose a completely new tradition, or an older one that has been modernized. You can do research if necessary.

A Work with a partner. Brainstorm current traditions that you are both interested in. Some examples are holidays, festivals, or traditions related to family, school, food, clothing, sports, or a life event (e.g., wedding, birthday, or graduation). Then decide on the tradition that you will present.

BRAINSTORMING

B Consider these points to help you research and organize your presentation:

- If it is a completely new tradition, describe how it began, its purpose, and how it is carried out.
- If it is an older tradition that has been modernized, provide background on the original tradition, how it has changed, and the reason for the change.
- Look for images or video that you might be able to use in your presentation. These may help you decide which details to include in your presentation.

C In your notebook, use an idea map to organize your ideas. Include the information from exercise B. Decide which parts each person will present.

D Add one or two rhetorical questions, as appropriate, for dramatic effect or to emphasize important points. If possible, create or obtain a visual related to the tradition to use in your presentation.

E Take turns rehearsing your presentation with your partner. After each turn, give each other feedback on how to improve.

PRESENTATION SKILL Speaking with Confidence

When speaking in front of a group, it is important to appear confident. This will give the impression that you know your topic well and that you believe in what you are saying. There are several things that you can do to feel more confident.

- Organize your notes well and practice your presentation at least once.
- Always have good posture and face the audience.
- Use hand gestures, eye contact, and body language, and smile when you can.
- Finally, remember to pause between sentences and to speak slowly and clearly.

F Give your presentation in front of the class, focusing on strategies for speaking with confidence.

REFLECTION

1. What information that you learned in this unit is likely to be the most useful to you? Why and how?

_____

_____

2. What information about different cultures are you likely to remember from this unit?

_____

_____

3. Here are the vocabulary words and phrases from the unit. Check (✓) the ones you can use.

☐ accustomed to	☐ hardship	☐ principle AWL
☐ assemble AWL	☐ heritage	☐ pursue AWL
☐ consent AWL	☐ insist on	☐ replicate
☐ contradiction AWL	☐ isolated AWL	☐ transition AWL
☐ diversity AWL	☐ livelihood	☐ ultimately AWL
☐ employ	☐ merit	☐ undertake AWL
☐ flourish	☐ preservation	

MONEY IN OUR LIVES

7

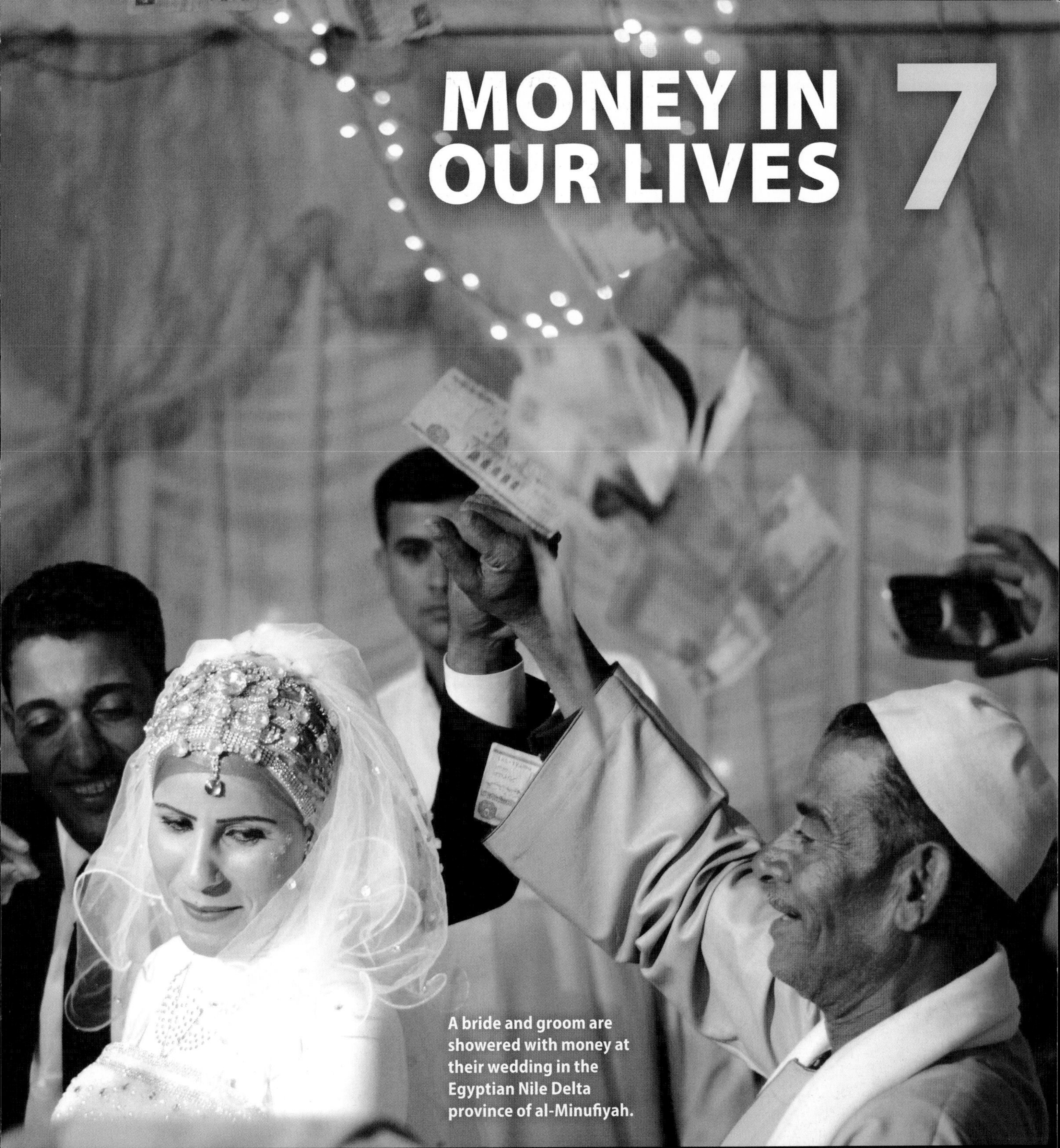

A bride and groom are showered with money at their wedding in the Egyptian Nile Delta province of al-Minufiyah.

ACADEMIC SKILLS

LISTENING   Listening for Shifts in Topic
               Summarizing
SPEAKING   Referencing Research Studies
               Linking Vowel Sounds

THINK AND DISCUSS

1   Look at the photo and read the caption. Does anything about it surprise you?

2   Why do you think money is a typical gift for a couple on their wedding day?

EXPLORE THE THEME

Look at the photo and the chart. Then discuss these questions.

1. What are the people in the photo spending money on?
2. Look at the chart. Which five countries spend the highest percentage of household budget on food?
3. Which categories do countries spend the lowest percentage of household budget on? Why do you think that is?
4. If your country is in the graph, does it accurately reflect your spending? If it isn't, which country's spending pattern is most similar to yours or your family's?

A cafe in New Orleans,
Louisiana, USA

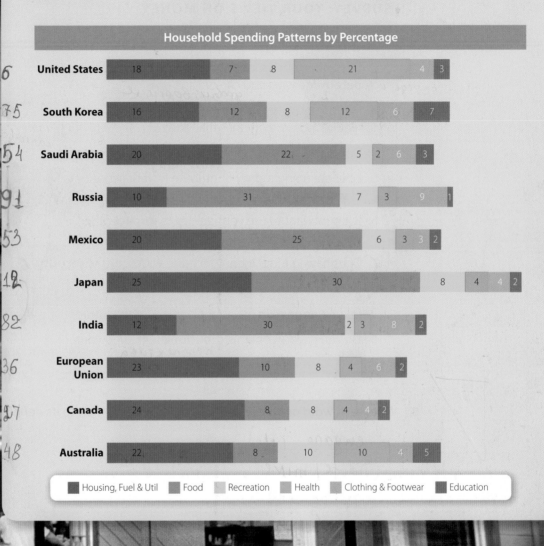

MONEY—HOW DO WE SPEND IT?

Household Spending Patterns by Percentage

Country	Housing, Fuel & Util	Food	Recreation	Health	Clothing & Footwear	Education
United States	18	7	8	21	4	3
South Korea	16	12	8	12	6	7
Saudi Arabia	20	22	5	2	6	3
Russia	10	31	7	3	9	1
Mexico	20	25	6	3	3	2
Japan	25	30	8	4	4	2
India	12	30	2	3	8	2
European Union	23	10	8	4	6	2
Canada	24	8	8	4	4	2
Australia	22	8	10	10	4	5

A Vocabulary

MEANING FROM
CONTEXT

A 🎧 **3.6** Read and listen to the survey from a study on money. Notice each word or phrase in **blue** and think about its meaning. Then choose your answers.

SURVEY: YOUR VIEWS ON MONEY	Yes	No
1. Do you **associate** a high salary with happiness?	☑	☐
2. Does how much money you have frequently **determine** what you can or can't do?	☑	☐
3. Do you find more **fulfillment** doing activities that require money than ones that don't?	☐	☑
4. Do you believe that saving money is a **virtue**?	☑	☐
5. Does spending money contribute to your sense of **well-being**?	☐	☑
6. Is it important to use your money to **impact** others' lives for the better?	☑	☐
7. Does having more money increase your sense of **security**?	☑	☐
8. Does having money **promote** independence?	☑	☐
9. Do you **engage in** financial planning for the future?	☑	☐
10. Do you have an optimistic **outlook** regarding your financial future?	☑	☐

Handwritten notes: определить (determine), удовлетворение (fulfillment), хорошее качество (virtue), делать вклад (contribute), влиять (impact), перспектива (outlook)

B Write each word or phrase in **blue** from exercise A next to its definition.

1. _engage in_ (v) to do (an activity)
2. _determine_ (v) to decide; influence
3. _associate_ (v) to connect in the mind
4. _impact_ (v) to have a direct effect on
5. _outlook_ (n) a point of view; attitude
6. _security_ (n) safety; protection from harm
7. _fulfillment_ (n) a feeling of achievement or satisfaction *удовлетворение*
8. _virtue_ (n) a positive personal characteristic
9. _promote_ (v) to help or encourage something to happen
10. _well-being_ (n) a state of happiness and health

C Work with a partner. Compare and discuss your answers in exercise A.

Many English words have more than one definition. When looking up words with multiple definitions, carefully examine the context for clues to the meaning.

For example, read the sentence and three possible definitions.

*I don't **associate** with my old coworkers anymore.*
1. (v) to connect ideas in one's mind
2. (v) to join as a friend or companion
3. (v) to connect logically

Because the meaning is clearly not related to things only in the mind or connections of logic, we know the correct definition must be number two.

D Choose the best definition for the **bold** word in each sentence.

1. I'd say her greatest **virtue** is patience.
   a. (n) a positive personal characteristic (I teach my son the virtue of honesty.)
   b. (n) an advantage or benefit (The virtue of toast is that it's easy to make.)
   c. (n) moral excellence (His mother is a model of virtue.)

2. Strict **security** is planned for the concert.
   a. (n) safety; protection from harm (The kitten sought security behind its mother.)
   b. (n) measures taken to protect a place (They are tightening security at the airport.)
   c. (n) a certificate proving investment (Securities are traded on Wall Street.)

3. The size of a piece of chicken **determines** its cooking time.
   a. (v) to choose or resolve to do (He'll do better once he determines to improve.)
   b. (v) to discover after investigation (Tests will determine the cause of his illness.)
   c. (v) to decide; influence (Years of service determine salary.)

4. The new president was able to **restore** confidence in the economy.
   a. (v) to repair and renovate (She's an expert in restoring paintings.)
   b. (v) to cause to possess again (The money must be restored to its owner.)
   c. (v) to cause to exist again (The revolution restored democracy.)

5. The economic **outlook** right now is relatively poor.
   a. (n) a forecast or prediction (The political outlook is rather unclear.)
   b. (n) a view (That hotel has a spectacular outlook on the lake.)
   c. (n) a point of view; attitude (I try to keep a positive outlook on life.)

E Complete the statements. Then discuss your answers with a partner.

1. The three factors that impact a person's well-being the most are ___health___,
   (poor) ___money,___ _____

2. I believe the most important virtue a person could have is ___family___

3. Engaging in activities such as ___eduction___ promotes ___working___

Listening An Interview about Money and Happiness

BEFORE LISTENING

CRITICAL THINKING: RANKING

A Read the phrases. How happy does each situation make you? Rank them from 1 (the happiest) to 6 (the least happy).

_1_ having money in the bank   _4_ earning money

_4_ spending money on items you want   _3_ receiving money as a gift

_2_ giving money to other people   _5_ spending money on travel

WHILE LISTENING

LISTENING FOR MAIN IDEAS

B 🎧 **3.7** Listen to the interview. Then choose the correct answers.

1. What does a recent study by psychologist Elizabeth Dunn show?
   a. Spending money brings us more happiness than saving money.
   b. Possessions determine our happiness level more than experiences do.
   c. Spending money on others makes you happier than spending it on yourself. •

2. What common error do people make when they try to buy happiness with money?
   a. They hesitate to buy the things that will really make them happy.
   b. They think major purchases such as houses will make them happy. •
   c. They don't spend freely enough when buying meaningful items.

3. What question did researchers Leaf Van Boven and Tom Gilovich want to answer?
   a. Do people feel happier possessing money or material goods?
   b. Does spending money on things increase people's sense of well-being?
   c. Which makes people happier: spending money on experiences or on items? •

4. What did Angus Deaton and Daniel Kahneman's study reveal?
   a. Making more than a certain amount of money doesn't affect happiness much.
   b. Making more than a certain amount of money causes unhappiness.
   c. Making more than a certain amount of money results in greater happiness. •

▼ **There are approximately 180 currencies recognized by the United Nations.**

NOTE-TAKING SKILL Summarizing

A summary is a shortened version of a passage. It contains the main ideas and some important details. Summarizing teaches you to distinguish between important and less important information, and writing a summary can improve your memory of information you read, listen to, or watch. When you summarize:

- start with a phrase or sentence describing the topic of the summary
- leave out unnecessary information and information that is repeated
- express ideas in as few words as possible, and combine ideas when possible

C 🎧 **3.7** Listen to the interview again. Complete the summaries of the three studies described by Dr. Simmons. Write no more than two words in each blank.

LISTENING FOR DETAILS

Study 1: A study by E. Dunn at the University of British Columbia determined that ___giving money___ away brings a greater sense of well-being than spending it on
                              1
oneself. Dunn gave money to two groups. Members of the first group spent money on
___others people___ ; members of the other spent it on ___themselves___ .
          2   3
Afterwards, the people were ___interviwed___ . The group that spent money on
                                            4
others was found to be ___happier___ .
                                  5

Study 2: L. Van Boven and T. Gilovich looked at the value of spending money on
___experiences___ versus material things. The scientists used ___serveys___
          6   7
to ask how people felt about each. They discovered that spending money on
___experiences___ made people happier than spending it on ___material goods___ .
          8   9
The reason is that experiences are more ___meaningfull___ and contribute to
                                                      10
___successful social___ relationships.
          11

Study 3: Economist A. Deaton and ___psyhologist___ D. Kahneman wanted to know
                                                12
whether more money means ___more happiness___ . They analyzed surveys filled out
                                        13
by ___thousands___ of people. They found that once a person earns $75,000/year,
          14
making more money doesn't ___significantly increase___ his or her happiness level.
                                        15

AFTER LISTENING

D In a group, discuss which option in each pair would result in more happiness according to the research studies you heard. Use *According to . . .* to start your sentences. Then discuss your opinions.

CRITICAL THINKING: SYNTHESIZING

- buying yourself a $1,000 coat/giving $1,000 to a charity
- taking a trip around the world/making an initial payment on a new house
- an easy job that pays $30,000 per year/a stressful job that pays $75,000 per year

A Speaking

SPEAKING SKILL Referencing Research Studies

Referencing research is a good way to support your message. When referring to studies, you can leave out the details and make a general reference instead. This is useful when there are too many studies to mention, when you can't remember the exact studies but know they exist, or when such details are unimportant. Here are some expressions you can use to reference research.

Research has proven/determined/demonstrated (that)...
(A number of/Various) studies show/have shown/suggest (that)...
Statistics show (that)...
According to (various) studies...

A 🎧 **3.8** Work with a partner. Take turns reading the excerpts from the interview about money and happiness. Use expressions from the Speaking Skill box. Then listen and complete each excerpt with the expression used.

1. But, you know, buying a home is a big financial commitment ... and, in fact, people often go deep into debt to buy one. Actually, _research suggests_ that owning your home brings no more happiness than renting.

2. People say that "the best things in life are free," which implies that money doesn't matter to happiness. But we all know that's not really true. _Studies show_ that debt has a negative effect on happiness, while savings and financial security tend to increase it.

3. What's important to remember is this: _research has determined_ that happiness isn't about how much money you have. It's what you do with the money that can promote happiness ...

REFERENCING
RESEARCH STUDIES

B With your partner, role-play a conversation between a college student and a student advisor using the information in the chart below. The advisor gives advice using expressions from the Speaking Skill box. Then switch roles.

Student's Questions	Research for Advisor's Answers
Should I get a part-time job on campus?	Working more than 15 hours a week lowers grades.
Should I apply for a credit card?	Credit cards make people spend more.
Should I quit school and work full time?	People with more education make more money.
Should I get financial advice from other students?	Young people don't always understand money.
Should I blame myself for not saving money?	Two-thirds of college students have little or no savings.

C Work with a partner. Study the chart. Then answer the questions below.

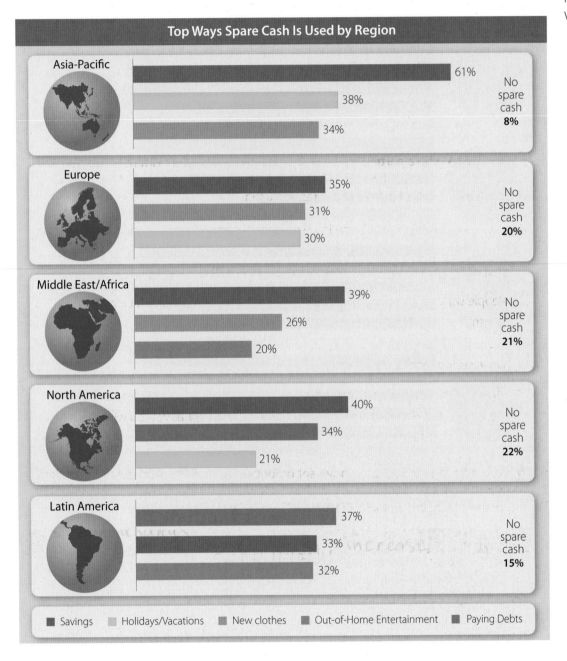

Top Ways Spare Cash Is Used by Region

Asia-Pacific
- 61%
- 38%
- 34%
- No spare cash **8%**

Europe
- 35%
- 31%
- 30%
- No spare cash **20%**

Middle East/Africa
- 39%
- 26%
- 20%
- No spare cash **21%**

North America
- 40%
- 34%
- 21%
- No spare cash **22%**

Latin America
- 37%
- 33%
- 32%
- No spare cash **15%**

■ Savings ■ Holidays/Vacations ■ New clothes ■ Out-of-Home Entertainment ■ Paying Debts

1. What do the different colors and bar lengths represent?
2. In which region do people tend to save the most?
3. In which regions do people use their spare cash to pay debts?
4. What conclusion(s) can you draw from this information?

D Work with a partner. Study the graph. Then answer the questions below.

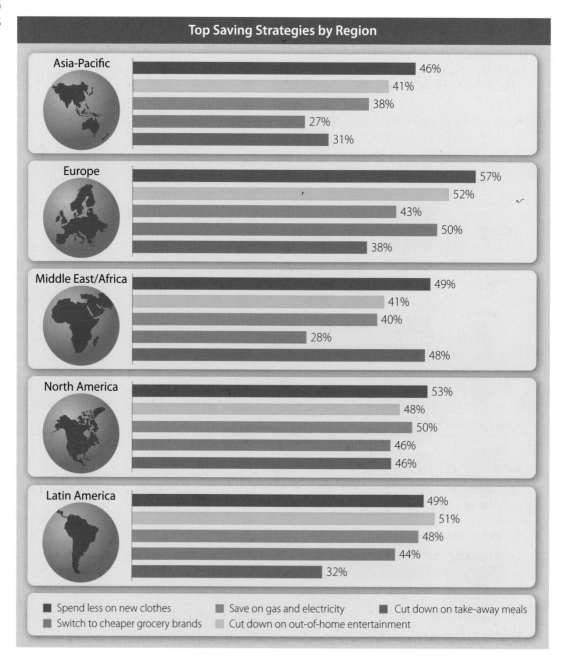

Top Saving Strategies by Region

Asia-Pacific
46%
41%
38%
27%
31%

Europe
57%
52%
43%
50%
38%

Middle East/Africa
49%
41%
40%
28%
48%

North America
53%
48%
50%
46%
46%

Latin America
49%
51%
48%
44%
32%

■ Spend less on new clothes   ■ Save on gas and electricity   ■ Cut down on take-away meals
■ Switch to cheaper grocery brands   ■ Cut down on out-of-home entertainment

1. What do the different colors and bar lengths represent?
2. Which region saves the most in each category?
3. Does the data for your region reflect your reality? Explain.

E Work in a small group. Discuss these questions.

1. Which of the five strategies for saving money would be easiest for you to implement? Which would be the most difficult?
2. What other strategies for saving money can you think of?

LESSON TASK Discussing Purchases and Happiness

A Write five of the most expensive items, services, or experiences that you have ever purchased. Then rank them in order of most expensive (1) to least expensive (5).

Purchase	Expense Rank	Happiness Rank
2. new car		
1. my daughter bought a new house		
3. traveling to the beach		
4. education		
5. clothes		

EVERYDAY LANGUAGE Asking and Answering Personal Questions

Asking

Can/May I ask you (about)…? Would you mind if I asked you (about)…?

Would you mind telling me (about)…? Is it all right/OK if I ask (about)…?

Answering

You certainly may./Of course. No, I don't/wouldn't mind.

Actually, I'd rather not talk about that. Sure./Of course.

B Work with a partner. Take turns sharing the items on your list and asking and answering questions about them. Find out if the items made your partner happy and why or why not. Use the expressions in the Everyday Language box.

A: *Do you mind if I ask you how expensive your watch was?*
B: *No, I don't mind. It was about $300. It's a Swiss watch.*
A: *Can I ask if it makes you happy?*

C Now go back to exercise A and rank your purchases in order of the happiness they gave you (1 = most happiness, 5 = least happiness).

CRITICAL THINKING: RANKING

D With your partner, discuss the questions.

CRITICAL THINKING: ANALYZING

1. How did your purchase lists and your happiness rankings compare? Describe the similarities or differences between you and your partner.
2. Does any of the research from the three studies discussed in the interview on money and happiness support your list and ranking? Explain.
3. Considering your purchase list and happiness ranking, what conclusions can you make about what brings you personal fulfillment? Explain.

Video

Bitcoin: The New Way to Pay

BEFORE VIEWING

PREDICTING

A Work in a small group. Discuss these questions. Predict answers if you are not sure.

1. What is virtual money, and how can people get it?
2. Can virtual money buy real-life objects and experiences?
3. Is virtual money regulated by a real-life bank?

B Match each word from the video to its definition. Use a dictionary to help you.

1. __e__ back up (v)　　　　　a. computer program instructions

2. __a__ code (n)　　　　　　b. limited in number

3. __c__ engrave (v)　　　　c. to cut or carve a design into something

4. __b__ finite (adj)　　　　d. to dig up, remove (from the earth)

5. __d__ mine (v)　　　　　　e. to support, help

1.
2.
3.

WHILE VIEWING

C ▶ 1.15 Watch the video. Which statement is the main idea?

1. Bitcoins are like gold—they are difficult to find, and their value changes daily.
2. Bitcoin is a valuable digital currency, but it has problems like all forms of money.
3. A major Bitcoin owner created a Web series about it to promote its use.
4. The use and security of Bitcoins are limited because they're not supported by a bank.

D Look back at your answers to exercise A. Were your predictions correct?

E ▶ 1.15 Watch the video again and complete the summary. Write no more than three words in each blank.

BITCOIN IN A NUTSHELL

Bitcoin is an Internet currency that gets its value from _the code itself_ [has real world value.]
1

There are two ways you can get Bitcoins: _mine for them_ like virtual or
2

gold or _buy them from_ another Bitcoin user. However, there is only a
3

finite amount of them online. People use Bitcoin to make big and
4

small purchases; there's _no limit_ to how much you can spend online
5

with Bitcoin. There's a risk in using Bitcoin because there's no central banking system

backing it up. While it's been associated with hacking and illegal activities,
6

most crimes are committed _cash_.
7

AFTER VIEWING

F Work in a small group. Discuss these questions.

1. How would you explain what Bitcoin is to a friend?
2. How do you usually pay for things such as food, phone and Internet service, eating out, rent, etc.?
3. Have you ever used Bitcoin? If not, would you ever? Explain.
4. What might be some of the benefits and drawbacks of using Bitcoin?
5. Do you think it would be fair for the creator of Bitcoin, who was anonymous, to use Bitcoin for personal financial gain? Why or why not?
6. Bitcoin is one form of cashless payment, which is becoming more and more popular. What do you think about the future of cash in your country?

B Vocabulary

MEANING FROM CONTEXT

A 🎧 **3.9** Read and listen to the personal finance tips. Notice each word or phrase in **blue** and think about its meaning.

NINE PERSONAL FINANCE TIPS

1. Don't trust yourself to remember to pay your bills on time. Instead, set up a bill pay **reminder** on your bank's website.

2. If your company offers direct deposit, **deposit** a percentage of your pay into a savings account. You'll be less tempted to spend money you never see.

3. Banking fees (monthly maintenance fees, ATM fees, foreign **transaction** fees) can add up. Consider opening an account with an online bank to save on fees.

4. **Allocate** at least 20 percent of your pay to financial priorities such as paying off debt and building your retirement **nest egg**.

5. It's possible to **overdo** saving money in the bank. If you have more than six months' savings in your account, then think about investing.

6. Pay attention to **seemingly** small daily expenses because they add up. Just giving up caffè lattes could save you hundreds every month.

7. College students: Be sure to apply for financial **aid** even if you think you won't get any. Last year, over a million students missed out on free money for school by not filling out the forms.

8. College graduates: Pay off your student loans quickly to avoid paying added **interest**. Making more than the minimum payment will help.

9. Don't **withdraw** money from retirement accounts unless absolutely necessary. It can mean paying high penalties. Instead, keep a separate fund for emergencies.

B Write the correct word or phrase in **blue** from exercise A to complete each definition.

1. _Interest_ is the fee you pay for borrowing money.

2. When you _deposit_ a sum of money, you put it into a bank account.

3. A(n) _transaction_ is an exchange of goods, services, or funds.

4. If you _withdraw_ money from a bank account, you take it out.

5. If you _allocate_ something, you dedicate it to a particular person or purpose.

6. A(n) _reminder_ is something that makes you not forget another thing.

7. _Aid_ is assistance in the form of money, equipment, or services.

8. A(n) _nest egg_ is a sum of money saved for the future.

9. If something is _seemingly_ true, it appears to be true.

10. If you _overdo_ an activity, you do it excessively.

C Work with a partner. Look back at the financial tips in exercise A. Tell your partner which tips you follow or have followed and how well they work or worked.

CRITICAL THINKING: REFLECTING

D Look at the pie chart. Then create a pie chart about your own spending. Share your chart with a partner. How are you similar to or different from the typical American?

ORGANIZING IDEAS

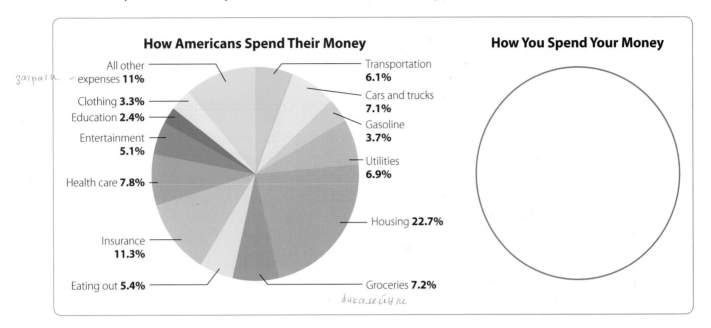

How Americans Spend Their Money

- All other expenses **11%**
- Clothing **3.3%**
- Education **2.4%**
- Entertainment **5.1%**
- Health care **7.8%**
- Insurance **11.3%**
- Eating out **5.4%**
- Transportation **6.1%**
- Cars and trucks **7.1%**
- Gasoline **3.7%**
- Utilities **6.9%**
- Housing **22.7%**
- Groceries **7.2%**

затраты

бакалейни

How You Spend Your Money

E Look at your pie chart. How could you better manage your money? Write five personal finance tips. Use vocabulary from exercise A. Then share your best tip with the class.

PERSONALIZING

B Listening A Conversation about Money

BEFORE LISTENING

PRIOR KNOWLEDGE

A Read about three types of payment cards and discuss the questions with a partner.

> **THREE TYPES OF PAYMENT CARDS**
>
> **Debit Cards:** Debit cards are directly connected to the money in your bank account. When you use your debit card, money is immediately withdrawn from your account.
>
> **Credit Cards:** When you use a credit card, you are borrowing money. The credit card company makes the payment for you, and you must pay the money back, usually with interest. If you don't make your payments on time, you can be charged late fees.
>
> **Stored-Value Cards:** Stored-value cards have electronic money stored right on the card. Anyone can use these cards, not just the person who originally bought the card. Examples are prepaid phone cards and gift cards.

1. Which of these payment cards do you use? When do you use them?
2. What other methods of payment do you regularly use?

WHILE LISTENING

LISTENING FOR MAIN IDEAS

B 🎧 3.10 Listen to the conversation. Choose the two main topics the speakers discuss.

1. the decreasing number of ATMs available in the city
2. the degree of safety of electronic transactions ·
3. when each method of payment was first used
4. the top reasons that credit cards are widely used
5. an alternative system for lending and borrowing money ·

A small business owner in Ghana, West Africa, was able to start her own business through micro loans.

C 🎧 3.10 Listen again. Then read the statements. Choose T for *True*, F for *False*, or NG for information *Not Given*.

1. The restaurant where they are doesn't accept debit cards.   T   (F)   NG

2. Both women feel that credit cards tempt them to spend too much.   (T)   F   NG

3. The man has probably lost a stored-value card in the past.   (T)   F   NG

4. Peer-to-peer lending services are offered by local banks.   T   (F)   NG

5. Peer-to-peer lending services allow international loans.   (T)   F   NG

6. The man has lent money through peer-to-peer lending.   T   F   (NG)

LISTENING SKILL Listening for Shifts in Topic

While talking about a topic, speakers sometimes remember a related topic that they want to mention. Recognizing when a speaker is shifting topics will help you follow the talk or discussion. Here are some expressions that signal a shift in topic:

> *Speaking of* [topic], . . .   *Incidentally,* . . .
>
> *Speaking of which,* . . .   *By the way,* . . .
>
> *That reminds me,* . . .

D 🎧 3.11 Listen to excerpts from the conversation. Match the expressions with the topics they introduce.

Expressions	Topics
1. __c__ Speaking of which, . . .	a. credit cards coming before debit cards 2
2. __a__ By the way, . . .	b. peer-to-peer lending 4
3. __e__ Incidentally, . . .	c. using credit cards 1
4. __b__ That reminds me, . . .	d. the service being slow 5
5. __d__ Speaking of helping people, . . .	e. taking out a car loan 3

AFTER LISTENING

E Work with a partner. Look at the topics in the box. Discuss the impact (if any) that each has had on your financial well-being. What changes would you like to make with how you use any of these? Explain.

cash	ATM machines	direct deposit	credit cards
debit cards	stored-value cards	peer-to-peer lending	interest

Speaking

PRONUNCIATION Linking Vowel Sounds

🎧 **3.12** When one word ends in a vowel sound and the next word begins with a vowel sound, we often add a slight *w* or *y* sound between the words.

1. Add a *w* sound when the first word ends in these sounds:

   /u/ overd**o**_it   /oʊ/ g**o**_**o**nline   /aʊ/ h**ow**_**a**bout

2. Add a *y* sound when the first word ends in these sounds:

   /i/ th**e**_**a**mount   /eɪ/ w**eigh**_**i**t   /aɪ/ l**ie**_**a**bout   /ɔɪ/ enj**oy**_**i**t

---

A 🎧 **3.13** Insert a *y* or *w* sound under each link. Then listen to check your answers.

1. I like the_idea of building affordable housing units.
2. The financial data are too_inaccurate to use.
3. The boss needs to_authorize your monthly_expense report.
4. I can see_it's going to be_immensely profitable.
5. The changes to_our financial situation worry me_a little.
6. She advised me to_engage in financial planning early_on.
7. It's so_easy to go_into debt when you spend excessively.
8. The trial of the_affluent doctor became a media event.

GRAMMAR FOR SPEAKING Connectors of Concession

Connectors of concession (*though, even though,* etc.) introduce information that is in contrast or contrary to what the listener might expect. Look at the underlined information introduced by the connectors of concession. Note how it contrasts with the information in the main clause.

> I don't want my nest egg stolen **even though** _it's not that big_.
> **Though** _they're really useful_, I find credit cards dangerous.

Use the connectors *although, even though,* or *though* in dependent clauses.

> **Although** _the dollar amount is small_, microloans can buy a lot.
> **Even though** _credit cards are convenient_, I prefer to pay with cash.

Use the connectors *even so, nonetheless,* or *nevertheless* in independent clauses:

> I don't have a big nest egg. **Even so**_, I want to keep what I have!_
> The restaurant only accepts cash. **Nevertheless**_, it's always busy at lunchtime._

The MoonDragon tiny house, Washington State, USA

B Work with a partner. Match the sentences that go together. Then take turns connecting the sentences with connectors of concession. Discuss which sentences you think are true and say why.

1. __b__ It's fun to daydream about being rich.

2. __c__ The cost of living is rising at an alarming rate.

3. __d__ You may or may not be able to make more money.

4. __a__ It's important to determine your budget ahead of time.

a. There are inevitably unplanned expenses to deal with.
b. Money doesn't guarantee one's happiness or well-being.
c. The increase has yet to impact the majority of the population.
d. Better use of the money you have can increase your happiness.

FINAL TASK A Role-Play about Financial Advice

> You will role-play a meeting between a financial advisor and a client to discuss ways that the client can save money. Then you will prepare and present a budget.

A Work with a partner. Read the roles and decide who will play each one.

Role #1: Financial Advisor

You are a financial professional. Discuss the client's budget with him or her, ask questions, and offer suggestions for reducing expenses and debt.

Role #2: Client

You recently moved into a new home, and now your expenses are more than your income. Explain the problem and ask about ways to reduce your expenses and debt.

B Study the client's monthly budget and prepare suggestions for reducing expenses and debt to fit a monthly income of $2,800. Use these questions to guide you.

Financial Advisor	Client
• Which expenses cannot be changed?	• Which expenses can be changed?
• Which items should the client allocate less money to? How much less?	• Of those expenses, which items are priorities for you?
• Which items should the client allocate more money to? How much more?	• Which items are you willing to spend less on? How much less?
• Which loan should be paid back first?	

Monthly Expenses		Debts		New Budget
Rent:	$1,040	Student loan balance: $10,500 (2% interest for 15 years)		
Food:	$300			
Heat and electricity:	$150			
Gas for car:	$120	Car loan balance: $4,600 (4% interest for 4 years)		
Entertainment:	$425			
Health insurance:	$450			
Charity donation:	$100	Credit card balance: $1,290 (18% interest per year)		
Credit card payment:	$400			
Student loan payment:	$100			
Car loan payment:	$140			
Total Expenses:	**$3,225**	**Total Debt:**	**$16,390**	**New Total Expenses:**

C Role-play a meeting between the financial advisor and client. Share your suggestions and come to an agreement on a budget so that the client's expenses are less than his or her income. Also include a plan for how to repay the client's debt.

D Decide on which parts of the budget you and your partner will each be responsible for presenting. Then present your budget to another pair of students.

REFLECTION

1. What skill in this unit do you think will be most useful to you?

_____

_____

2. What is the most useful information related to money that you learned in this unit?

_____

_____

3. Here are the vocabulary words and phrases from the unit. Check (✔) the ones you can use.

☐ aid AWL   ☐ impact AWL   ☐ security AWL

☐ allocate AWL   ☐ interest   ☐ seemingly

☐ associate   ☐ nest egg   ☐ transaction

☐ deposit   ☐ outlook   ☐ virtue

☐ determine   ☐ overdo   ☐ well-being

☐ engage in   ☐ promote AWL   ☐ withdraw

☐ fulfillment   ☐ reminder

HEALTH AND TECHNOLOGY 8

Students react while watching a robot practice surgical techniques at a hospital in Pennsylvania, USA.

Look at the photo and read the information. Then discuss the questions.

1. What are the devices shown in the photo and what are they used for?

2. What other functions do you think these devices could have?

3. What kinds of information related to the environment, health, or fitness can be monitored by technology?

INNOVATIONS IN MEDICINE

Innovation and advances in medical technology are at the heart of modern medicine and have led to life-changing treatments and cures for patients around the world. Technology is also transforming the way health care information is accessed and communicated. It has impacted everything from better diagnostic, therapeutic, and surgical procedures to preventative medicine and disease management. It has also allowed individuals to take a more active role in monitoring their own health through the

Employees of Japanese weather forecasting company Weathernews display the "Pollen-robot" in Tokyo. These pollen-detecting robots will be set up at 1,000 points across Japan to observe pollen levels and send reports back to the company. This information will help people with allergies and breathing problems avoid unhealthy areas.

A Vocabulary

A 🎧 3.14 Read and listen to this information from a health management company. Notice each word or phrase in **blue** and think about its meaning.

HEALTH DATA: MAKE USE OF IT!

The use of technology to manage personal health is growing **by leaps and bounds**! It's easy to wear a cool **gadget** to help you **keep track of** your activity, blood pressure, or body weight. And many of us surf the Web for health tips. There is a great deal of health information available, but studies show that most people are **reluctant** to take advantage of it. Many people have a **tendency** to put off taking care of their health, and often wait until a serious problem comes up to **consult** a doctor. With our service, we keep all of your information strictly **confidential**. We analyze your data and send you health reminders. In addition, if you have a problem, we have health professionals who can discuss a possible **diagnosis** and **clarify** any issues. Remember, prevention is **comparatively** cheap when you think of the alternative! Let us help you manage your health data today!

B Match each word or phrase with its definition.

1. __g__ by leaps and bounds (adv phr)
2. __j__ gadget (n)
3. __a__ keep track of (v)
4. __h__ reluctant (adj)
5. __d__ tendency (n)
6. __i__ consult (v)
7. __e__ confidential (adj)
8. __f__ diagnosis (n)
9. __b__ clarify (v)
10. __c__ comparatively (adv)

a. to monitor
b. to make something easier to understand; explain
c. in relation to something else; relatively
d. a habit of acting or thinking in a certain way
e. meant to be kept secret or private
f. a medical assessment of a disease or condition
g. with rapid progress; at a rapid pace
h. unwilling; not enthusiastic
i. to seek advice or information from; refer to
j. a small and useful device or tool

C Discuss the questions with a partner.

1. How do you keep track of your finances?

2. Have you ever been reluctant to try something new? Explain.

3. What kinds of things do you have a tendency to put off doing?

4. In what situations do you consult a dictionary? A grammar book?

5. What is something that you keep confidential?

D 🎧 3.15 Work with a partner. Listen to part of a conversation between a manager of a health club and a member. Complete the statements with words from exercise B.

1. At first, Jessica feels _reluctant_ about participating in the survey.
2. Jessica is concerned that her information won't be kept _confidential_.
3. Jessica feels her fitness has improved _by leaps and bounds_.
4. When Jessica joined, she received a _gadget_ to track her activity.
5. She doesn't usually _keep track of_ her workouts.
6. Jessica thinks the monthly fee is _comparatively_ higher than other clubs' fees.
7. Jessica has a _tendency_ to work late, so she likes the health club's late hours.
8. Mike offers to _clarify_ the contract for Jessica when she finishes the survey.
9. Jessica went to the wellness center to _consult_ with a doctor about her back.
10. The doctor's _diagnosis_ was that Jessica had strained her back.

VOCABULARY SKILL Using Synonyms

Synonyms are words with the same meaning or very similar meanings. Learning synonyms enables you to use a greater variety of words and avoid sounding repetitious. It is important to be aware of any differences in meaning and usage between synonyms. For example, *tall* and *high* are synonyms, but we say *tall building* or *person* but *high mountain* or *ceiling*. You can find examples of usage in a dictionary, or by searching online.

E Choose the word or phrase that best completes each sentence. Choose both choices if they are both appropriate. Use a dictionary or other resource to help you.

1. The best therapy for your elbow is to move it back and forth (by leaps and bounds / at a rapid pace).
2. All construction workers on this site must wear a helmet and a (tool / gadget) belt.
3. Where are your keys? Why is it so hard for you to (keep track of / monitor) them?
4. I buy the store brand medicine because it's (comparatively / relatively) inexpensive.
5. He said he's (slow / reluctant) to go, but I still think we can convince him.
6. If your blood pressure is still too high, you should (consult / refer to) a doctor.
7. If you are concerned about your information being kept (private / confidential), we can assure you that our servers follow the highest levels of security.
8. My art teacher told me his general (diagnosis / assessment) of my painting.
9. In my family, excellent health and long life seem to be genetic (tendencies / habits).
10. Our meeting was helpful and (clarified / explained) my understanding of the problem.
11. This is a (confidential / private) club—you can only join if invited by a member.
12. Companies, from Apple to small startups, are creating (gadgets / devices) that monitor and track health data.

Listening A Lecture about Big Data in Health Care

BEFORE LISTENING

PRIOR KNOWLEDGE **A** Work in a small group. Discuss the questions.

1. What kind of medical data about patients do doctors need?
2. Do you think health data should be kept confidential? Explain.
3. What do you think the term *big data* means?

WHILE LISTENING

B 🎧 3.16 Listen to the first part of the lecture. Was your understanding of big data correct?

LISTENING FOR
MAIN IDEAS
C 🎧 3.17 ▶ 1.16 Listen to the lecture. Which of these points does the lecturer make? Put a check (✓) in the correct column.

	Yes	No
1. Advertisers are reluctant to use big data because of consumer concerns. *рекламодатели*	☐	☑
2. Until recently, health care data has had a tendency to be unreliable. *ненадежными*	☑	☐
3. Health care data has focused on collection and storage rather than analysis.	☑	☐
4. It is predicted that artificial intelligence will one day replace doctors.	☐	☑
5. Big data can enhance patient health even after patients leave the hospital. *улучшить*	☑	☐

> ### NOTE-TAKING SKILL Using a T-Chart
>
> A T-chart can be an effective note-taking tool when a lecture or presentation deals with two sides of a topic (e.g., advantages and disadvantages, challenges and solutions, causes and effects). Placing these aspects on the same line on either side of a chart creates a visually clear arrangement that helps both comprehension and memory.

▶ **Students visit Corporea, an interactive museum in Naples, Italy, devoted entirely to the subject of health, science and biomedical technologies, and prevention.**

3.18 Listen again to part of the lecture. As you listen, complete the notes related to challenges in the left column. Then listen again, and complete the notes related to solutions in the right column. Write no more than two words in each blank.

Big Data and Health Care	
Challenges	**Solutions**
Patients have tendency to be __dishonest__ when reporting their health data 1	Collect __factual information__ only, from dr. appts, lab tests, devices 8
Patients afraid data won't be kept __confidential__ 2	Dev. of better & better __data security__ technlgy 9
Medical data useless unless in a form that doctors __can use__ 3	Pittsburgh Health Data Alliance's profiles give docs info in form that's easy __to access__ 10
The amount of patient data is becoming __overwhelming__ 4	Use artificial intell. (AI) to __analyze__ & interpret data 11
Even ideas suggested by __AI programs__ can't be trusted 5	These new ideas must be tested in studies supervised __by doctors__ 12
Some patients are __reluctant__ or unable to follow doc's orders 6	Big data being used to determine who these __patients are__ 13
Traditionally, it's been difficult to __monitor patients__ in follow-up care 7	New __apps__ keep track of patient location, meds, sleep, psych. state 14

AFTER LISTENING

E Work in a small group. Discuss the questions.

1. The speaker says that for big data to be useful, it needs to be analyzed and distributed to the "right people." Who are the "right people" to receive big data in this context?

2. The speaker says, "We haven't yet reached the point where a computer can replace a doctor." Does his lecture imply that will happen someday? Explain.

3. What does the speaker imply about patients' use of new apps when he says, "And while it has traditionally been difficult to monitor patients in follow-up care, new apps keep track of where they are, whether they're taking their medicine, how well they're sleeping, and even their psychological state after they've left the hospital"?

A Speaking

> **SPEAKING SKILL** Emphasizing Important Information
>
> When you want to make a point and be sure that your listeners don't miss it, you need to emphasize that point. You can use these expressions to emphasize important information.
>
> *It's important to note/remember/keep in mind that...* 1
>
> *We need to remember/keep in mind that...*
>
> 2 *Let me point out/stress/highlight that...*
>
> *I'd like to emphasize/point out/stress that...*

A 🎧 3.19 Listen to the excerpts from the lecture. Write the information the speaker emphasizes. With a partner, discuss why this information is important.

1. _We need to keep in mind_

2. _the computer_

3. _the more_

B With a partner, discuss the positive and negative implications of institutions having unlimited access to data about a person's health, diet, and daily activities. Write your ideas in the T-chart. Then share your ideas with another pair.

Full Access to Data	
Positive Implications	**Negative Implications**
Doctors needs Learn about family history. diagnosis easyly	to take for advertising dishonest

A noun clause functions as a noun in a sentence. *That* can introduce a noun clause, but is often omitted in speaking. Noun clauses can come:

After *be* + certain adjectives, such as *sure, concerned, interesting, true,* and *worried.*

> I'm *sure* (that) we'll see a lot more collaboration in the future.
>
> It's *true* (that) advertisers use big data about people's shopping habits.

After verbs related to thinking, such as *agree, keep in mind, realize,* and *worry.*

> Many people *agree* (that) big data has immense potential.

C 🎧 3.20 Listen to Dr. Stafford's answer to a student's question after the lecture. Match each main clause with the noun clause the doctor uses.

1. _____ This leads some people to worry

    a. that there are more opportunities for their data to be unprotected.

2. _____ . . . some people are worried

    b. that these new methods of recording and sharing health data will also require new security measures.

3. _____ It is obvious

    c. that the wireless networks used by health institutes could present security issues.

D With a partner, take turns creating sentences. Combine main clauses from the first column with noun clauses in the second to express your opinions on information from the lecture. Explain your reasons.

I (don't) agree	(that) health care professionals should trust big data
I (don't) think	(that) AI can be trusted to analyze big data
I (don't) feel	(that) drug companies should share their data with each other
I am (not) sure	(that) big data has immense potential to treat and monitor patients

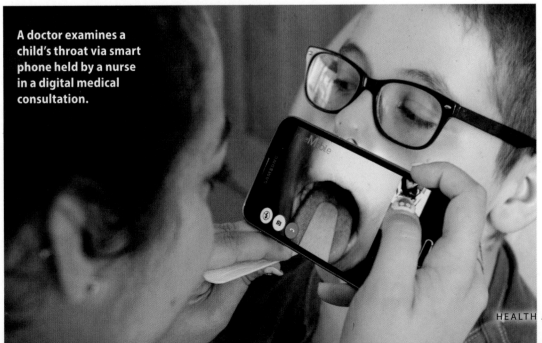

A doctor examines a child's throat via smart phone held by a nurse in a digital medical consultation.

E Form a small group and discuss the situation below. Was the company's decision the right one? Explain.

> Two equally qualified candidates were being considered for one position at a company. The company used big data to determine that one of the candidates could suffer from a serious health problem in the future. This candidate was not offered the job.

CRITICAL THINKING Synthesizing Information

When we synthesize information, we make connections among different ideas. For example, in academic classes, you will be asked to combine information from multiple sources such as a reading and a lecture to gain a deeper understanding of a topic.

F With a partner, synthesize the information you learned in Lesson A about health care and the use of big data. Create a T-chart and list the pros and cons. Discuss your ideas and give examples.

Dubai has launched a smart city initiative to explore energy, environment, infrastructure, and mobility. Its goal: to be the world's happiest and smartest city.

LESSON TASK Assessing a City's Health

A Work in a small group. Read this definition of a healthy city. Discuss whether your city or town fits the description.

> *опредеяеl*   *беспрестанно*
> The World Health Organization defines a healthy city as one that is continually
> creating and improving physical and social environments in order to support
> personal health. A healthy city enables residents to support each other in daily
> *создавать возможность*
> activities and to reach their maximum potential.

B With your group, discuss how a city you know is doing in the areas listed below. Then decide on the area that is most important to improve.

- air / water / noise pollution
- parks / green space
- sports / exercise facilities
- public transportation cost / availability

- stress at home / in the workplace
- food prices / quality
- health care costs / availability / quality
- unhealthy lifestyles

EVERYDAY LANGUAGE   Evaluating Ideas

Positive Evaluation: *I'd say that (idea) has a lot of potential.*
                          I think that (idea) could/might work.
                          That (idea) sounds good/That sounds like a good idea.

Uncertain Evaluation: *I'm not sure how well that (idea) would work.*
                          I don't know if that's the best way to do it/go.
                          That might not be the best solution/plan/idea.

C With your group, brainstorm methods of improving the area you chose in exercise B. Use expressions for evaluating ideas.

A: *One way to improve public transportation is to bring in experts to analyze the situation.*
B: *That sounds like a good idea. What's another idea?*

D Choose one person to report your ideas to the class.

Video

Bikers squeeze between cars and buses in Tokyo, Japan.

Biking in the City

Tuck aerial

BEFORE VIEWING

PRIOR KNOWLEDGE

A You are going to watch a video about a small study that is collecting health data from bicyclists in the city. Discuss the questions with a partner.

1. In Lesson A, you learned about big data and health. What kinds of data would help the well-being of bicyclists riding in cities?
2. Are you concerned about the health effects of air pollution on the streets of your city or town?
3. Is biking in polluted city air better or worse for your health than just staying home?

B Match each word from the video with its definition. Use a dictionary as needed.

1. __c__ deploy (v)   a. to produce or send out (a sound, signal, etc.) 2
2. __a__ emit (v)   b. a bit of material as small as or smaller than a piece of dust 4
3. __e__ optimize (v)   c. to put something into use 1
4. __b__ particle (n)   d. how near a thing or place is to another 5
5. __d__ proximity (n)   e. to make the best or most effective use of 3

WHILE VIEWING

C ▶ 1.17 Watch the video. Read the statements. Choose T for *True*, F for *False*, or NG for information *Not Given*.

UNDERSTANDING MAIN IDEAS

notauotue

1. The health study is attempting to clarify a question about exercising in close proximity to traffic. — (T) F NG

2. Pollution from vehicles on the road is increasing. — T (F) NG

3. Participants wear clothing and gadgets that take measurements. — (T) F NG

4. Information collected about participants is kept confidential. — T F (NG)

5. Pollution and smoking can lead to a similar disease diagnosis. — (T) F NG

6. The researchers' goal is to create an app that bicyclists can consult for the quietest route. — T (F) NG

D ▶ 1.17 Preview the questions. Then watch the video again. Take notes as you watch. Write no more than three words for each answer.

UNDERSTANDING DETAILS

1. What does the study want to find new ways of measuring? __air pollution__

   zacto
2. How frequently does the blood pressure monitor take a measurement? __every half hour__

   boūTy
3. What device do the participants use to log their location? __GPS device__

4. How long do the researchers have to prove the success of their study? __two years__

   zacTuyn
5. When particles of pollution are breathed in, where in the body do they go? __in lungs and bloodstream__

6. The planned app would balance less pollution with what other factor? __saving time__

AFTER VIEWING

E Work with a partner. Think about the study in the video and answer the questions.

1. What was the research question that inspired the study? *take measuring air pollution*
2. How was the research carried out? *onновиеничи monitor, GPS*
3. What will the researchers do after this study is completed? *They take the information and keep in confidential*
4. In Lesson B, you will learn about various devices related to health maintenance. Would you use a pollution tracking app? Why or why not?

B Vocabulary

A 🎧 3.21 Read and listen to this email. Notice each word or phrase in **blue** and think about its meaning.

From: Human Resources

To: All employees

Subject: Technology and Service Upgrades

Plans to update our office technologies and services are moving forward! Below is a list of suggestions for equipment upgrades and new services that we would like your feedback on. Please rank them from 1 to 10 (1 = most important, 10 = least important) and send this form back to HR at your earliest convenience.

_____ Replace standard keyboards and mouse devices with ergonomic¹ ones to reduce and prevent injuries caused by **repetitive** movements. _10_
повторяющие   обнаружить

_____ Supply employees with monitors that **detect** _9_ steps taken, calories burned, activity level, etc.

_____ Provide "smart chairs" that monitor worker **posture** and sitting time. _1_
поза   уведомляет

_____ Equip desks with emotion monitors that **notify** _3_ employees of high levels of stress and anxiety.
прослеживать

_____ Provide wearable gadgets to **track** blood _7_ pressure, blood sugar levels, heart rate, temperature, etc.

_____ Install apps on office computers to provide information about the **nutritional** value of _6_ different foods.
питательные

_____ Institute game breaks with fitness videos to fight the negative effects of **sedentary** time. _2_
сидячее

_____ Give employees sleep monitors to use at home to check for sleep-related health issues that can impact **productivity** at the office. _5_
производительность

_____ Equip computers with anti-glare² screen protectors and provide special eyewear for employees who are **prone to** eye strain. _4_
склонны к

_____ Set up a technology hotline to take questions on using new technology and services and to help _8_ **resolve** any issues that employees may have.
разрешить

¹**ergonomic** (adj): designed for health and comfort
²**glare** (n): light that is very bright and difficult to look at

B Write each word or phrase in **blue** from exercise A next to its definition.

1. _posture_ (n) the position in which you stand or sit
2. _sedentary_ (adj) sitting down a lot and getting little physical exercise
3. _notify_ (v) to inform someone about something
4. _prone to_ (adj) having a tendency, usually negative
5. _productivity_ (n) effectiveness of workers at getting things done
6. _nutritional_ (adj) related to the health benefits of food and drink
7. _track_ (v) to regularly check the value or position of something
8. _resolve_ (v) to find a solution to a problem or difficulty
9. _detect_ (v) to find or discover by investigating
10. _repetitive_ (adj) occurring again and again, sometimes in a boring way

C Choose the word that forms a correct collocation with the word in **bold**. Use a dictionary or other resource to help you.

USING COLLOCATIONS

1. People who use computers a lot are prone to **repetitive** (stress / tension) injuries.
2. I avoid working in an office because I don't want a **sedentary** (livelihood / lifestyle).
3. Eating foods with a high **nutritional** (value / amount) will improve your health.
4. A healthy diet, exercise, and sleep can **resolve** many (issues / topics) with one's health.
5. All the hospitals were **notified** (on / of) the new data privacy legislation.
6. What are the legal implications of so much **tracking** (of / to) personal data?
7. The new workflow is the reason for our team's (increased / multiplied) **productivity**.
8. I keep track of my calories because I (am / have) **prone** to overdoing it whenever I eat out.
9. Marco had (poor / serious) **posture** until he bought an ergonomic chair.
10. The gadget was so small that it (escaped / exited) **detection** by the authorities.

D Work with a partner. Imagine you work at the company in exercise A. Discuss the importance of the suggestions to you and rank them from 1 to 10.

CRITICAL THINKING: RANKING

E Work with a partner. Use the vocabulary words to describe or make suggestions to improve your own work, school, or home life.

PERSONALIZING

> _I want an app that notifies me whenever I make a mistake in English!_

Listening A Podcast about Fitness Gadgets

BEFORE LISTENING

PRIOR KNOWLEDGE **A** Work with a partner. Think of three gadgets, apps, or websites related to fitness that you have owned or know about. What functions do they perform? How do they work? Write them in the chart.

Gadgets	Functions

WHILE LISTENING

LISTENING FOR
MAIN IDEAS
B 🎧 3.22 Listen to a podcast reviewing five gadgets related to health and fitness. Check (✓) the ones that Tyler and Hannah would recommend to their listeners.

Gadget	Recommended by Tyler	Recommended by Hannah
FitterYet	✓	
Smarty Sleep Mask	✓	✓
Sun Disc 3		✓
e-Beverage System		✓
BestPosture	✓	✓

An athlete gets ready for a run with her fitness smartwatch.

When reviewing products or services, people often make positive or negative assessments. Listening for assessments allows you to understand what the speaker perceives to be the pros and cons of the topic of discussion.

Positive Assessments	Negative Assessments
What I like about it is (that)… *I'm impressed with…* *On the plus side/positive side/upside,…* *A/One (big/major/significant/important) advantage/benefit is (that)…*	*What I don't like about it is (that)…* *I'm not impressed with…* *On the minus side/negative side/ downside,…* *A/One (big/major/significant/important) disadvantage/drawback is (that)…*

C 🎧 3.22 Listen again. What features of the gadgets were positively or negatively assessed by the speakers? Take notes in the chart.

LISTENING FOR DETAILS

Gadget	Pros	Cons
FitterYet	– accurately tracks how far you walk – inexpensive	– big and unattractive
Smarty Sleep Mask	– hleps help to sleep faster, be fiter – really works – comftobale – analyzes sleep, patterns	– need to be conected to the internet – battery life is poor
Sun Disc 3	measures strength of sun accurately	– breaks easely – made of thin plastic
e-Beverage System	– notifies you if you haven't had enough to drink – dishwasher safe – atractive design	– leaks into backpack
BestPosture	– work well since small device not expensive	– only works within a short range – doesn't work with loose clothing

AFTER LISTENING

D Work in a small group. Discuss the questions.

PERSONALIZING

1. Of the gadgets you heard about, which ones would you be interested in using? Which ones don't interest you?
2. Do you think fitness gadgets are a passing trend or are they here to stay? Explain.

Speaking

PRONUNCIATION Dropped Syllables

🎧 **3.23** We sometimes drop a vowel sound in words with three syllables or more. In these words, the vowel sound that comes after a stressed syllable is dropped.

Maybe it's unattractive, but then, it's not a piece of **jewelry**, is it?

I was very **interested** in trying this one out because I have a tendency to burn.

It also analyzes the nutritional profile of the **beverage** you're drinking.

It's a **mystery** to me how it works . . .

A 🎧 **3.24** One or two words in each sentence has a syllable where the vowel sound can be dropped. Cross out the vowels that are dropped. Then listen to check your answers.

1. The laboratory was open during renovation.
2. I was able to internalize what I learned in my mathematics class.
3. I find it easy to conform to the corporate culture.
4. I think it's undeniable that broccoli improves one's memory.
5. To me, vegetable juice is just cold soup.
6. The drop in sales was disastrous for our restaurant.
7. We're planning to initiate several new projects every year.
8. Did you know that I actually daydream about chocolate?
9. My family takes a two-week vacation each year.
10. Success in business is always a collaborative effort.

B 🎧 **3.25** Practice saying the following words that are often pronounced with a dropped syllable. Then listen and check your pronunciation.

1. average
2. deliberately
3. elementary
4. desperate
5. federal

6. different
7. preference
8. reference
9. temperature
10. traveler

C Work with a partner. Make your own sentences using words with dropped syllables from this page. Say them with and without dropping the syllables, and ask your partner if he or she can hear the difference.

> I deliberately try to avoid being sedentary on the weekends.

D Work in a small group. Look at the graphic and discuss the questions.

CRITICAL THINKING: INTERPRETING VISUALS

1. Where do people prefer to attach health/fitness gadgets? Why do you think that is?
2. What might be the advantage of a device worn in contact lenses?
3. Where would you prefer to wear a health/fitness gadget?

Where Would You Wear A Health/Fitness Gadget?

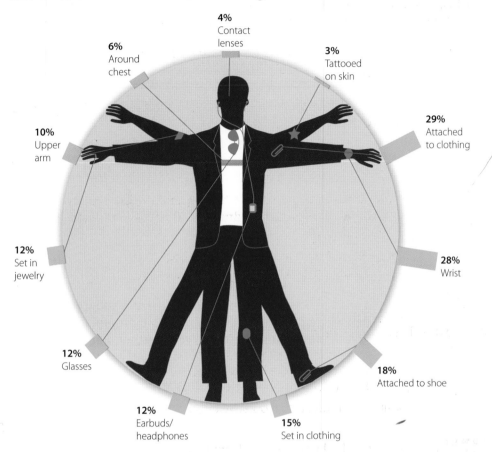

6%
Around chest

4%
Contact lenses

3%
Tattooed on skin

10%
Upper arm

29%
Attached to clothing

12%
Set in jewelry

28%
Wrist

12%
Glasses

12%
Earbuds/ headphones

15%
Set in clothing

18%
Attached to shoe

FINAL TASK Presenting on a Health Tech Product

> You will give an individual presentation on a health/fitness technology product.

A Research a health/fitness tech product that has some product reviews available.

B Use these questions to guide your research:

- Is there a story behind the invention?
- What company makes it?
- Is there anything interesting or notable about it?
- What does the device look like and how is it used?
- Where do you wear it?
- What kinds of information does it track?
- What features does it offer?
- Are there any competing brands?

C Analyze online reviews of the product. As you read the reviews, take notes in a T-chart on the positive and negative assessments.

ORGANIZING IDEAS **D** Organize your notes for the presentation. Highlight the important information. Review the expressions for emphasizing important information in the Speaking Skill box, and the expressions for making assessments in the Listening Skill box. Choose an appropriate picture of the product, and prepare a T-chart of the pros and cons to use as visuals or handouts.

PRESENTATION SKILL Engaging Your Audience

Here are some suggestions to help you engage your audience.
- At the beginning of your presentation, ask some questions that can be answered by a show of hands.
- As appropriate during your presentation, ask for one or more volunteers to assist you or to provide an example for a point.
- Focus on how the points you are making can benefit your audience. When you do, check if they agree.
- Use rhetorical questions to encourage your audience to think about something, to invite them to agree with you, or to ask questions you think your audience would like to ask.

E Prepare questions to engage your audience and plan where in your presentation you will ask them. Then with a partner, practice giving your presentations. Provide feedback and modify your presentation based on your partner's feedback.

PRESENTING **F** Give your presentation to the class. Invite audience questions at the end of your presentation.

[Handwritten notes:]
1) Humans show their abilities to make decisions, to learn, understand, apply logic, to recognize patterns, comprehend ideas, plan, solve problems, retain information, use language to communicate. Humans are conscious of the presence, thoughts and feelings of others. solving problems – problem-solving skills. we're creative. We think abstractly. communication skills.

2) Chimpanzees, dolphins, crows, dogs, cats
hunting, organized groups, make and use tools, self-awareness, are able to identify each other using their own signature whistles. To create booms exceeding 230 decibels. To think and reason, remember their pasts and plan their futures.

– Dogs have advanced memory skills, are able to read, react appropriately to human body language, to understand human voice commands
– Cats – to solve problems, adapt to their environment

REFLECTION

1. What skill in this unit do you think will be most useful to you? In what way?

_____

_____

2. Which technological gadget in this unit interested you most? Why?

_____

_____

3. Here are the vocabulary words and phrases from the unit. Check (✓) the ones you can use.

☐ by leaps and bounds	☐ gadget	☐ reluctant AWL
☐ clarify AWL	☐ keep track of	☐ repetitive
☐ comparatively	☐ notify	☐ resolve AWL
☐ confidential	☐ nutritional	☐ sedentary
☐ consult AWL	☐ posture	☐ tendency
☐ detect AWL	☐ productivity	☐ track
☐ diagnosis	☐ prone to	

[Handwritten:] 3. Long term memory is good.

[Handwritten:] My short term memory is good too.

THE MYSTERIOUS MIND 9

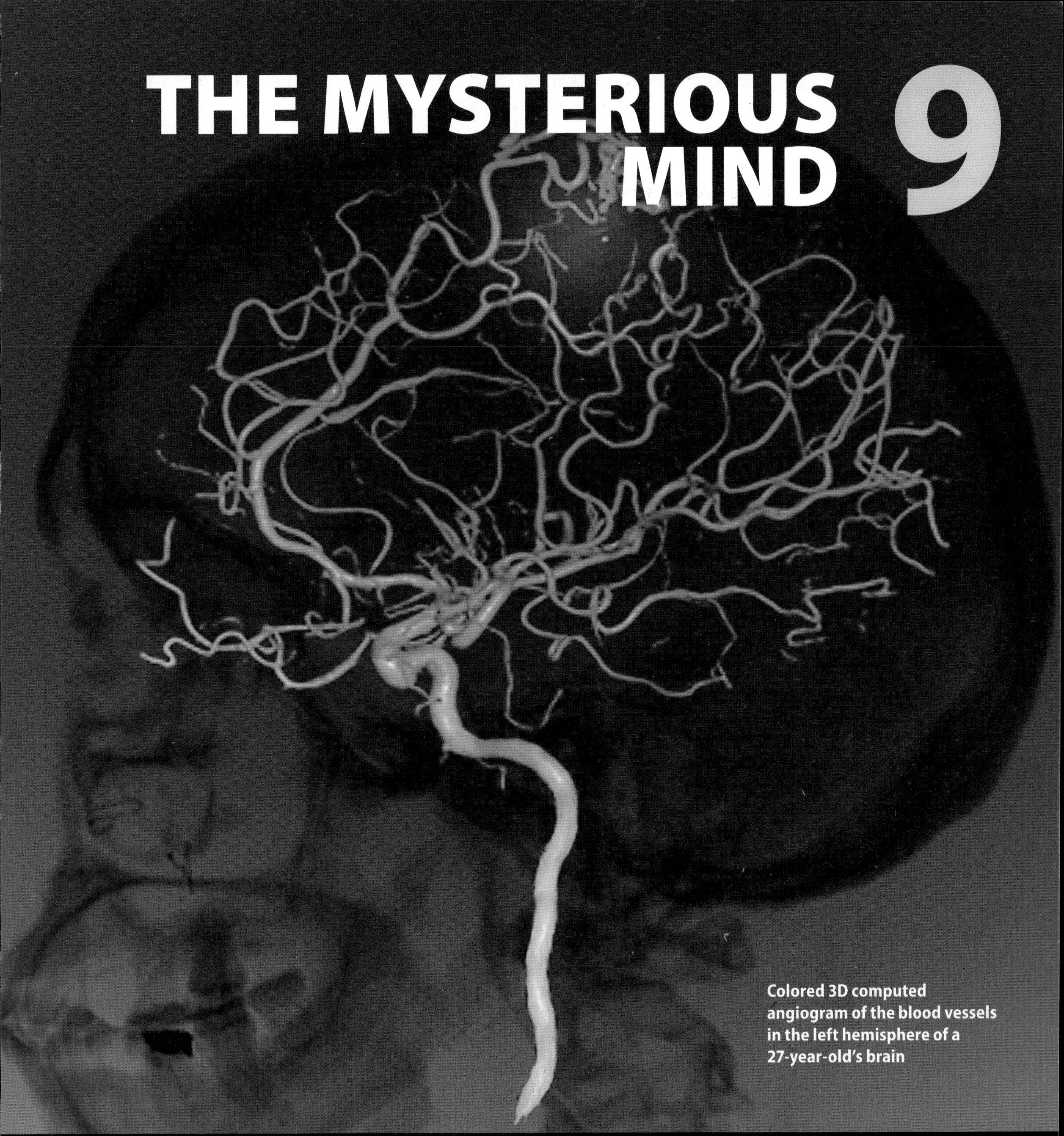

Colored 3D computed
angiogram of the blood vessels
in the left hemisphere of a
27-year-old's brain

ACADEMIC SKILLS

LISTENING   Recognizing Appositives
            Highlighting Conclusions
SPEAKING   Expressing Causal Relationships
            Reduced Function Words
CRITICAL THINKING Evaluating Conclusions

THINK AND DISCUSS

1 How do humans show intelligence?
2 Besides humans, what animals do you think
   are intelligent? Why?
3 How good is your memory? Explain.

EXPLORE THE THEME

Look at the images and read the text. Then discuss these questions.

1. What would be an advantage of having a fully developed frontal lobe? — *critical thinking would be an advantage.*
2. Which parts do you think are probably the most developed in a professional athlete's brain? Why?
3. Think of activities that you are able to do well. Which areas of your brain do you think are the most developed?

cerebellum is at the back of the brain. It controls balance, movement, coordination.

THE AMAZING MIND

The brain consists of six major parts, each responsible for certain functions. A comprehensive list of all the functions would fill a book. However, to gain a better understanding of this remarkable organ, it is useful to look at where some essential functions are located. Keep in mind, though, that the parts of your brain don't work in isolation. Rather, they work together through an intricate network of nerves to communicate to all parts of your body.

Frontal Lobe

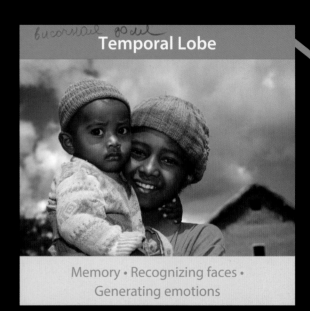

Reasoning · Speaking · Problem solving

Temporal Lobe

Memory · Recognizing faces · Generating emotions

Brain Stem

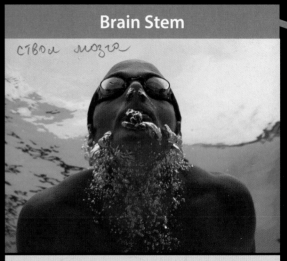

Breathing · Heartbeat · Body temperature

Parietal Lobe

Sensation • Reading • Body orientation

Occipital Lobe

Vision • Color perception • Light perception

Cerebellum

Balance • Coordination •
Fine muscle control

A Vocabulary

MEANING FROM
CONTEXT

A 🎧 **4.2** Read and listen to the information. Notice each word or phrase in **blue** and think about its meaning.

WHAT DOES IT MEAN TO BE INTELLIGENT?

Traditionally, a person who could solve problems, use **logic**, or think critically was considered smart. However, that understanding has changed over time, thanks in part to the work of Professor Howard Gardner of Harvard University. In the 1980s, Gardner made the surprising claim that there are at least seven "intelligences," **namely** logical, linguistic, visual/spatial, musical, kinesthetic, interpersonal, and intrapersonal—in other words, there are "multiple intelligences." Which intelligences do *you* have?

LOGICAL
- approaches problems using rules of math or logic
- prefers to work with **objective** facts rather than **subjective** opinions

LINGUISTIC
- is skilled at **verbal** expression
- has a large vocabulary
- has a talent for languages

VISUAL/SPATIAL
- understands **spatial** relationships
- can easily **visualize** and move objects in the mind
- works well with charts, graphs, and visuals

INTRAPERSONAL
- is highly **analytical** with his own feelings
- has a deep understanding of self

MULTIPLE INTELLIGENCES

MUSICAL
- is comfortable with sound, music, and rhythm
- can memorize music, sing, or play instruments
- can distinguish between tones

INTERPERSONAL
- has excellent **intuition** about others' feelings
- is happy to be around other people and **vice versa**

KINESTHETIC
- has control over body movements
- is skilled with hands
- is often a good dancer

B Complete each sentence with the correct word or phrase in **blue** from exercise A.

1. _objective / ~~analytical~~_ information is true from a scientific point of view.

2. "_vice versa_" is used to say that the reverse of a statement is also true.

3. "_spatial_" describes things related to size, shape, area, and position.

4. If you are a(n) _analytical / ~~logic~~_ person, you think about things in a logical way.

5. "_namely_" is a word that introduces specific information or examples.

6. If you _visualize_ something, you form a picture of it in your mind.

7. Something that is _subjective_ is based on personal opinions and feelings.

8. Something that is _verbal_ has to do with words and language.

9. Our _intuition_ tells us something is true though we have no proof that it is.

10. _logic / ~~logic~~_ is a thought process based on good judgment and common sense.

VOCABULARY SKILL Suffixes –al, –tial, and –ical

The suffixes –al, –tial, and –ical are used to create adjectives from nouns.

- With many nouns, the suffix –al is added directly with no changes in spelling.
  logic → logic**al**   nutrition → nutrition**al**   verb → verb**al**

- With some nouns, adding –al involves slight changes in spelling.
  contrové**rsy** → contrové**rsial**   trib**e** → trib**al**   benefi**t** → benefi**cial**

- Nouns ending in –ce often take the suffix –tial in their adjective form.
  confiden**ce** → confiden**tial**   referen**ce** → referen**tial**   spa**ce** → spa**tial**

- Some adjectives are formed by adding the suffix –ical with other spelling changes.
  analy**sis** → analy**tical**   hypothe**sis** → hypothe**tical**   ecolo**gy** → ecolo**gical**

C Complete each question with the correct form of the word in parentheses. Use the suffix –al, –tial, or –ical. Use a dictionary as needed.

ESL classes have been most useful to me.

1. Which of your _educational_ (education) experiences has been most useful to you?

I have a logical mind

2. Do you have a _mathematical_ (math) mind?   _No, I do not have a mathematical mind._

My writing's teacher has been the most influential in my life.

3. Which of your teachers has been the most _influential_ (influence) in your life?

I prefer historical books

4. Do you prefer books that are _historical_ (history) or ones that are _biographical_ (biography)?

5. What is one _practical_ (practice) strategy you use when preparing for a test?

D Work with a partner. Take turns asking and answering the questions from exercise C.   PERSONALIZING

A Listening A Podcast on the Brain and Intelligence

[handwritten notes:] A person who is Left brained hemisphere is said to be more logical, analitical, objective.   Right brained hemispere is intuitive, thoughtful, and subjec[...]

[handwritten labels around image:] number, language, reasoning, logic, science, math, analitical thin[king]   —   Idea!   —   emotional intelligence, imagination, expression, art awareness, intuition, creativity

BEFORE LISTENING

PRIOR KNOWLEDGE   **A**   Work in a small group. Look at the photo. What do you know about the two sides of the brain? Discuss with your group and write down your ideas.

WHILE LISTENING

LISTENING FOR MAIN IDEAS   **B**   🎧 4.3 ▶ 1.18 Listen to the podcast. Does the speaker make these points? Check (✓) *Yes* or *No*.

	Yes	No
1. Experiments have shown differences in the two halves of the brain.	☑	☐
2. The experiments of early brain researchers were not scientific.	☐	☑
3. People have drawn incorrect conclusions about the brain in the past.	☑	☐
4. Right-brained and left-brained personalities are scientific facts.	☐	☑
5. Modern brain science has cleared up some confusion about the brain.	☑	☐

NOTE-TAKING SKILL Highlighting Conclusions

The details of scientific experiments are not usually as important as the conclusions. When you take notes, highlight or underline the conclusions so that they stand out. Later, it will be simple to review these key pieces of information. Here are some expressions to listen for.

> *… it can be concluded that …*
>
> *… we came to/reached/arrived at/drew the conclusion that …*
>
> *It is clear that …*

4.4 **1.19** Listen to the main portion of the podcast. Complete the notes with no NOTE TAKING more than two words in each blank, and underline the conclusions.

1861, France, P. P. Broca

Examined brain damage that affected _verbal ability_ [1]

Discovered damage was on left side of brain

Seemed obvious that _speech_ [2] problms = result of L-brain damage

1960s, California, R. Sperry

Expermnts on patients whose R&L-brains were surgically _seperated_ [3]

Exper. #1: Patients saw words on R of screen easily, but didn't see on L

Concl. L-brain is dominant in _verbal proccessing_ [4]

Exper. #2: Patients arrange shapes & patterns on objects to match cards

Easy w/their _left_ [5] hand, diffclt w/their

right [6] hand

Concl: spatial abilities are in the _right brain_ [7]

Psychology & Education

L-brain has language, & lang. is brain's most imp. capability

Concl: L-brain is the _dominant half_ [8]

Educational ideas: brain-balancing activities

Sit up straight and do _maths_ [9] problems (to help L-brain)

Lie down and draw _diograms_ [10] (to help R-brain)

Modern Brain Science

Electrical actvty exists in _both_ [11] halves of brain during all thinking

Clear that the _two halves_ [12] of brain always work together

AFTER LISTENING

CRITICAL THINKING   Evaluating Conclusions

Different conclusions can be drawn using the same information. To judge if a conclusion is reasonable, check whether it is objective, analytical, and based on available facts. Poor or unreasonable conclusions are based on assumptions that are not sufficiently supported, that attempt to fit information to expectations or desires, or that are from a subjective point of view.

D Work in a small group. Look back at the conclusions you underlined in exercise C. Discuss why they seem reasonable or unreasonable.

CRITICAL THINKING: EVALUATING CONCLUSIONS

A Speaking

> **SPEAKING SKILL** Expressing Causal Relationships

Many verb phrases express causal, or cause and effect, relationships.

- Cause before Effect

  Damage to the left brain ***can result in*** *speech problems.*

- Cause after Effect

  Speech problems ***can be a result of*** *damage to the left brain.*

Here are some verb phrases for talking about causal relationships:

Cause before Effect	Cause after Effect
. . . causes . . .	. . . is caused by . . .
. . . results in . . .	. . . is a result of . . .
. . . leads to . . .	. . . is due to . . .
. . . is responsible for . . .	. . . results from . . .
. . . produces . . .	. . . is produced by . . .

A 🎧 4.5 *впереписи* Listen to three excerpts from the podcast about the brain. Match the statements about cause and effect. Underline the cause in each statement.

1. __C__ It seemed obvious that the speech problems

2. __a__ Unfortunately, the fascinating scientific discoveries of Broca, Sperry, and others

3. __b__ In education, the right-brain/left-brain model

a. led to some less-than-scientific conclusions about the brain in the fields of psychology *2* and education.

b. resulted in the idea that "brain-balancing" activities could strengthen the less *3* dominant side of the brain.

c. were a direct result of the damage. *1*

EXPRESSING CAUSAL RELATIONSHIPS

B Work in a small group. Discuss possible causes and effects for each of these topics related to psychology, and write them in the chart.

> *A self-confident personality is usually a result of having successful or positive experiences. I think it can lead to more leadership opportunities.*

reason *result*

Topics	Causes	Effects
1. A self-confident personality	is caused by childhood accomplishments	boosts performance
2. Computer game addiction	provides with a high amount of dopamine	can cause structural changes to our brain
3. A positive outlook on life	causes happiness	creats an upbeat attitude
4. Stress in the workplace	are caused by heavy workloads	affects performance, anxiety
5. Strong social connections	are important to our well-being	boost our mental health

A baby listens to music with headphones.

C Look at this list of popular ideas related to psychology and the mind. Do you think they are probably true or probably false, or are you unsure? Mark T for *Probably True*, F for *Probably False*, and U for *Unsure*.

CRITICAL THINKING: EVALUATING

1. Playing classical music to babies increases their level of intelligence.   T   F   U

2. Human beings normally use only 10 percent of their brain.   T   F   U

3. People with opposite personalities find each other attractive.   T   F   U

4. When the moon is full, there is an increase in crime and crazy behavior.   T   F   U

5. Repeating new words is the most effective way to learn them.   T   F   U

6. If you let yourself occasionally show a little anger, you will avoid getting very angry.   T   F   U

D Work in a small group. Compare and discuss your answers from exercise C.

E Now read the explanations below and check your answers from exercise C. With your group, discuss any facts that surprise you.

1. Two recent studies determined that playing classical music to babies produces no clear measurable effect on their intelligence.

2. Although the entire brain isn't used all the time, modern brain imaging techniques have shown that all parts of the brain are regularly active and no part is left unused.

3. Research has shown that people are more often attracted to people with whom they share various similarities.

4. Physics tells us that the pull of the moon has almost no effect on our brains, and studies show that there is no more crime during full moons than at other times.

5. Research has shown that effective vocabulary learning is the result of encountering new vocabulary in various meaningful ways, and not the result of simple repetition.

6. Recent scientific studies show that people who allow themselves to show their anger actually become angrier, which leads to negative consequences.

F Work with a partner. Read about four psychological experiments. Then discuss the question below each.

1. Participants are shown a short video of six people passing basketballs back and forth. Three of the people are wearing white, and three are wearing black. The participants are asked to count the number of passes between the people wearing white. At one point during the video, a person dressed in a gorilla costume walks through the people passing basketballs.
Question: How do you think the participants reacted?

2. In a subway station in Washington, D.C., world-famous violinist Joshua Bell played his 3.5 million-dollar violin during rush hour for people walking by. He had recently played in Boston at $100 a ticket, but in the station he put his open violin case in front of him to collect donations.
Question: What do you think happened?

3. In a 150-seat movie theater, all the seats except two in the middle are taken by people who look like members of a motorcycle gang. They are, in fact, paid actors. A real couple walks into the theater. The experiment is repeated with several couples.
Question: What do you think most couples did?

4. Three groups of people were given simple word problems. Group 1 had words like *polite*, *patient*, and *courtesy*. Group 2 had words like *bother*, *disturb*, and *bold*. A third group had random words. They were then told to go talk with the experimenter, but they found him deep in conversation with someone.
Question: How do you think the behavior of the people in the groups differed?

G 🎧 4.6 Now listen to the results of the experiments and take notes. What conclusion can you make about human psychology based on each experiment? Discuss your ideas with the class.

LESSON TASK Discussing Learning Styles

A Psychology tells us that different people prefer to learn in different ways. Look at these seven learning styles. Which styles do you prefer? Check (✓) Y for *Yes*, N for *No*, or NS for *Not Sure*.

Learning Style	Description	Preferred		
visual	prefer to take in information by seeing it	☐ Y	☐ N	☐ NS
audio	receive information best through sound	☐ Y	☐ N	☐ NS
verbal	focus best on words—written, spoken, or recorded	☐ Y	☐ N	☐ NS
physical	eager to get the body in action when learning	☐ Y	☐ N	☐ NS
logical	like numbers, rules, logic, and solving problems	☐ Y	☐ N	☐ NS
social	prefer group work and interacting with others	☐ Y	☐ N	☐ NS
solitary	focused and productive in individual activities	☐ Y	☐ N	☐ NS

▲ **Students creating a robotic arm**

B Work in a small group. Compare your learning style preferences from exercise A.

EVERYDAY LANGUAGE   Making Recommendations

I (would) recommend (that) . . .	*It would be a good idea to . . .*
I think (that) . . .	*. . . would/could/might be a good idea.*
Why don't you/we . . . ?	*I suggest (that) . . .*

C Work in a group. For each group member, discuss ideas for studying effectively. Consider their preferred learning styles from exercise A. Use expressions for making recommendations. Take notes in the chart on the suggestions made for you.

CRITICAL THINKING: SYNTHESIZING

A: *Since Sung-min is a visual learner, I think studying grammar charts would be a good idea.*
B: *Yes, and for vocabulary, flash cards with pictures might be good.*

Subject Area	Study Suggestions
Grammar	Reading improves grammar skills.
Vocabulary Building	Keeping dictionary handy helps to build vocabulary.
Listening and/or Speaking	Trying to picture what the speaker is saying helps with listening skills
Reading and/or Writing	Reading regulary helps with reading skills.

Memory Man

▲ An exhibit of neurobiological memory processes at the Deutsches Hygiene Museum, Dresden, Germany

BEFORE VIEWING

A Work with a partner. Discuss the questions.

1. What kinds of things are easy for you to remember? Difficult?
2. How far back can you remember? Describe your earliest memory.
3. What are some techniques you use when you need to remember something?

WHILE VIEWING

UNDERSTANDING
MAIN IDEAS

B ▶ 1.20 Watch the video about an amazing man named Gianni Golfera. Are these points made in the video? Check (✓) *Yes* or *No*.

	Yes	No
1. Gianni Golfera's memory attracts popular and scientific attention.	✓	☐
2. Some people question whether Golfera's memory abilities are real.	☐	✓
3. Scientists are working to discover a genetic component to memory.	✓	☐
4. Golfera's great memory skill is due in part to his own efforts.	✓	☐
5. Doctors can improve memory by making changes to the brain.	☐	✓

C ▶ 1.20 Watch the video again. Complete the facts about Gianni Golfera. Write one word or a number for each answer.

1. Gianni Golfera can remember _____sixty_____ numbers and repeat them forward and backward.

2. Gianni has memorized over 250 _____books_____ .

3. Gianni can remember every _____detail_____ of every day of his life.

4. Dr. Malgaroli will compare the Golfera family's _____genes_____ with those of other families.

5. Researchers are investigating how memory and learning _____change_____ the brain.

6. Dr. Malgaroli says that remembering well is just a matter of _____exesise_____ .

7. Gianni has been training his brain since he was _____11_____ years old.

8. Gianni has memorized a series of _____historical_____ books.

9. For Gianni, working to improve his memory is like a _____full-time_____ job.

10. Despite his obvious gift, Gianni has a relatively _____normal_____ life.

AFTER VIEWING

D Look at this list of strategies for improving memory. Rank them according to how effective you think they would be for you, from 1 (most effective) to 5 (least effective). Then share your ranking with a partner.

_____ Eat memory-enhancing foods, such as avocado, berries, coconut, oily fish, nuts, and dark chocolate, frequently.

_____ Strengthen your memory by not using a GPS for directions, learning a new language, trying an online brain-training game, or starting a new hobby.

_____ Get physical exercise to clear your mind and provide oxygen to your brain, and do mind-body exercises such as yoga, which has a proven positive impact on memory.

_____ Live a healthy lifestyle that improves memory by getting eight hours of sleep, socializing with friends regularly, and avoiding junk food and unhealthy snacks.

_____ Use memory techniques such as making words from the first letters of the words you need to remember, making lists, and drawing mind maps to connect ideas.

E Work with a partner. Discuss these questions.

1. Sometimes something you see, taste, touch, hear, or smell causes you to have a certain memory. From your experience, which of the senses (sight, hearing, taste, smell, and touch) do you think is linked most closely to memory? Explain.

2. After watching the video, are you inspired to improve your memory? If so, would you like to try one of the strategies from exercise D? Which one(s)?

B Vocabulary

A 🎧 4.7 Listen and check (✓) the words or phrases you already know. Use a dictionary to help you with any new words.

угрубляешь — ☑ **deepen** (v)   *этический* ☑ **ethical** (adj)   *хорошей* *низший* ☑ **inferior** (adj)   *врожденный* ☑ **innate** (adj)

устарелый — ☑ **obsolete** (adj)   ☑ **radical** (adj)   ☑ **stemmed from** (v phr)   ☑ **superior** (adj)

норма; стандарт — ☑ **norm** (n)   ☑ **unprecedented** (adj)   *вытекает из*   *превосходящий*

беспрецедентный

MEANING FROM
CONTEXT

B 🎧 4.8 Read the blog post and fill in each blank with the correct word or phrase from exercise A. Then listen and check your answers.

THE ANIMAL MIND

Do animals think and feel like we do? Are they similar to or completely different from humans? In the early 20th century, British psychologist C. L. Morgan claimed that animal behavior could only be interpreted in terms of lower mental faculties.[1] This guideline _stemmed from_ (1) the ideas that 17th century thinkers had about the animal mind. At that time, the _norm_ (2) was to see animals as living machines. The French philosopher Nicolas Malebranche wrote that animals "eat without pleasure, cry without pain, grow without knowing it: they desire nothing, fear nothing, know nothing." For Malebranche, the animal mind seemed _inferior_ (3) to the human mind in every way.

Today there has been a(n) _radical_ (4) change in the way scientists view the animal mind, and the ideas of Malebranche have become _obsolete_ (5). No longer are all animal behaviors regarded as _innate_ (6); examples of learning in birds, dolphins, and apes have proven that point of view to be false. On the contrary, there have been _unprecedented_ (7) discoveries of language abilities in parrots and apes. In one experiment, a kind of memory competition between humans and apes, apes demonstrated _superior_ (8) memory skills by defeating their human opponents. In addition, evidence of empathy[2] among animals has been observed in the wild. As scientists' understanding of the animal mind continues to _deepen_ (9), it is becoming clear that various characteristics once thought to be uniquely human actually are not. This is leading some to ask serious _ethical_ (10) questions about the treatment of animals and their rights in the human-dominated world.

[1] **faculty** (n): power, capability
[2] **empathy** (n): the ability to share another person's feelings and emotions as if they were your own

A blue and yellow macaw performs a trick at the KL Bird Park in Kuala Lumpur, Malaysia.

C Match each word or phrase with its <u>opposite</u> meaning.

1. _c/d_ unprecedented
2. _b/f_ superior
3. _a_ norm
4. _j_ stem from
5. _i_ radical
6. _d_ ethical
7. _f_ inferior
8. _g_ obsolete
9. _e_ deepen
10. _h_ innate

a. a strange or unusual situation
b. of lower status or importance
c. having happened before
d. dishonest; immoral
e. decrease; weaken; lighten
f. of higher status or importance
g. current and up-to-date
h. acquired or learned *эквайерд – приобретенный*
i. modest or balanced
j. cause; produce

D Work with a partner. Discuss the questions.

CRITICAL THINKING: ANALYZING

1. What are some examples of innate abilities in humans or animals?
2. In what ways might some animal minds be superior to human minds? *smell*
3. What are some of the benefits of pet ownership?
4. In 2004, the city of Reggio Emilia in Italy passed unprecedented regulations that made it illegal to boil lobsters alive, to keep goldfish in glass bowls, or for amusement parks to give customers live rabbits as prizes. What is your opinion of these regulations?

Listening A Conversation about Memory

BEFORE LISTENING

PREDICTING **A** You are going to listen to a conversation about memory. Guess the meanings of two terms you will hear discussed.

угадай

1. What is *superior autobiographic memory*?

   _____ to remember everything clearly_____

   лосай
2. What is the *method of loci* used for? (*Loci* means *locations* or *places*.)

   _____

WHILE LISTENING

CHECKING
PREDICTIONS
B 🎧 **4.9** Listen to the conversation and check if your predictions were correct.

> **LISTENING SKILL** Recognizing Appositives
>
> An appositive is a noun or noun phrase that identifies or gives more information about another noun or noun phrase. An appositive usually follows the noun or noun phrase it modifies.
>
> > Have you ever heard of "superior autobiographical memory," **an incredibly accurate memory for past events**?
>
> The slight pause a speaker makes before an appositive can help you identify it.

C 🎧 **4.10** Listen to excerpts from the conversation. Write the appositives you hear in these sentences. Then underline the noun/noun phrase that it identifies.

1. Oh, wait. I saw a TV show about that, _amazing science_.

2. Oh, and I know the meaning stems from two ancient Greek words, _hippo meaning horse, campus meaning sea monster._

3. You could try this approach to remembering things that began in ancient Greece, _the method of loci._

▶ **The hippocampus is a part of the brain that is vital for memory creation.**

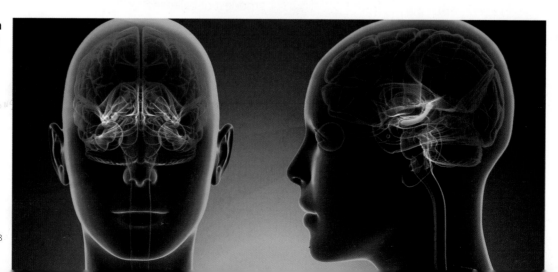

D 🎧 4.11 Preview the questions. Then listen again to part of the conversation. Take notes as you listen. Write no more than three words or a number for each answer.

LISTENING FOR DETAILS

1. What institution were the researchers studying superior autobiographic memory from? _University of California_

2. How many people with superior autobiographic memory did the researchers find?
   8 people

3. What career did one person with superior autobiographical memory have?
   TV star

4. What was different about some parts of the brains of people with superior autobiographical memory? _They were bigger_

5. In what year did Dr. Scoville's famous operation take place?
   _in 1953_

6. What was the major negative result of the operation for the patient?
   a patient lost his memory

E 🎧 4.12 Listen to the last part of the conversation. Complete the outline with information from the conversation. Write no more than three words in each blank.

NOTE TAKING

I. The method of loci
   A. Began in ancient Greece; a way to remember ___list of words___
      1
   B. How it works
      a. Picture a path that ___you know well___.
         2
      b. Look at a list of words and ___create image in your mind___ for each.
         3
      c. Put those ___images___ @ places along the path.
         4
      d. Later, you ___visualize___ walking along the path.
         5
      e. The images will ___remind you of___ the words.
         6

AFTER LISTENING

F Work with a partner. Discuss these questions.

1. Trying to help, Dr. Scoville permanently damaged his patient's memory. However, as a result, scientists learned a great deal about the brain. Do you think Dr. Scoville's actions were ethical?

2. Try to remember the Lesson A or Lesson B vocabulary words using the method of loci. Your partner will try to remember the other list. Check the vocabulary lists as you recite the words to each other.

Speaking

PRONUNCIATION Reduced Function Words

🎧 **4.13** Function words are words that show grammatical relationships in a sentence. They include: auxiliary verbs, prepositions, pronouns, conjunctions, and articles.

Function words are not usually stressed. Often, the vowel sounds are reduced to a schwa sound (/ə /), and certain consonants may be dropped. Notice the pronunciation of the underlined function words.

Prepositions:	*We went <u>to</u> the center <u>of</u> town <u>for</u> the lesson.*
Pronouns / Possessive Adjectives:	*Did you give <u>him</u> <u>his</u> award for winning <u>your</u> memory contest?*
Auxiliary Verbs:	*The test will be hard. <u>Can</u> we study together?*
	She <u>couldn't have</u> seen the answers.
Conjunctions:	*My memory is better <u>than</u> my brother's <u>and</u> sister's.*
Articles:	*Give me <u>the</u> test again. I have <u>an</u> hour.*

A 🎧 **4.14** Underline the function words that you think are reduced in these sentences from the conversation. Then listen and repeat to check your answers.

1. People with superior autobiographical memory can remember virtually everything that's ever happened to them.
2. It's a part of the brain that's really important for memory function.
3. I have a huge history exam next week, and I have to memorize a ton of information.
4. Having a good memory isn't an innate skill, you know.
5. In your mind, you need to visualize a path that you know well, like the way to school.

B Practice the conversation with a partner. Reduce the function words. Then switch roles.

A: Hey, how have you been?

B: Um, I've been a little depressed. Can you tell?

A: Yeah, I knew something or other was wrong. You know, I know a great doctor. Do you want his number? I highly recommend him!

B: No, it's something that will pass. It always happens in January and February.

A: Oh, the *winter blues*! That's what my mom calls them, anyway. She sits under a special lamp for half an hour a day and says it's better than medicine.

B: Really? Can I have her email? I want to ask her about her lamp so I can get one, too.

When using quantifiers with a noun, be sure to check for subject-verb agreement.

- With *all*, *a lot*, *some*, *a few*, *both*, and *most* + *of* + a plural count noun, use a plural verb.

    And **some** of the **methods** <u>work</u> surprisingly well.

    All of the **questions** <u>were</u> incredibly difficult.

- With *one*, *none*, *each*, *neither*, and *every one* + *of* + a plural count noun, use a singular verb.

    Anyway, **one** of the most famous **case studies** <u>was</u> in 1953, in Connecticut.

C Work with a partner. Take turns using quantifiers from the Grammar for Speaking box to make sentences with the following topics.

> *Some of the parrots I've seen on YouTube videos speak surprisingly well.*

abilities that animals have	methods for memory improvement	my parents
learning styles	the people I know	my friends
standardized English tests	the students in the class	my memories
the lessons in this unit		

FINAL TASK Speaking about a "Life Hack"

You are going to research and give a speech about three psychological "life hacks," or strategies we use to manage our time and daily lives in a more efficient way.

A Work with a partner. Read the information and discuss how useful you think this psychological life hack is.

CRITICAL THINKING: EVALUATING

LIFE HACK

At the supermarket, we all want to choose the fastest line. If you are like most people, you would get in line behind three people with 10 items each instead of someone with a cart containing 50 items—but you would be wrong! Research shows that each individual takes about 41 seconds while each item takes only three seconds. The total time is the individual time plus the time for each item.

> 3 shoppers with 10 items each = (41 sec. × 3) + (10 items × 3 sec. × 3) = 213 seconds
> 1 shopper with 50 items = 41 sec. + (50 items × 3 sec.) = 191 seconds

So next time, don't be afraid to get behind a shopper with a full cart!

B Look online and make a list of four to six psychological life hacks that sound interesting. Then work in a small group and share your lists. Choose three life hacks that you would like to research for your speech.

C Research your three life hacks. For each, take notes on the information below.

- a description of the life hack
- the problem it is designed to solve (if any) and/or who it might benefit
- an explanation of how the hack is implemented
- an explanation of why it works (include a psychological explanation, if appropriate)
- whether you have tried it or would like to try it, and why

PRESENTATION SKILL Using Gestures

Gestures can be very useful in a presentation. Keep your hands and body mainly in a neutral position until you want to make a gesture. Here are some ways to gesture:

- Use your hands and fingers to show size, speed, location, or numbers
- Raise or lower your shoulders to express doubt or sadness, raise or open your arms to show strength or openness, and use your face to show a variety of expressions
- Raise your hand and say, "Raise your hand if . . ." to get your audience involved

---

D With a partner, practice your speech. Remember to use gestures. Give each other feedback on your speeches and on any gestures used, and adjust your speech as needed.

PRESENTING **E** Give your speech to your group. When you finish, invite and answer questions from the group.

REFLECTION

1. Which language skill in this unit do you think will be most useful to you? In what situation(s)?

_____

_____

2. What did you learn about the mind, the brain, or memory that you didn't know before?

_____

_____

3. Here are the vocabulary words and phrases from the unit. Check (✓) the ones you can use.

☐ analytical AWL	☐ namely	☐ subjective
☐ deepen	☐ norm AWL	☐ superior
☐ ethical AWL	☐ objective AWL	☐ unprecedented AWL
☐ inferior	☐ obsolete	☐ verbal
☐ innate	☐ radical AWL	☐ vice versa
☐ intuition	☐ spatial	☐ visualize AWL
☐ logic AWL	☐ stem from	

THE FUTURE OF FOOD 10

A drought-tolerant tomato photographed with sand illustrates the research of Dan Chitwood. Chitwood grows these tomatoes by crossing standard tomato plants with wild tomato plants from the Atacama Desert, the driest place on earth.

ACADEMIC SKILLS

LISTENING	Listening for Suggestions
	The Cornell Method
SPEAKING	Referring to Group Opinions
	Reduced Auxiliary Phrases
CRITICAL THINKING	Categorizing

THINK AND DISCUSS

1 How do you choose the food you buy? What types of things do you think about before you buy food? What are some things you always buy? Never buy?

2 What do you think it means when we say food is genetically modified?

SAVING FOR THE FUTURE

EXPLORE THE THEME

Look at the photo and read the information. Then discuss the questions.

1. What is the goal of the Svalbard Global Seed Bank?

2. Why might a remote location have been chosen for this seed bank?

3. What does *doomsday* mean, and why do you think this name was given to the seed bank?

4. Name some crops that you would like to see saved in a seed bank. Why are they important?

WHAT: The Svalbard Global Seed Vault, called the "Doomsday Seed Vault" by some, was created to preserve samples of seeds from around the world. More than two billion seeds can be stored in the vault in case of natural or man-made disaster.

HOW: The climate and the thick rock surrounding the vault will ensure that even without electricity the samples will remain frozen.

WHEN: Building started June 19, 2006.

WHERE: It's north of the Arctic Circle on the island of Spitsbergen in the Arctic Ocean, 621 miles (1,000 km) north of mainland Norway. It is the northernmost part of the Kingdom of Norway.

WHY: It's being built to protect the earth's crop diversity.

American agriculturalist Cary Fowler holds vials of peas at the Svalbard Global Seed Bank in Longyearbyen, Svalbard, Norway.

Vocabulary

A 🎧 **4.15** Read and listen to the article about the world's food supply. Notice each word or phrase in **blue** and think about its meaning.

WHY PUT SEEDS IN A BANK?

Cary Fowler inside the seed bank

The world population is now over seven billion people and growing, and the pressure on world food suppliers is more **intense** than ever. Many large farms now **cultivate** only a small number of crops such as corn, wheat, or rice over vast areas. This type of agriculture is known as monoculture. While experts acknowledge how well it maximizes harvests, **skeptics** say that this benefit is **offset** by its negative effects.

One serious **drawback** of monoculture is the effect it has on the number of vegetable varieties grown by farmers. The diversity of crops has greatly diminished since the beginning of the 10th century, and many crop species no longer exist. We are moving toward a risky situation in which global agriculture relies on too few crops. If existing crop species get diseases against which they have no **resistance**, they could be wiped out. This would be **detrimental** to the world's food supply.

To save vegetable varieties from extinction, many experts **advocate** for the preservation of seeds **by means of** "seed banks." There are farmers and scientists who devote themselves to setting up such facilities. At last count, there were about 1,400 seed banks around the world. The seeds inside these seed banks could be **invaluable** in the future.

B Write each word or phrase in **blue** from exercise A next to its definition.

1. _by means of_ (prep phr) with the use of (a tool, method, idea, etc.)
2. _offset_ (v) to act to balance another action or effect
3. _intense_ (adj) high in energy or degree
4. _invaluable_ (adj) extremely useful
5. _detrimental_ (adj) having a harmful or damaging effect
6. _skeptics_ (n) people who doubt things that others believe
7. _resistance_ (n) the act of fighting against something
8. _cultivate_ (v) to prepare land and grow crops there
9. _advocate_ (v) to publicly recommend something
10. _drawback_ (n) a negative or unwanted aspect or feature

VOCABULARY SKILL Investigating Authentic Language

One way to investigate authentic examples of words and phrases is to do an Internet search. If you put multiple words in quotation marks, search engines will return many examples of the exact phrase. Another way to find authentic examples is to use online concordancers. Concordancers also reveal word collocations.

C Read these sample lines from a concordancer and answer the questions.

> government resources proved **invaluable** to private sector corporations
> stoves that have proven **invaluable** for preparing food that is sub
> thank John, whose efforts were **invaluable** to bringing this project to a

1. What verb is a strong collocation with *invaluable*? _have proven_

2. What prepositions are used after *invaluable*? _to / for_

> the problem had a clearly **detrimental** effect on the remaining part
> against its potentially **detrimental** impact on sources of clean
> that has a particularly **detrimental** effect in areas that have been

3. What adverbs are used with *detrimental*? _clearly, potentiaally, particularly_

4. What noun is a strong collocation after *detrimental*? _impact_

> which exposed a serious **drawback** of the envisioned plan, namely
> investors of a potential **drawback** to leaving funds in an account
> covered yet another serious **drawback** to the strategy of planting crop

5. What prepositions are used after *drawback*? _of / to_

6. What adjective is a strong collocation with *drawback*? _serious_

> sufficient period to build up **resistance** to recently developed pesticide
> disease has shown unusual **resistance** to treatment with conventional
> which continues to show **resistance** to GM corn varieties designed

7. What preposition is a strong collocation with *resistance*? _to_

8. What verb is a strong collocation with *resistance*? _to show_

D Complete the statements. Use a dictionary or a concordancer to help you. Discuss your answers with a partner.   PERSONALIZING

1. I tend to be a skeptic _about the news I wach on TV._

2. I generally advocate _for a healthy lifestyle._

3. A drawback _of this car_ is _the price_.

4. _Social media_ has a detrimental _impact_ on my studies. (бредной)

5. _His support_ has been invaluable _for my future life._

Listening A Lecture about GM Foods

BEFORE LISTENING

PRIOR KNOWLEDGE **A** Work in a small group. In what ways are specific crops and animals (for food) altered by genetic modifications? Discuss your ideas and take notes in the chart.

Plants	Animals
Apples are altered to last longer.	Cows are altered to produce more milk. ~изменено~
Tomatoes are altered to with stand diseases	Pigs are altered to grow up faster.
Cucumbers are altered to be bigger	Chickens are altered to produce more eggs.
Grapes are altered to be sweeter	Fish are altered to grow bigger in size and mass.
Grains are altered to be more resistant to pests.	

WHILE LISTENING

LISTENING FOR MAIN IDEAS

B ∩ 4.16 ▶ 1.21 Listen to a lecture about genetically modified (GM) foods. Which points does the speaker make? Put a check (✓) in the correct column.

chop- gnc kyccar

	Yes	No
1. There is controversy around the issue of genetically modified foods.	☑	☐
2. The government has acted in response to concerns about GM foods.	☑	☐
3. The dangers of GM foods mentioned have been scientifically proven.	☐	☑
4. There have been some promising developments in GM food research.	☑	☐
5. The professor feels that GM foods are a little too risky.	☐	☑

NOTE-TAKING SKILL The Cornell Method

The Cornell method of note taking, invented by an education professor at Cornell University, is a three-step note-taking method.

Step 1: Take detailed notes as you listen.

Step 2: After listening, write main points or questions for the different parts of your notes in a column to the left of your notes.

Step 3: Write a short summary of the notes at the bottom of your paper.

The advantage of the Cornell method is that it keeps your notes organized and turns them into an efficient study sheet.

▶ **These two Coho salmon are 18 months old, but one was genetically modified to be larger than the other.**

C 🎧 **4.16** Listen again and complete the notes section below. Write only one word or number for each answer. You will complete the summary section in exercise D.

GM Foods

Main Points	Notes
What are GM foods?	Foods made from animals & plants with modified __genes__ [1] Ex: Rat gene into __lettuce__ [2] = vit. C
Concerns about GM foods	Weeds pick up resist. to weed __killers__ [3] → "super weeds" Detrimental effects of GM plants on __insects__ [4] & animals Mixing GM plants w/conventional ones could impact gene __flow__ [5] If insects become __accustomed__ [6] to GM crops → super pests
Eating GM foods	GM __vegetables__ [7] sold in U.S. & planted in Argentina, Canada, China, S. Africa, Australia, Germany & Spain GM salmon declared safe in __2010__ [8] but didn't sell GM animals may be in markets w/in next __five__ [9] yrs.
Golden rice	Golden rice = rice w/beta-carotene, needed to produce vitamin A 100–140 mil __children__ [10] suffer from lack of vitamin A __sceptics__ [11] say it may not raise vit. A levels in pop.
Benefits of GM foods	↑ food production; crops w/ __resistance__ [12] to pests & disease; ways to cultivate crops on ↓ quality land

Summary

The __genes__ [1] of any animal and plant can be mixed and matched to create useful __characteristics__ [2]. Although there are __concerns__ [3] about the dangers of GM plants, such as super weeds and gene flow, we are already eating them. __Approval__ [4] for various GM animals is taking longer but will likely happen. A type of __GM salmon__ [5] was declared safe, but it wasn't __popular__ [6]. The __benefits__ [7] of GM foods include more food, __resistant__ [8] crops, and useable farmable land.

AFTER LISTENING

D Now complete the summary section in the lecture notes in exercise C with the words and phrases in the box.

approval	resistant	GM salmon	characteristics
benefits	concerns	genes	popular

1. genes
2. lettuce
3. killers
4. insects
5. flow
6. accustomed

7 vegetables have been
8. 2010
9. five
10. children in the world
11. skeptics
12. resistant

Speaking

A

SPEAKING SKILL Referring to Group Opinions

You can support an opinion with the opinion of a knowledgeable group. You do not have to name a specific person or organization. Instead you refer to the group in general.

> ***Many scientists*** *are optimistic about the technology and feel that GM foods could be the key to significant advances in agriculture and health.*

> ***Researchers*** *haven't been able to demonstrate that GM crops are detrimental to human health or to the environment.*

Groups (often used with *some, many*, etc.):

advocates (of/for…)	experts (on…)	journalists	doctors
proponents (of…)	critics (of…)	scientists	researchers

сторонер р

Verbs/Verb phrases:

be pessimistic	be certain	agree	admit	feel
be concerned	point out	think	insist	fear страх
be optimistic	believe	claim	warn	say

предупредить

CRITICAL THINKING:
EVALUATING

A Work in a small group. The lecturer refers to general advocates and critics of GM foods. Discuss which specific people, groups of people, and organizations might belong to each general group and why. List your ideas in the chart.

Advocates	Critics
Farmers with low-quality farmland	Organic farmers
Farmers with harsh environment	People who are concerned about the
Farmers who live in hot climate	negative effect of GM foods
People who do not have a lot of farmland	Naturalists who want to save nature the way it is.

B Work with a partner. Role-play a conversation at a grocery store between roommates. Take turns suggesting the grocery items in the chart below, referring to a positive then a negative group opinion. You can also make other suggestions using your own ideas.

A: *How about we get some of this fruit juice? It looks really fresh.*
B: *I'm not sure. Some experts say it can have as much sugar as soda.*
A: *Yeah, some juice does. But doctors point out that it contains a lot of vitamins.*

Grocery Item	Positives	Negatives
fruit juice	contains a lot of vitamins	can have as much sugar as soda
tomatoes	may fight some kinds of cancer	tomato farm workers not always well paid
GM salmon	completely safe to eat	likely to escape into the environment
beef	high in protein	raising beef may harm the environment
organic apples	fight tooth decay	go bad faster than conventional apples

скрещивание

C Work with a partner. Read about three methods of breeding and modifying crops. Then, discuss the benefits and drawbacks of each.

Breeding Better Crops

Genetic modification gets the public attention—and the controversy—but plant breeders today have numerous tools for creating crops with new traits[1]. The goal: continually increasing yields[2] in an increasingly challenging climate.

отдача — урожаи   сложный

Traditional Breeding	Interspecies Crosses	Genetic Modification
Desired traits are identified in separate individuals of the same species, which are then bred to combine those traits in a new hybrid[3] variety.	Breeders can also cross different species. Modern wheat comes from such hybridizations, some of which happened naturally.	Genes identified in one species can be transferred directly to an unrelated species, giving it an entirely new trait—resistance to a pest, say, or to a weed killer.

ухаживает

[1] **trait** (n): a genetic characteristic
[2] **yield** (n): the amount of food produced by crops
[3] **hybrid** (adj): bred by combining two different species

▼ **Javier Alcantar tends to corn crops at the Monsanto test field in California, where the crop is from genetically modified seed.**

CRITICAL THINKING:
CATEGORIZING

D **Read about these crops and animals. Decide if each was created by traditional breeding (TB), interspecies cross (IC), or genetic modification (GM). Write the appropriate abbreviation. You will use each one twice.**

1. _IC_ The tangelo fruit is a cross between a grapefruit and a tangerine. It has characteristics of both species and is extremely popular.

2. _GM_ GloFish® are brightly colored red, green, and orange fish sold as pets. They were created by inserting genes from a colorful jellyfish into black and white zebra fish.

3. _TB_ Since the 1930s, the yield of corn plants has greatly increased because farmers have bred the most productive plants of that species in each generation.

4. _GM_ To wipe out dangerous mosquito populations, scientists "programmed" their genes to make them die before becoming adults. The young bred from "programmed" and wild mosquitoes also die early.

5. _TB_ Wheat has been improving for over 10,000 years because farmers have selected the healthiest and largest plants to pass on their genetic characteristics to future generations.

6. _IC_ When the wild South American strawberry was bred with the North American strawberry, the result was the pineberry, a fruit that looks like a white strawberry but tastes like a pineapple.

E Work with a partner. Compare and explain the reasons for your answers in exercise D.

GloFish® were genetically engineered to glow in order to help scientists study pollution.

LESSON TASK Role-playing a Town Hall Meeting

A Work with a partner. Prepare to role-play a question-and-answer (Q&A) session at a town hall meeting (a public meeting where people can ask officials questions). Choose a role and read the information.

Role #1: Leader of a Farmers' Association

You are the leader of a farmers' association in a country that uses traditional farming methods. Recent problems of drought, crop disease, and insect pests have caused farmers to consider using GM crops. You are attending a town hall meeting to ask an official from GM Industries, a company that wants to supply GM crops to your country, about the concerns of the farmers.

<u>Notes for Questions</u>
- GM crops harmful to animals and humans?
- Insects develop resistance to GM crops, become more difficult to control?
- Genes from GM plants flow to other plant populations, create "super weeds"?
- GM crop seed too expensive?

Role #2: Spokesperson for GM Industries

You are a spokesperson for GM products in this country and believe they will dramatically improve the situation of its farmers. You are participating in a town hall meeting to answer questions and reduce fears that local farmers have about using GM crops.

<u>Notes for Answers</u>
- GM crops tested for safety more than other crops
- Insect resistance to GM crops can occur; will teach how to avoid
- Information about gene flow and "super weeds" scarce, being studied
- Initial cost of GM crop seed is more, but yields, quality, reliability are higher

---

EVERYDAY LANGUAGE Inviting Responses

Once you present an idea, you often want others to respond. Use these phrases.

What do you say to that?
Can/How do you respond to that issue/claim/concern?
What's your response to that issue/claim/concern?
Can you address that/those issue(s)/claim(s)/concern(s)?

B Role-play the town hall Q&A with your partner. Try not to read your notes as you speak. Invite responses using the expressions above, and refer to group opinions as appropriate.

CRITICAL THINKING: APPLYING

A: *Critics of GM crop companies say that you always put profits ahead of people. What do you say to that?*

B: *I understand your concern, but GM Industries is different. That's why we're having this meeting—we're here to show you that we care about farmers.*

A fish farm in
Colon, Panama

Panama

Farming the Open Ocean

BEFORE VIEWING

A Read the information about fish farming. Then answer the questions with a partner.

> **FISH FARMS** About half of the world's seafood comes from fish farms, and in 15 years that amount will rise to about two-thirds. Unfortunately, fish farms have problems due to: diseases created by crowded, stressful conditions; pollution caused by drugs and chemicals put in the water to fight those diseases; and too much waste in the area. In open-ocean fish farms, however, increased space reduces stress on the fish, and the constant movement of water keeps the area clean.

1. The video you are going to watch is about Open Blue, the world's largest open-ocean fish farm. What are some similarities and differences between farming crops and farming fish?

2. Open Blue fish farm is located in Panama. Why do you think Open Blue is located there?

WHILE VIEWING

UNDERSTANDING
MAIN IDEAS

B ▶ 1.22 Watch the video. Which of these points does Brian O'Hanlon make? Put a check (✓) in the correct column.

	Yes	No
1. The open ocean provides a clean environment for fish farming.	✓	
2. The techniques used in open-ocean farming are still evolving.	✓	
3. O'Hanlon plans to manufacture open-ocean farming equipment.		✓
4. Cobia are the most suitable type of fish to farm in the open ocean.		✓
5. O'Hanlon hopes to expand his fish farming business in the future.	✓	

C ▶ 1.22 Watch the video again. Complete this summary. Write one word only in each blank.

OPEN BLUE SEA FARMS

The open ocean is pristine and not impacted by ___land___ -based activities,
so the fish produced there are very clean. Brian O'Hanlon is the ___founder___
of Open Blue sea farms. Panama offers efficiency of transportation for bringing in raw
___materials___ and transporting finished products to the ___markets___.

The busy fish farm is 7.5 to 8 miles out in the ocean. It has mooring grid structures
that are one-kilometer long with fish pens inside. One harvest of fish is 20 to 25
___tones___. The process is still ___labor___ intensive, but they are
working on streamlining and automating it. Farming the ocean has greater potential for
___productivity___ than farming on land because it's three-dimensional. They farm cobia,
a fast-growing fish. O'Hanlon sees the open ocean as a huge ___opportunity___ in
the future.

D ▶ 1.22 Watch the video again. Complete each sentence with a word or phrase from the box.

посредством by means of 5	detrimental 1	intense 2
cultivating 4	drawback	invaluable

1. The _detrimental_ effects of pollution don't affect the open ocean very much.
2. The _intense_ activity over the fish farm makes it look like a little town.
3. One current _drawback_ to fish farming work is that it requires a lot of labor.
4. The potential for farming the ocean is much greater than for _cultivating_ land.
5. The fish are kept from escaping _by means of_ enormous pens made of netting.
6. The fast-growing cobia have clearly been _invaluable_ to Open Blue's success.

AFTER VIEWING

E Work with a partner. Discuss the questions.

1. Is open-ocean fish farming a good alternative to traditional fish farming? Explain.
2. Sometimes a solution to a specific problem may have unintended consequences. What might be some unintended consequences of open-ocean fish farming?

B Vocabulary

A **4.17** Listen and check (✓) the words and phrases you already know.

☐ **ample** (adj) 10 ☐ **call for** (v) 5 ☐ **coincide** (v) 2 ☐ **exceed** (v) 4
☐ **inadequate** (adj) 7 ☐ **opt** (v) 9 ☐ **output** (n) 1 ☐ **root** (n) 3
☐ **scenario** (n) 6 ☐ **surge** (n) 8

MEANING FROM
CONTEXT

B **4.18** Read the article and fill in each blank with the correct form of a word or phrase from exercise A. Then listen and check your answers.

The Next "Green Revolution"

The increase in agricultural ___output___ of the late 1900s is sometimes referred
to as the "Green Revolution." During this period, four important farming technologies
___coincided___, bringing immense benefits. They are:

- irrigation, a technology that brings water to crops;
- chemical pesticides to help kill or control insects;
- fertilizers, which give plants what they need to grow;
- smaller plants that produce as much food as larger plants.

Unfortunately, we can no longer depend on agricultural production rates to continue to
increase as they have in the past. This puts us in a dangerous situation. The ___root___
of the problem is the rising global population, which threatens to ___exceed___ nine
billion by the year 2050. Many are now ___calling for___ a second "Green Revolution" that
will help the world avoid a future nightmare ___scenario___ with excessively high food
prices, ___inadequate___ food supplies, and their disastrous consequences.

On the other hand, many experts remain optimistic that another ___surge___
in agricultural productivity will occur if farmers ___opt___ to use GM crops and
sustainable farming methods. Only time will tell if this second "Green Revolution" can
ensure ___ample___ food for future generations.

▼ **Urban farm on
rooftop in New
York City, USA**

C Match the words and phrases with their synonyms. Use a dictionary if needed.

1. __d__ ample   a. coexist
2. __h__ call for   b. go beyond
3. __a__ coincide   c. insufficient
4. __b__ exceed   d. abundant
5. __c__ inadequate   e. yield
6. __i__ opt   f. rise
7. __e__ output   g. situation
8. __j__ root   h. demand
9. __g__ scenario   i. choose
10. __f__ surge   j. cause

D Choose the correct collocation for the word or phrase in **bold**. Use a dictionary or concordancer to help you.

1. The funds for the seed program were (darkly / emptily / hopelessly) **inadequate**.
2. The **root** (to / of / for) the extinction was the modification of the birds' habitat.
3. The winner shouted, "This **calls for** (celebrating / a celebration / celebrations)!"
4. After the fire, the diversity of plants will return given **ample** (period / age / time).
5. The merits of the plants **exceeded** (confidence / expectations / hypotheses).
6. A flood wiping out the crops would be a worst (model / state / case) **scenario**.
7. The warm, wet spring ultimately caused a **surge** (up / at / in) the insect population.
8. The tribal ceremonies **coincide** (with / as / to) the beginning of the corn harvest.
9. Multiple storms were the reason for the (low / bare / cheap) **output** of farms that year.
10. The farmer **opted** (on / for / to) a variety of rice with exceptional resistance to disease.

E With a partner, make sentences about food issues with collocations from exercise D.

> *The choice of restaurants in my neighborhood is hopelessly inadequate.*

F Work with a partner. Discuss the questions.   PERSONALIZING

1. When shopping for vegetables, do you opt for organic varieties? Explain.
2. In your opinion, what is the root of the world hunger issue?
3. Have you ever had a restaurant experience when the food, the service, or something else was inadequate? How about an experience that exceeded your expectations?

Listening A Conversation about Food Prices

BEFORE LISTENING

PRIOR KNOWLEDGE **A** Work with a partner. Discuss the questions.

1. Study the bar chart below. What are some possible reasons for the difference between the percentage of income spent on food in the United States and Singapore and the other countries shown?
2. What percentage of your income do you or your family spend on food? Is the percentage increasing or decreasing? Explain.
3. What are some reasons for changes in food prices?

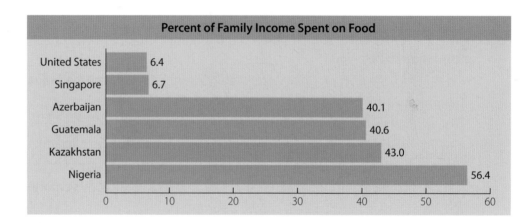

Percent of Family Income Spent on Food

United States	6.4
Singapore	6.7
Azerbaijan	40.1
Guatemala	40.6
Kazakhstan	43.0
Nigeria	56.4

WHILE LISTENING

LISTENING FOR
MAIN IDEAS

B 🎧 4.19 Listen to a conversation about food issues. Then read the statements. Choose T for *True*, F for *False*, or NG for information *Not Given*.

1. Emily says there are multiple factors affecting food prices.   T✓   F   NG
2. Economic success in certain countries is affecting food prices.   T✓   F   NG
3. The habit of eating meat and dairy pushes grain prices down.   T   F✓ NG
4. Governments are planning food aid for parts of Africa and Asia.   T   F   NG✓
5. Lucas feels the current food shortages are a hopeless situation.   T   F✓ NG

LISTENING SKILL Listening for Suggestions

Sometimes speakers make suggestions about changes they would like to see happen in the world around them but don't mention who will actually make the change. To recognize these kinds of suggestions, listen for:

- the pronouns *they, somebody, someone* + *should, have/has to, need(s) to* + verb
- negative questions with *Why don't they ...?* or *Why doesn't somebody/someone ...?*
- the passive voice of *should, have to, need to,* without an agent (e.g., *This problem really needs to be solved.*)

отрывки
багерзики

C 🎧 4.20 Listen to four excerpts. For each, write the problem and suggestion you hear.

1. _Prices are out of control (food)._

2. _Food supplis uaq._
   Plant food

3. _____
   Reseonable pri_

4. _Africa and Asia become desert._
   Something find to gid

D 🎧 4.19 Preview the questions. Then listen again to the conversation. Take notes as you listen. Write no more than three words or a number for each answer.

LISTENING FOR DETAILS

1. What does Emily believe is the basic cause of rising food prices?
   food shortages.

2. About how much cultivatable farmland has been lost in the past 40 years?
   losiny landir

3. What kinds of foods do middle classes tend to eat more of?
   _____

4. What amount of meat can be produced with 3.2 kilograms of grain?
   _____

5. About what percent of their calories do humans derive from grain?
   _____

6. What have some governments called for to ensure people have enough food to eat?
   _____

7. Which continents may see large areas become deserts in the future?
   _____

8. Where do scientists suggest increasing the quantity of food grown?
   kwä late
   _____

AFTER LISTENING

E Work in a small group. Discuss the questions.

CRTICAL THINKING: ANALYZING

1. What are some specific trends in food prices that you've noticed? What changes in the availability of food have you noticed?
2. Where are the vegetables and fruits you eat grown? Where is the meat raised? Do you expect the supplies to remain steady in the future? Explain. *устойчиво*
3. How has your diet changed over the years? Have your food choices been affected by your income or lifestyle?

Speaking

GRAMMAR FOR SPEAKING Subjunctive Verbs in *That* Clauses

To give advice in a formal context, we can use a *that* clause with a subjunctive verb. The subjunctive verb is always in the base form.

> *For now, I think it's best* **that we <u>stick</u> to our budget**.
>
> *They recommend* **that every country <u>increase</u> agricultural output**.

сослагательное наклонение

Use a *that* clause with the subjunctive after certain verbs and expressions:

советовать
консультировать —

- Verbs of advice

~ advise	recommend	suggest
~ insist	propose	request

утверждать
настоять

предложить
выдвинуть

- Expressions

It is vital (that) …	*It is essential (that)* …	*It is important (that)* …
It is best (that) …	*It is crucial (that)* …	*It is imperative (that)* …

A Work in a small group. Imagine you are advisors to the president of a small island nation. The president has sent you a letter asking for advice. Read the letter and prepare as many suggestions as you can. Use subjunctive verbs in *that* clauses.

> *It is crucial that we stop using monoculture and increase crop diversity!*

> To My Trusted Advisors:
>
> Please advise me on how to deal with the following issues:
>
> - Agricultural output is low due to insect pests and plant diseases.
> - We need to let the world know about our delicious agricultural products.
> - The amount of seafood caught around the island is diminishing every year.
> - Tourists have been complaining about the quality of island restaurants.
> - Islanders are suffering from health problems due to poor nutrition.
> - There is a scarcity of young people who want to pursue farming as a career.
>
> I look forward to hearing your invaluable suggestions.

▼ **Blueberries displayed at an organic farmers market in Maine, USA**

⌒ 4.21 Auxiliary verbs, such as modals or other helping verbs, are commonly reduced. The vowels in these unstressed words reduce to schwa (/ə/), and certain consonant sounds are changed or dropped. Listen to these examples.

have to → /ˈhæftə/	should have → /ˈʃʊdəv/	must have → /ˈmʌstəv/
has to → /ˈhæstə/	would have → /ˈwʊdəv/	may have → /ˈmeɪyəv/
want to → /ˈwʌnə/	could have → /ˈkʊdəv/	might have → /ˈmaɪdəv/
going to → /ˈgʌnə/	shouldn't have → /ˈʃʊdnəv/	don't know → /dəˈnoʊ/
ought to → /ˈɔdə/	wouldn't have → /ˈwʊdnəv/	
supposed to → /səˈpoʊstə/	couldn't have → /ˈkʊdnəv/	

Note: In casual speech, the /v/ sound is often dropped from *have*. For example, *should have* sounds like *shoulda* (/ˈʃʊdə/).

B ⌒ 4.22 Read the sentences. Underline the auxiliary phrases. Then listen and repeat the sentences. Notice the reduced phrases.

1. I could have told you it was going to rain.
2. They must have raised the price again.
3. I'll have to get some next time.
4. I could have told you that.
5. Someone really has to do something about it.
6. I would have brought home lamb for dinner.
7. And I certainly wouldn't have had any trouble buying rice!
8. We're going to be in trouble.

C With a partner, practice the conversation using reduced auxiliary phrases. Then switch roles and repeat.

A: Did you check out the farmers' market on Sunday? The vegetables were amazing.
B: I didn't know about it. But I couldn't have gone anyway. I was studying for a test.
A: How did you do on the test?
B: I could have done better, but I was tired. I shouldn't have stayed up so late.
A: You know what might have helped? Blueberries from the farmers' market.
B: Blueberries? I don't know how those would have helped.
A: Well, they're supposed to be really good for the brain.
B: Really? You should have told me that before the test. I love blueberries!

FINAL TASK Making a Formal Proposal

You and your group members are part of a government-appointed team assigned to create a program to address a particular food or nutrition issue. This will require identifying a population with unmet nutritional or other food-related needs, finding solutions to meet those needs, and preparing a proposal to submit to the appropriate government agency for approval.

A Work in a small group. Look at the chart and decide the population you will target and the types of assistance you will provide. Check your choices.

Populations in Need	Types of Assistance
Elderly in community living settings	Funds to purchase food
Elderly living alone	Food giveaways and distribution
Limited-income families/individuals	Kitchen appliances and tools
Homeless families/individuals	Assistance with food-related transportation
Schoolchildren	Assistance with food preparation
People with mobility/transportation issues	Organizing farmers' markets
Other:	Other:

BRAINSTORMING **B** Read the four sections that your proposal should include. With your group, brainstorm ideas and prepare the information needed for each section.

1. **Provide an overview:** Give a brief description of your program.
2. **Describe the problem:** What need(s) is your program attempting to meet? What type(s) of assistance will you provide? Who is the target population?
3. **Describe the solution:** What will you do to meet the need(s)? How will you accomplish this? What problems do you expect to face? How will you solve them?
4. **Describe the resources needed:** What resources will you need—money, people, other materials? How will these resources be used?

C With your group, prepare a presentation of your proposal to an appropriate government agency. Decide who will present each section. Include statements using the subjunctive, and support your ideas with others' opinions as appropriate. Practice your presentation as needed.

PRESENTING **D** Present your proposal to the class. After each group has presented, discuss what was the strongest point in each proposal.

REFLECTION

1. Which skill in the unit do you think you will be able to use in the future?

_____

_____

2. What aspects of the modern food industry do you see differently after finishing this unit?

_____

_____

3. Here are the vocabulary words and phrases from the unit. Check (✓) the ones you can use.

☐ advocate AWL   ☐ drawback   ☐ output AWL

☐ ample   ☐ exceed AWL   ☐ resistance

☐ by means of   ☐ inadequate AWL   ☐ root

☐ call for   ☐ intense AWL   ☐ scenario AWL

☐ coincide AWL   ☐ invaluable   ☐ skeptic

☐ cultivate   ☐ offset AWL   ☐ surge

☐ detrimental   ☐ opt

Independent Student Handbook

Table of Contents

Listening Skills .... page 201
Note-Taking Skills .... page 203
Organizing Information .... page 204
Speaking: Phrases for Classroom Communication .... page 206
Speaking: Phrases for Presenting .... page 208
Presentation Strategies .... page 209
Presentation Outline .... page 211
Pronunciation Guide .... page 212
Vocabulary Building Strategies .... page 213

LISTENING SKILLS

Predicting

Speakers giving formal talks usually begin by introducing themselves and their topic. Listen carefully to the introduction of the topic so that you can predict what the talk will be about.

Strategies:

- Use visual information including titles on the board or on presentation slides.
- Think about what you already know about the topic.
- Ask yourself questions that you think the speaker might answer.
- Listen for specific phrases that indicate an introduction (e.g., *My topic is…*).

Listening for Main Ideas

It is important to be able to tell the difference between a speaker's main ideas and supporting details. It is more common for teachers to test understanding of main ideas than of specific details.

Strategies:

- Listen carefully to the introduction. Speakers often state the main idea in the introduction.
- Listen for rhetorical questions, or questions that the speaker asks, and then answers. Often the answer is the statement of the main idea.
- Notice words and phrases that the speaker repeats. Repetition often signals main ideas.

Listening for Details (Examples)

A speaker often provides examples that support a main idea. A good example can help you understand and remember the main idea better.

Strategies:

- Listen for specific phrases that introduce examples.
- Listen for general statements. Examples often follow general statements.

Listening for Details (Cause and Effect)

Speakers often give reasons or list causes and/or effects to support their ideas.

Strategies:

- Notice nouns that might signal causes/reasons (e.g., *factors, influences, causes, reasons*) or effects/results (e.g., *effects, results, outcomes, consequences*).
- Notice verbs that might signal causes/reasons (e.g., *contribute to, affect, influence, determine, produce, result in*) or effects/results (often these are passive, e.g., *is affected by*).

Understanding the Structure of a Presentation

An organized speaker uses expressions to alert the audience to important information that will follow. Recognizing signal words and phrases will help you understand how a presentation is organized and the relationship between ideas.

Introduction

A good introduction identifies the topic and gives an idea of how the lecture or presentation will be organized. Here are some expressions to introduce a topic:

I'll be talking about . . .   *My topic is* . . .

There are basically two groups . . .   *There are three reasons* . . .

Body

In the body of a lecture, speakers usually expand upon the topic. They often use phrases that signal the order of events or subtopics and their relationship to each other. Here are some expressions to help listeners follow the body of a lecture:

The first/next/final (point/reason) is . . .   *First/Next/Finally, let's look at* . . .

Another reason is . . .   *However,* . . .

Conclusion

In the conclusion of a lecture, speakers often summarize what they have said. They may also make predictions or suggestions. Sometimes they ask a question in the conclusion to get the audience to think more about the topic. Here are some expressions to give a conclusion:

In conclusion, . . .   *In summary,* . . .

As you can see. . .   *To review, + (restatement of main points)*

Understanding Meaning from Context

When you are not familiar with a word that a speaker says, you can sometimes guess the meaning of the word or fill in the gaps using the context or situation itself.

Strategies:

- Don't panic. You don't always understand every word of what a speaker says in your first language, either.
- Use context clues to fill in the blanks. What did you understand just before or just after the missing part? What did the speaker probably say?
- Listen for words and phrases that signal a definition or explanation (e.g., *What that means is…*).

Recognizing a Speaker's Bias

Speakers often have an opinion about the topic they are discussing. It's important for you to know if they are objective or subjective about the topic. Objective speakers do not express an opinion. Subjective speakers have a bias or a strong feeling about the topic.

Strategies:

- Notice words like adjectives, adverbs, and modals that the speaker uses (e.g., *ideal, horribly, should, shouldn't*). These suggest that the speaker has a bias.
- Listen to the speaker's voice. Does he or she sound excited, angry, or bored?
- Notice if the speaker gives more weight or attention to one point of view over another.
- Listen for words that signal opinions (e.g., *I think…*).

NOTE-TAKING SKILLS

Taking notes is a personalized skill. It is important to develop a note-taking system that works for you. However, there are some common strategies to improve your note taking.

Before You Listen

Focus

Try to clear your mind before the speaker begins so you can pay attention. If possible, review previous notes or think about what you already know about the topic.

Predict

If you know the topic of the talk, think about what you might hear.

Listen

Take Notes by Hand

Research suggests that taking notes by hand rather than on a computer is more effective. Taking notes by hand requires you to summarize, rephrase, and synthesize information. This helps you *encode* the information, or put it into a form that you can understand and remember.

Listen for Signal Words and Phrases

Speakers often use signal words and phrases (e.g., *Today we're going to talk about…*) to organize their ideas and show relationships between them. Listening for signal words and phrases can help you decide what information to write in your notes.

Condense (Shorten) Information

- As you listen, focus on the most important ideas. The speaker will usually repeat, define, explain, and/or give examples of these ideas. Take notes on these ideas.

    Speaker: *The Itaipu Dam provides about 20% of the electricity used in Brazil and about 75% of the electricity used in Paraguay. That electricity goes to millions of homes and businesses, so it's good for the economy of both countries.*

    Notes: Itaipu Dam → electricity: Brazil 20%, Paraguay 75%

- Don't write full sentences. Write only key words (nouns, verbs, adjectives, and adverbs), phrases, or short sentences.

    Full sentence: *Teachers are normally at the top of the list of happiest jobs.*

    Notes: teachers happiest

- Leave out information that is obvious.

  Full sentence: *Photographer Annie Griffiths is famous for her beautiful photographs. She travels all over the world to take photos.*

  Notes: *A. Griffiths famous for photos; travels world*
- Write numbers and statistics using numerals. (9 bil; 35%)
- Use abbreviations (e.g., *ft., min., yr*) and symbols (=, ≠, >, <, %, →)
- Use indenting. Write main ideas on left side of paper. Indent details.
  Benefits of eating ugly foods
  Save $
  10-20% on ugly fruits & vegs. at market
- Write details under key terms to help you remember them.
- Write the definitions of important new words.

After You Listen

- Review your notes soon after the lecture or presentation. Add any details you missed.
- Clarify anything you don't understand in your notes with a classmate or teacher.
- Add or highlight main ideas. Cross out details that aren't important or necessary.
- Rewrite anything that is hard to read or understand. Rewrite your notes in an outline or other graphic organizer to organize the information more clearly.
- Use arrows, boxes, diagrams, or other visual cues to show relationships between ideas.

ORGANIZING INFORMATION

You can use a graphic organizer to take notes while you are listening, or to organize your notes after you listen. Here are some examples of graphic organizers:

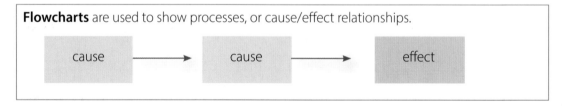

Flowcharts are used to show processes, or cause/effect relationships.

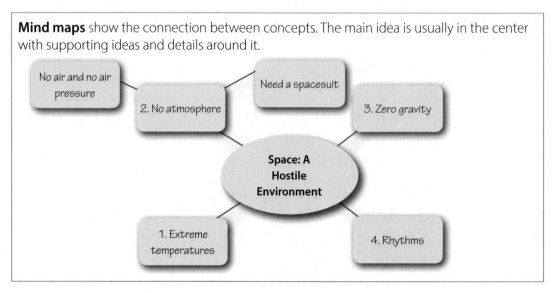

Mind maps show the connection between concepts. The main idea is usually in the center with supporting ideas and details around it.

Outlines show the relationship between main ideas and details.

To use an outline for taking notes, write the main ideas at the left margin of your paper. Below the main ideas, indent and write the supporting ideas and details. You may do this as you listen, or go back and rewrite your notes as an outline later.

I. Introduction: How to feed the world

II. Steps

Step One: Stop deforestation

a. stop burning rainforests

b. grow crops on land size of South America

T-charts compare two topics.

Climate Change in Greenland	
Benefits	**Drawbacks**
shorter winters	rising sea levels

Timelines show a sequence of events.

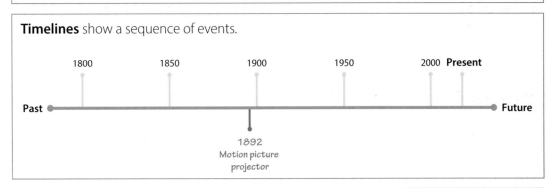

Venn diagrams compare and contrast two or more topics. The overlapping areas show similarities.

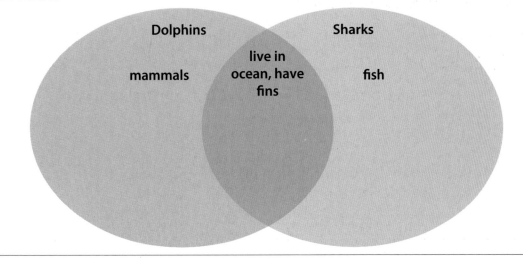

SPEAKING: COMMON PHRASES

Phrases for Expressing Yourself

Expressing Opinions
I think…
I believe…
I'm sure…
In my opinion/view…
If you ask me,…
Personally,…
To me,…

Expressing Likes and Dislikes
I like…
I prefer…
I love…
I can't stand…
I hate…
I really don't like…
I don't care for…

Giving Facts
There is evidence/proof…
Experts claim/argue…
Studies show…
Researchers found…
The record shows…

Giving Tips or Suggestions
Imperatives (e.g., Try to get more sleep.)
You/We should/shouldn't…
You/We ought to…
It's (not) a good idea to…
I suggest (that)…
Let's…
How about… + (noun/gerund)
What about… + (noun/gerund)
Why don't we/you…
You/We could…

Agreeing
I agree.
True.
Good point.
Exactly.
Absolutely.
I was just about to say that.
Definitely.
Right!

Disagreeing
I disagree.
I'm not so sure about that.
I don't know.
That's a good point, but I don't agree.
I see what you mean, but I think that…

Phrases for Interacting with Others

Clarifying/Checking Your Understanding

So are you saying that…?
So what you mean is…?
What do you mean?
How's that?
How so?
I'm not sure I understand/follow.
Do you mean…?
I'm not sure what you mean.

Asking for Clarification/Confirming Understanding

Sorry, I didn't catch that. Could you repeat it?
I'm not sure I understand the question.
I'm not sure I understand what you mean.
Sorry, I'm not following you.
Are you saying that…?
If I understand correctly, you're saying that…
Oh, now I get it. You're talking about…, right?

Checking Others' Understanding

Does that make sense?
Do you understand?
Do you see what I mean?
Is that clear?
Are you following/with me?
Do you have any questions?

Asking for Opinions

What do you think?
We haven't heard from you in a while.
Do you have anything to add?
What are your thoughts?
How do you feel?
What's your opinion?

Taking Turns

Can/May I say something?
Could I add something?
Can I just say…?
May I continue?
Can I finish what I was saying?
Did you finish your thought?
Let me finish.
Let's get back to…

Interrupting Politely

Excuse me.
Pardon me.
Forgive me for interrupting…
I hate to interrupt but…
Can I stop you for a second?

Asking for Repetition

Could you say that again?
I'm sorry?
I didn't catch what you said.
I'm sorry. I missed that. What did you say?
Could you repeat that please?

Showing Interest

I see.	*Good for you.*
Really?	*Seriously?*
Um-hmm.	*No kidding!*
Wow.	*And? (Then what?)*
That's funny / amazing / incredible / awful!	

SPEAKING: PHRASES FOR PRESENTING

Introduction

Introducing a Topic

I'm going to talk about…
My topic is…
I'm going to present…
I plan to discuss…
Let's start with…

Today we're going to talk about…
So we're going to show you…
Now/Right/So/Well, (pause), let's look at…
There are three groups/reasons/effects/ factors…
There are four steps in this process.

Body

Listing or Sequencing

First/First of all/The first (noun)/To start/To begin,…
Second/Secondly/The second/Next/Another/ Also/Then/In addition,…
Last/The last/Finally,…
There are many/several/three types/kinds of/ ways,…

Signaling Problems/Solutions

The one problem/issue/challenge is…
The one solution/answer/response is…

Giving Reasons or Causes

Because + (clause): Because the climate is changing…
Because of + (noun phrase): Because of climate change…
Due to + (noun phrase)…
Since + (clause)
The reason that I like hip-hop is…
One reason that people listen to music is…
One factor is + (noun phrase)
The main reason that…

Giving Results or Effects

so + (clause): so I went to the symphony
Therefore, + (sentence): Therefore, I went to the symphony.
As a result, + (sentence)
Consequently, + (sentence)
…causes + (noun phrase)
…leads to + (noun phrase)
…had an impact/effect on + (noun phrase)
If…then…

Giving Examples

The first example is…
Here's an example of what I mean…
For instance,…
For example,…
Let me give you an example…
…such as…
…like…

Repeating and Rephrasing

What you need to know is…
I'll say this again…
So again, let me repeat…
The most important point is…

Signaling Additional Examples or Ideas	Signaling to Stop Taking Notes
Not only…but, besides	*You don't need this for the test.*
Besides…	*This information is in your books/on your handout/on the website.*
Not only do…, but also	*You don't have to write all this down.*
Identifying a Side Track	**Returning to a Previous Topic**
This is off-topic,…	*Getting back to our previous discussion,…*
On a different subject,…	*To return to our earlier topic…*
As an aside, …	*OK, getting back on topic…*
That reminds me…	*So to return to what we were saying,…*
Signaling a Definition	**Talking about Visuals**
Which means…	*This graph/infographic/diagram shows/explains…*
What that means is…	*The line/box/image represents…*
Or…	*The main point of this visual is…*
In other words,…	*You can see…*
Another way to say that is…	*From this we can see…*
That is…	
That is to say…	

Conclusion

Concluding	
Well/So, that's how I see it.	*To sum up,*
In conclusion,	*As you can see,…*
In summary,	*At the end,…*
	To review, (+ restatement of main points)

PRESENTATION STRATEGIES

You will often have to give individual or group presentations in your class. The strategies below will help you to prepare, present, and reflect on your presentations.

Prepare

As you prepare your presentation:

Consider Your Topic

- **Choose a topic you feel passionate about.** If you are passionate about your topic, your audience will be more interested and excited about your topic, too. Focus on one major idea that you can bring to life. The best ideas are the ones your audience wants to experience.

Consider Your Purpose

- **Have a strong start.** Use an effective hook, such as a quote, an interesting example, a rhetorical question, or a powerful image to get your audience's attention. Include one sentence that explains what you will do in your presentation and why.

- **Stay focused.** Make sure your details and examples support your main points. Avoid sidetracks or unnecessary information that takes you away from your topic.

- **Use visuals that relate to your ideas.** Drawings, photos, video clips, infographics, charts, maps, slides, and physical objects can get your audience's attention and explain ideas effectively. For example, a photo or map of a location you mention can help your audience picture a place they have never been. Slides with only key words and phrases can help emphasize your main points. Visuals should be bright, clear, and simple.

- **Have a strong conclusion.** A strong conclusion should serve the same purpose as a strong start—to get your audience's attention and make them think. Good conclusions often refer back to the introduction, or beginning of the presentation. For example, if you ask a question in the beginning, you can answer it in the conclusion. Remember to restate your main points, and add a conclusion device such as a question, a call to action, or a quote.

Consider your Audience

- **Use familiar concepts.** Think about the people in your audience. Ask yourself these questions: Where are they from? How old are they? What is their background? What do they already know about my topic? What information do I need to explain? Use language and concepts they will understand.

- **Share a personal story.** Consider presenting information that will get an emotional reaction; for example, information that will make your audience feel surprised, curious, worried, or upset. This will help your audience relate to you and your topic.

- **Be authentic (be yourself!).** Write your presentation yourself. Use words that you know and are comfortable using.

Rehearse

- **Make an outline** to help you organize your ideas.

- **Write notes on notecards.** Do not write full sentences, just key words and phrases to help you remember important ideas. Mark the words you should stress and places to pause.

- **Review pronunciation.** Check the pronunciation of words you are uncertain about with a classmate, a teacher, or in a dictionary. Note and practice the pronunciation of difficult words.

- **Memorize the introduction and conclusion.** Rehearse your presentation several times. Practice saying it out loud to yourself (perhaps in front of a mirror or video recorder) and in front of others.

- **Ask for feedback.** Note and revise information that doesn't flow smoothly based on feedback and on your own performance in rehearsal. If specific words or phrases are still a problem, rephrase them.

Present

As you present:

- **Pay attention to your pacing** (how fast or slow you speak). Remember to speak slowly and clearly. Pause to allow your audience to process information.

- **Speak at a volume loud enough to be heard** by everyone in the audience, but not too loud. Ask the audience if your volume is OK at the beginning of your talk.

- **Vary your intonation.** Don't speak in the same tone throughout the talk. Your audience will be more interested if your voice rises and falls, speeds up and slows down to match the ideas you are talking about.
- **Be friendly and relaxed with your audience**—remember to smile!
- **Show enthusiasm for your topic.** Use humor if appropriate.
- **Have a relaxed body posture.** Don't stand with your arms folded, or look down at your notes. Use gestures when helpful to emphasize your points.
- **Don't read directly from your notes.** Use them to help you remember ideas.
- **Don't look at or read from your visuals too much.** Use them to support your ideas.
- **Make frequent eye contact** with the entire audience.

Reflect

As you reflect on your presentation:

- **Consider what you think went well** during your presentation and what areas you can improve upon.
- **Get feedback** from your classmates and teacher. How do their comments relate to your own thoughts about your presentation? Did they notice things you didn't? How can you use their feedback in your next presentation?

PRESENTATION OUTLINE

When you are planning a presentation, you may find it helpful to use an outline. If it is a group presentation, the outline can provide an easy way to divide the content. For example, one student can do the introduction, another student the first idea in the body, and so on.

1. Introduction

Topic: _____

Hook: _____

Statement of main idea: _____

2. Body

First step/example/reason: _____

  Supporting details: _____ _____ _____

Second step/example/reason: _____

  Supporting details: _____ _____ _____

Third step/example/reason: _____ _____ _____

  Supporting details: _____ _____ _____

3. Conclusion

Main points to summarize: _____ _____

Suggestions/Predictions: _____ _____

Closing comments/summary: _____ _____

PRONUNCIATION GUIDE

Sounds and Symbols

Vowels

Symbol	Key Words
/ɑ/	hot, stop
/æ/	cat, ran
/aɪ/	fine, nice
/i/	eat, need
/ɪ/	sit, him
/eɪ/	name, say
/ɛ/	get, bed
/ʌ/	cup, what
/ə/	about, lesson
/u/	boot, new
/ʊ/	book, could
/oʊ/	go, road
/ɔ/	law, walk
/aʊ/	house, now
/ɔɪ/	toy, coin

Consonants

Symbol	Key Word	Symbol	Key Word
/b/	boy	/t/	tea
/d/	day	/tʃ/	cheap
/dʒ/	job, bridge	/v/	vote
/f/	face	/w/	we
/g/	go	/y/	yes
/h/	hat	/z/	zoo
/k/	key, car		
/l/	love	/ð/	they
/m/	my	/θ/	think
/n/	nine	/ʃ/	shoe
/ŋ/	sing	/ʒ/	measure
/p/	pen		
/r/	right		
/s/	see		

Source: *The Newbury House Dictionary plus Grammar Reference,* Fifth Edition, National Geographic Learning/ Cengage Learning, 2014.

Rhythm

The rhythm of English involves stress and pausing.

Stress

- English words are based on syllables—units of sound that include one vowel sound.
- In every word in English, one syllable has the primary stress.
- In English, speakers group words that go together based on the meaning and context of the sentence. These groups of words are called *thought groups*. In each thought group, one word is stressed more than the others—the stress is placed on the syllable with the primary stress in this word.
- In general, new ideas and information are stressed.

Pausing

- Pauses in English can be divided into two groups: long and short pauses.
- English speakers use long pauses to mark the conclusion of a thought, items in a list, or choices given.
- Short pauses are used in between thought groups to break up the ideas in sentences into smaller, more manageable chunks of information.

Intonation

English speakers use intonation, or pitch (the rise and fall of their voice), to help express meaning. For example, speakers usually use a rising intonation at the end of *yes/no* questions, and a falling intonation at the end of *wh-* questions and statements.

VOCABULARY BUILDING STRATEGIES

Vocabulary learning is an on-going process. The strategies below will help you learn and remember new vocabulary words.

Guessing Meaning from Context

You can often guess the meaning of an unfamiliar word by looking at or listening to the words and sentences around it. Speakers usually know when a word is unfamiliar to the audience, or is essential to understanding the main ideas, and often provide clues to its meaning.

- Repetition: A speaker may use the same key word or phrase, or use another form of the same word.
- Restatement or synonym: A speaker may give a synonym to explain the meaning of a word, using phrases such as *in other words, also called, or…, also known as.*
- Antonyms: A speaker may define a word by explaining what it is NOT. The speaker may say *Unlike A/In contrast to A, B is…*
- Definition: Listen for signals such as *which means* or *is defined as*. Definitions can also be signaled by a pause.
- Examples: A speaker may provide examples that can help you figure out what something is. For example, ***Mascots*** *are a very popular marketing tool. You've seen them on commercials and in ads on social media –* **cute, brightly colored creatures that help sell a product**.

Understanding Word Families: Stems, Prefixes, and Suffixes

Use your understanding of stems, prefixes, and suffixes to recognize unfamiliar words and to expand your vocabulary. The stem is the root part of the word, which provides the main meaning. A prefix comes before the stem and usually modifies meaning (e.g., adding *re-* to a word means "again" or "back"). A suffix comes after the stem and usually changes the part of speech (e.g., adding *-ion, -tion,* or *-ation* to a verb changes it to a noun). Words that share the same stem or root belong to the same word family (e.g., *event, eventful, uneventful, uneventfully*).

Word Stem	Meaning	Example
ann, enn	year	anniversary, millennium
chron(o)	time	chronological, synchronize
flex, flect	bend	flexible, reflection
graph	draw, write	graphics, paragraph
lab	work	labor, collaborate
mob, mot, mov	move	automobile, motivate, mover
port	carry	transport, import
sect	cut	sector, bisect

Prefix	Meaning	Example
dis-	not, opposite of	disappear, disadvantages
in-, im-, il-, ir-	not	inconsistent, immature, illegal, irresponsible
inter-	between	Internet, international
mis-	bad, badly, incorrectly	misunderstand, misjudge
pre-	before	prehistoric, preheat
re-	again; back	repeat; return
trans-	across, beyond	transfer, translate
un-	not	uncooked, unfair

Suffix	Meaning	Example
-able, -ible	worth, ability	believable, impossible
-en	to cause to become; made of	lengthen, strengthen; golden
-er, -or	one who	teacher, director
-ful	full of	beautiful, successful
-ify, -fy	to make or become	simplify, satisfy
-ion, -tion, -ation	condition, action	occasion, education, foundation
-ize	cause	modernize, summarize
-ly	in the manner of	carefully, happily
-ment	condition or result	assignment, statement
-ness	state of being	happiness, sadness

Using a Dictionary

Here are some tips for using a dictionary:

- When you see or hear a new word, try to guess its part of speech (noun, verb, adjective, etc.) and meaning, then look it up in a dictionary.
- Some words have multiple meanings. Look up a new word in the dictionary and try to choose the correct meaning for the context. Then see if it makes sense within the context.
- When you look up a word, look at all the definitions to see if there is a basic core meaning. This will help you understand the word when it is used in a different context. Also look at all the related words, or words in the same family. This can help you expand your vocabulary. For example, the core meaning of *structure* involves something built or put together.

structure /ˈstrʌktʃər/ *n.* **1** [C] a building of any kind: *A new structure is being built on the corner.* **2** [C] any architectural object of any kind: *The Eiffel Tower is a famous Parisian structure.* **3** [U] the way parts are put together or organized: *the structure of a song||a business's structure*
–v. [T] **-tured, -turing, -tures** to put together or organize parts of s.t.: *We are structuring a plan to hire new teachers.*
-adj. **structural.**

Source: *The Newbury House Dictionary plus Grammar Reference*, Fifth Edition, National Geographic Learning/Cengage Learning, 2014

Multi-Word Units

You can improve your fluency if you learn and use vocabulary as multi-word units: idioms (*go the extra mile*), collocations (*wide range*), and fixed expressions (*in other words*). Some multi-word units can only be understood as a chunk—the individual words do not add up to the same overall meaning. Keep track of multi-word units in a notebook or on notecards.

Vocabulary Note Cards

You can expand your vocabulary by using vocabulary note cards or a vocabulary building app. Write the word, expression, or sentence that you want to learn on one side. On the other, draw a four-square grid and write the following information in the squares: definition; translation (in your first language); sample sentence; synonyms. Choose words that are high frequency or on the academic word list. If you have looked a word up a few times, you should make a card for it.

definition:	first language translation:
sample sentence:	synonyms:

Organize the cards in review sets so you can practice them. Don't put words that are similar in spelling or meaning in the same review set as you may get them mixed up. Go through the cards and test yourself on the words or expressions. You can also practice with a partner.

VOCABULARY INDEX

Word	Page	CEFR† Level	Word	Page	CEFR† Level	Word	Page	CEFR† Level
accustomed to	104	C1	descendant	84	C2	innate	174	C2
advocate	184	C2	detect	154	C1	innovative	4	C1
affluent	14	C1	determine	124	C1	insert	54	C1
affordable	4	C1	detrimental	184	C2	insist on	104	C1
aid	134	C1	diagnosis	144	C2	integrate	54	C1
alarming	44	C1	diminish	94	C1	intense	184	C1
allocate	134	C1	displace	94	C1	interest	134	C1
ample	194	C1	distinct	44	C1	interfere	94	C1
analytical	164	C1	diversity	114	C1	internalize/	14	off-list
anticipate	74	C1	dominant	14	C1	internalise		
application	74	C2	drawback	184	C1	intuition	164	C2
archaeologist	84	C1	ecology	94	C1	invaluable	184	C1
assemble	104	C2	emerging	74	C1	isolated	104	C1
associate	124	C1	employ	104	C1	keep track of	144	C1
authority	34	C1	enforce	14	C1	labor / labour	64	C1
authorize /	4	C1	engage in	124	C2	legislation	94	C2
authorise			enrich	74	C1	livelihood	114	off-list
be derived from	54	C1	envision	44	C1	logic	164	C1
be to blame	24	C1	ethical	174	C2	mass	74	C1
be unique to	14	C1	ethnic	14	C1	maximize /	4	C2
by leaps and	144	C2	evolve	44	C1	maximise		
bounds			exceed	194	C1	merit	114	C1
by means of	184	C1	excessively	44	off-list	migrate	84	C1
call for	194	C2	exclusively	44	C1	modify	24	C1
clarify	144	C1	exhibit	54	C1	monitor	94	C1
coincide	194	C2	extinct	24	C1	namely	164	C1
collaborate	74	C1	facilitate	64	C1	neglect	34	C1
comparatively	144	C1	flourish	114	C2	nest egg	134	C2
competence	64	C1	fulfillment /	124	C2	norm	174	C1
component	64	C1	fulfilment			notable	84	C1
confidential	144	C1	funds	4	C1	notify	154	C1
conform	14	off-list	gadget	144	C1	nutritional	154	C1
confront	94	C2	genetic	84	C1	objective	164	B2
consent	114	C1	habitat	24	C1	obsolete	174	C1
constitute	44	C1	hardship	114	C1	offset	184	C2
constructive	54	C1	heritage	114	C2	ongoing	24	C2
consult	144	C1	hypothesis	84	C2	opt	194	C1
contradiction	104	C2	immense	84	C1	outlook	124	C2
contrary (to)	34	C1	impact	124	C1	output	194	C2
controversy	34	C1	implication	74	C1	overdo	134	C1
cultivate	184	C1	impose	24	C1	overwhelming	94	C1
daydream	54	C1	inadequate	194	C1	perceive	44	C1
debatable	14	off-list	inevitably	64	C1	perspective	84	C1
dedicated (to)	94	C1	inferior	174	C1	persuasive	54	C1
deepen	174	C1	influential	74	C1	pertain (to)	64	off-list
deposit	134	C1	initiate	34	C2	portable	74	C1

Word	Page	CEFR† Level	Word	Page	CEFR† Level	Word	Page	CEFR† Level
posture	154	C1	replicate	114	off-list	tendency	144	C1
practical	54	C1	resistance	184	C2	threaten	24	C1
predator	34	C1	resolve	154	C1	thrive	24	C1
preservation	104	C1	restrict	14	C1	track	154	C2
prey on	34	off-list	retain	64	C2	transaction	134	C1
principle	104	C2	root	194	C1	transition	104	C2
prioritize /	4	off-list	scarcity	4	C2	tribal	94	C2
prioritise			scenario	194	C2	ultimately	114	C1
productivity	154	C1	sector	64	C1	undeniable	34	C1
prominent	74	C2	security	124	C1	undertake	114	C1
promising	64	C1	sedentary	154	C2	unprecedented	174	C2
promote	124	C1	seemingly	134	C1	unquestionably	54	C1
prone to	154	C2	skeptic / sceptic	184	off-list	upkeep	34	C2
pursue	104	C1	spatial	164	off-list	venture	84	C2
radical	174	C1	status	24	C1	verbal	164	C2
random	44	C1	stem from	174	C1	vice versa	164	C1
rank	14	C1	stroll	4	C1	virtue	124	C2
ratio	44	C1	subjective	164	C1	visualize /	164	off-list
regulate	4	C1	subsequently	84	C1	visualise		
reluctant	144	C1	substantially	54	C1	well-being	124	C1
reminder	134	C1	superior	174	C1	widespread	64	C1
renovation	4	C1	surge	194	C1	wipe out	24	C2
repetitive	154	C1	sustainable	34	C1	withdraw	134	C1

†The Common European Framework of Reference for Languages (CEFR) is an international standard for describing language proficiency. Pathways Level 4 is intended for students at CEFR level C1. The target vocabulary is at the following CEFR levels:

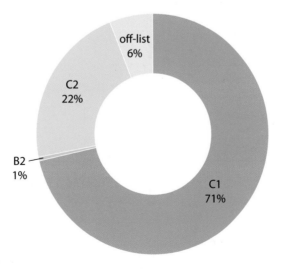

off-list 6%

C2 22%

B2 1%

C1 71%

*These words are on the Academic Word List (AWL). The AWL is a list of the 570 highest-frequency academic word families that regularly appear in academic texts. The AWL was compiled by researcher Averil Coxhead based on her analysis of a 3.5-million-word corpus (Coxhead, 2000).

RUBRICS

UNIT 1   Lesson B Lesson Task

Check (✓) if the presenter did the following:	Name		
	___	___	___
1. described a problem affecting a city and its causes	☐	☐	☐
2. proposed possible solutions to the problem	☐	☐	☐
3. used signal phrases to introduce additional aspects of the topic	☐	☐	☐
4. divided the presentation appropriately	☐	☐	☐
5. spoke clearly and at an appropriate pace	☐	☐	☐
6. used appropriate vocabulary	☐	☐	☐
OVERALL RATING Note: 1 = lowest; 5 = highest	1 2 3 4 5	1 2 3 4 5	1 2 3 4 5
Notes:			

UNIT 2   Lesson B Final Task

Check (✓) if the presenters did the following:	Name		
	___	___	___
1. provided appropriate support in favor of or against the argument	☐	☐	☐
2. responded to arguments appropriately	☐	☐	☐
3. debated for three to five minutes	☐	☐	☐
4. spoke clearly and at an appropriate pace	☐	☐	☐
5. used appropriate vocabulary	☐	☐	☐
OVERALL RATING Note: 1 = lowest; 5 = highest	1 2 3 4 5	1 2 3 4 5	1 2 3 4 5
Notes:			

UNIT 3   Lesson B Final Task

Check (✓) if the presenter did the following:	Name		
	_____	_____	_____
1. described fashion trends in a particular location in detail	☐	☐	☐
2. displayed appropriate visuals	☐	☐	☐
3. organized the presentation appropriately	☐	☐	☐
4. paraphrased new or difficult information	☐	☐	☐
5. spoke clearly and at an appropriate pace	☐	☐	☐
6. used appropriate vocabulary	☐	☐	☐
OVERALL RATING Note: 1 = lowest; 5 = highest	1 2 3 4 5	1 2 3 4 5	1 2 3 4 5
Notes:			

UNIT 4   Lesson B Lesson Task

Check (✓) if the presenters did the following:	Name		
	_____	_____	_____
1. described a social media platform and its history	☐	☐	☐
2. discussed the advantages of the platform and how it compares to others	☐	☐	☐
3. evaluated the platform in terms of its effect on globalization and its future prospects	☐	☐	☐
4. clarified terms/ideas with definitions	☐	☐	☐
5. spoke slowly and confidently	☐	☐	☐
6. used appropriate vocabulary	☐	☐	☐
OVERALL RATING Note: 1 = lowest; 5 = highest	1 2 3 4 5	1 2 3 4 5	1 2 3 4 5
Notes:			

UNIT 5 Lesson B Final Task

Check (✓) if the presenters did the following:	Name		
	_____	_____	_____
1. explained the animal migration clearly	☐	☐	☐
2. displayed a time line of the animal migration	☐	☐	☐
3. handled audience questions appropriately	☐	☐	☐
4. spoke clearly and at an appropriate pace	☐	☐	☐
5. used appropriate vocabulary	☐	☐	☐
OVERALL RATING Note: 1 = lowest; 5 = highest	1 2 3 4 5	1 2 3 4 5	1 2 3 4 5
Notes:			

UNIT 6 Lesson B Final Task

Check (✓) if the presenters did the following:	Name		
	_____	_____	_____
1. described a current tradition in detail	☐	☐	☐
2. organized ideas effectively	☐	☐	☐
3. used rhetorical questions appropriately	☐	☐	☐
4. used strategies to appear confident when speaking	☐	☐	☐
5. used appropriate vocabulary	☐	☐	☐
OVERALL RATING Note: 1 = lowest; 5 = highest	1 2 3 4 5	1 2 3 4 5	1 2 3 4 5
Notes:			

UNIT 7   Lesson B Final Task

Check (✓) if the presenter did the following:	Name		
	_____	_____	_____
1. presented a balanced budget	☐	☐	☐
2. described a plan to repay the client's debt	☐	☐	☐
3. used appropriate connectors to organize ideas	☐	☐	☐
4. spoke clearly and at an appropriate pace	☐	☐	☐
5. used appropriate vocabulary	☐	☐	☐
OVERALL RATING Note: 1 = lowest; 5 = highest	1 2 3 4 5	1 2 3 4 5	1 2 3 4 5
Notes:			

UNIT 8   Lesson B Final Task

Check (✓) if the presenter did the following:	Name		
	_____	_____	_____
1. described a health/fitness technology product	☐	☐	☐
2. emphasized important information	☐	☐	☐
3. discussed the positive and negative assessments of the product	☐	☐	☐
4. presented a pros and cons chart for the product	☐	☐	☐
5. used questions to engage the audience	☐	☐	☐
6. used appropriate vocabulary	☐	☐	☐
OVERALL RATING Note: 1 = lowest; 5 = highest	1 2 3 4 5	1 2 3 4 5	1 2 3 4 5
Notes:			

UNIT 9   Lesson B Final Task

Check (✓) if the presenters did the following:	Name		
	_____	_____	_____
1. described three life hacks, the problems they solve, and/or who they benefit	☐	☐	☐
2. discussed his/her personal experience with and/or opinions of the life hacks	☐	☐	☐
3. used appropriate gestures	☐	☐	☐
4. spoke clearly and at an appropriate pace	☐	☐	☐
5. used appropriate vocabulary	☐	☐	☐
OVERALL RATING Note: 1 = lowest; 5 = highest	1 2 3 4 5	1 2 3 4 5	1 2 3 4 5
Notes:			

UNIT 10   Lesson B Final Task

Check (✓) if the presenters did the following:	Name		
	_____	_____	_____
1. explained how the program solves a problem	☐	☐	☐
2. described the resources needed to implement the program	☐	☐	☐
3. supported ideas with others' opinions when appropriate	☐	☐	☐
4. spoke clearly and at an appropriate pace	☐	☐	☐
5. used appropriate vocabulary	☐	☐	☐
OVERALL RATING Note: 1 = lowest; 5 = highest	1 2 3 4 5	1 2 3 4 5	1 2 3 4 5
Notes:			

ACKNOWLEDGEMENTS

The Authors and Publisher would like to acknowledge the teachers around the world who participated in the development of the second edition of *Pathways*.

A special thanks to our Advisory Board for their valuable input during the development of this series.

ADVISORY BOARD

Mahmoud Al Hosni, Modern College of Business and Science, Muscat; **Safaa Al-Salim**, Kuwait University, Kuwait City; **Laila AlQadhi**, Kuwait University, Kuwait City; **Julie Bird**, RMIT University Vietnam, Ho Chi Minh City; **Elizabeth Bowles**, Virginia Tech Language and Culture Institute, Blacksburg, VA; **Rachel Bricker**, Arizona State University, Tempe, AZ; **James Broadbridge**, J.F. Oberlin University, Tokyo; **Marina Broeder**, Mission College, Santa Clara, CA; **Shawn Campbell**, Hangzhou High School, Hangzhou; **Trevor Carty**, James Cook University, Singapore; **Jindarat De Vleeschauwer**, Chiang Mai University, Chiang Mai; **Wai-Si El Hassan**, Prince Mohammad Bin Fahd University, Dhahran; **Jennifer Farnell**, University of Bridgeport, Bridgeport, CT; **Rasha Gazzaz**, King Abdulaziz University, Jeddah; **Keith Graziadei**, Santa Monica College, Santa Monica, CA; **Janet Harclerode**, Santa Monica Community College, Santa Monica, CA; **Anna Hasper**, TeacherTrain, Dubai; **Phoebe Kamel Yacob Hindi**, Abu Dhabi Vocational Education and Training Institute, Abu Dhabi; **Kuei-ping Hsu**, National Tsing Hua University, Hsinchu; **Greg Jewell**, Drexel University, Philadelphia, PA; **Adisra Katib**, Chulalongkorn University Language Institute, Bangkok; **Wayne Kennedy**, LaGuardia Community College, Long Island City, NY; **Beth Koo**, Central Piedmont Community College, Charlotte, NC; **Denise Kray**, Bridge School, Denver, CO; **Chantal Kruger**, ILA Vietnam, Ho Chi Minh City; **William P. Kyzner**, Fuyang AP Center, Fuyang; **Becky Lawrence**, Massachusetts International Academy, Marlborough, MA; **Deborah McGraw**, Syracuse University, Syracuse, NY; **Mary Moore**, University of Puerto Rico, San Juan; **Raymond Purdy**, ELS Language Centers, Princeton, NJ; **Anouchka Rachelson**, Miami Dade College, Miami, FL; **Fathimah Razman**, Universiti Utara Malaysia, Sintok; **Phil Rice**, University of Delaware ELI, Newark, DE; **Scott Rousseau**, American University of Sharjah, Sharjah; **Verna Santos-Nafrada**, King Saud University, Riyadh; **Eugene Sidwell**, American Intercon Institute, Phnom Penh; **Gemma Thorp**, Monash University English Language Centre, Melbourne; **Matt Thurston**, University of Central Lancashire, Preston; **Christine Tierney**, Houston Community College, Houston, TX; **Jet Robredillo Tonogbanua**, FPT University, Hanoi.

GLOBAL REVIEWERS

ASIA

Antonia Cavcic, Asia University, Tokyo; **Soyhan Egitim**, Tokyo University of Science, Tokyo; **Caroline Handley**, Asia University, Tokyo; **Patrizia Hayashi**, Meikai University, Urayasu; **Greg Holloway**, University of Kitakyushu, Kitakyushu; **Anne C. Ihata**, Musashino University, Tokyo; **Kathryn Mabe**, Asia University, Tokyo; **Frederick Navarro Bacala**, Yokohama City University, Yokohama; **Tyson Rode**, Meikai University, Urayasu; **Scott Shelton-Strong**, Asia University, Tokyo; **Brooks Slaybaugh**, Yokohama City University, Yokohama; **Susanto Sugiharto**, Sutomo Senior High School, Medan; **Andrew Zitzmann**, University of Kitakyushu, Kitakyushu

LATIN AMERICA AND THE CARIBBEAN

Raul Bilini, ProLingua, Dominican Republic; **Alejandro Garcia**, Collegio Marcelina, Mexico; **Humberto Guevara**, Tec de Monterrey, Campus Monterrey, Mexico; **Romina Olga Planas**, Centro Cultural Paraguayo Americano, Paraguay; **Carlos Rico-Troncoso**, Pontificia Universidad Javeriana, Colombia; **Ialê Schetty**, Enjoy English, Brazil; **Aline Simoes**, Way To Go Private English, Brazil; **Paulo Cezar Lira Torres**, APenglish, Brazil; **Rosa Enilda Vasquez**, Swisher Dominicana, Dominican Republic; **Terry Whitty**, LDN Language School, Brazil.

MIDDLE EAST AND NORTH AFRICA

Susan Daniels, Kuwait University, Kuwait; **Mahmoud Mohammadi Khomeini**, Sokhane Ashna Language School, Iran; **Müge Lenbet**, Koç University, Turkey; **Robert Anthony Lowman**, Prince Mohammad bin Fahd University, Saudi Arabia; **Simon Mackay**, Prince Mohammad bin Fahd University, Saudi Arabia.

USA AND CANADA

Frank Abbot, Houston Community College, Houston, TX; **Hossein Aksari**, Bilingual Education Institute and Houston Community College, Houston, TX; **Sudie Allen-Henn**, North Seattle College, Seattle, WA; **Sharon Allie**, Santa Monica Community College, Santa Monica, CA; **Jerry Archer**, Oregon State University, Corvallis, OR; **Nicole Ashton**, Central Piedmont Community College, Charlotte, NC; **Barbara Barrett**, University of Miami, Coral Gables, FL; **Maria Bazan-Myrick**, Houston Community College, Houston, TX; **Rebecca Beal**, Colleges of Marin, Kentfield, CA; **Marlene Beck**, Eastern Michigan University, Ypsilanti, MI; **Michelle Bell**, University of Southern California, Los Angeles, CA; **Linda Bolet**, Houston Community College, Houston, TX; **Jenna Bollinger**, Eastern Michigan University, Ypsilanti, MI; **Monica Boney**, Houston Community College, Houston, TX; **Nanette Bouvier**, Rutgers University – Newark, Newark, NJ; **Nancy Boyer**, Golden West College, Huntington Beach, CA; **Lia Brenneman**, University of Florida English Language Institute, Gainesville, FL; **Colleen Brice**, Grand Valley State University, Allendale, MI; **Kristen Brown**, Massachusetts International Academy, Marlborough, MA; **Philip Brown**, Houston Community

College, Houston, TX; **Dongmei Cao**, San Jose City College, San Jose, CA; **Molly Cheney**, University of Washington, Seattle, WA; **Emily Clark**, The University of Kansas, Lawrence, KS; **Luke Coffelt**, International English Center, Boulder, CO; **William C Cole-French**, MCPHS University, Boston, MA; **Charles Colson**, English Language Institute at Sam Houston State University, Huntsville, TX; **Lucy Condon**, Bilingual Education Institute, Houston, TX; **Janice Crouch**, Internexus Indiana, Indianapolis, IN; **Charlene Dandrow**, Virginia Tech Language and Culture Institute, Blacksburg, VA; **Loretta Davis**, Coastline Community College, Westminster, CA; **Marta Dmytrenko-Ahrabian**, Wayne State University, Detroit, MI; **Bonnie Duhart**, Houston Community College, Houston, TX; **Karen Eichhorn**, International English Center, Boulder, CO; **Tracey Ellis**, Santa Monica Community College, Santa Monica, CA; **Jennifer Evans**, University of Washington, Seattle, WA; **Marla Ewart**, Bilingual Education Institute, Houston, TX; **Rhoda Fagerland**, St. Cloud State University, St. Cloud, MN; **Kelly Montijo Fink**, Kirkwood Community College, Cedar Rapids, IA; **Celeste Flowers**, University of Central Arkansas, Conway, AR; **Kurtis Foster**, Missouri State University, Springfield, MO; **Rachel Garcia**, Bilingual Education Institute, Houston, TX; **Thomas Germain**, University of Colorado Boulder, Boulder, CO; **Claire Gimble**, Virginia International University, Fairfax, VA; **Marilyn Glazer-Weisner**, Middlesex Community College, Lowell, MA; **Amber Goodall**, South Piedmont Community College, Charlotte, NC; **Katya Goussakova**, Seminole State College of Florida, Sanford, FL; **Jane Granado**, Texas State University, San Marcos, TX; **Therea Hampton**, Mercer County Community College, West Windsor Township, NJ; **Jane Hanson**, University of Nebraska – Lincoln, Lincoln, NE; **Lauren Heather**, University of Texas at San Antonio, San Antonio, TX; **Jannette Hermina**, Saginaw Valley State University, Saginaw, MI; **Gail Hernandez**, College of Staten Island, Staten Island, NY; **Beverly Hobbs**, Clark University, Worcester, MA; **Kristin Homuth**, Language Center International, Southfield, MI; **Tim Hooker**, Campbellsville University, Campbellsville, KY; **Raylene Houck**, Idaho State University, Pocatello, ID; **Karen L. Howling**, University of Bridgeport, Bridgeport, CT; **Sharon Jaffe**, Santa Monica Community College, Santa Monica, CA; **Andrea Kahn**, Santa Monica Community College, Santa Monica, CA; **Eden Bradshaw Kaiser**, Massachusetts International Academy, Marlborough, MA; **Mandy Kama**, Georgetown University, Washington, D.C.; **Andrea Kaminski**, University of Michigan – Dearborn, Dearborn, MI; **Phoebe Kang**, Brock University, Ontario; **Eileen Kramer**, Boston University CELOP, Brookline, MA; **Rachel Lachance**, University of New Hampshire, Durham, NH; **Janet Langon**, Glendale Community College, Glendale, CA; **Frances Le Grand**, University of Houston, Houston, TX; **Esther Lee**, California State University, Fullerton, CA; **Helen S. Mays Lefal**, American Learning Institute, Dallas, TX; **Oranit Limmaneeprasert**, American River College, Sacramento, CA; **Dhammika Liyanage**, Bilingual Education Institute, Houston, TX; **Emily Lodmer**, Santa Monica Community College, Santa Monica Community College, CA; **Ari Lopez**, American Learning Institute Dallas, TX; **Nichole Lukas**, University of Dayton, Dayton, OH; **Undarmaa Maamuujav**, California State University, Los Angeles, CA; **Diane Mahin**, University of Miami, Coral Gables, FL; **Melanie Majeski**, Naugatuck Valley Community College, Waterbury, CT; **Judy Marasco**, Santa Monica Community College, Santa Monica, CA; **Murray McMahan**, University of Alberta, Alberta; **Deirdre McMurtry**, University of Nebraska Omaha, Omaha, NE; **Suzanne Meyer**, University of Pittsburgh, Pittsburgh, PA; **Cynthia Miller**, Richland College, Dallas, TX; **Sara Miller**, Houston Community College, Houston, TX; **Gwendolyn Miraglia**, Houston Community College, Houston, TX; **Katie Mitchell**, International English Center, Boulder, CO; **Ruth Williams Moore**, University of Colorado Boulder, Boulder, CO; **Kathy Najafi**, Houston Community College, Houston, TX; **Sandra Navarro**, Glendale Community College, Glendale, CA; **Stephanie Ngom**, Boston University, Boston MA; **Barbara Niemczyk**, University of Bridgeport, Bridgeport, CT; **Melody Nightingale**, Santa Monica Community College, Santa Monica, CA; **Alissa Olgun**, California Language Academy, Los Angeles, CA; **Kimberly Oliver**, Austin Community College, Austin, TX; **Steven Olson**, International English Center, Boulder, CO; **Fernanda Ortiz**, University of Arizona, Tucson, AZ; **Joel Ozretich**, University of Washington, Seattle, WA; **Erin Pak**, Schoolcraft College, Livonia, MI; **Geri Pappas**, University of Michigan – Dearborn, Dearborn, MI; **Eleanor Paterson**, Erie Community College, Buffalo, NY; **Sumeeta Patnaik**, Marshall University, Huntington, WV; **Mary Peacock**, Richland College, Dallas, TX; **Kathryn Porter**, University of Houston, Houston, TX; **Eileen Prince**, Prince Language Associates, Newton Highlands, MA; **Marina Ramirez**, Houston Community College, Houston, TX; **Laura Ramm**, Michigan State University, East Lansing, MI; **Chi Rehg**, University of South Florida, Tampa, FL; **Cyndy Reimer**, Douglas College, New Westminster, British Columbia; **Sydney Rice**, Imperial Valley College, Imperial, CA; **Lynnette Robson**, Mercer University, Macon, GA; **Helen E. Roland**, Miami Dade College, Miami, FL; **Maria Paula Carreira Rolim**, Southeast Missouri State University, Cape Girardeau, MO; **Jill Rolston-Yates**, Texas State University, San Marcos, TX; **David Ross**, Houston Community College, Houston, TX; **Rachel Scheiner**, Seattle Central College, Seattle, WA; **John Schmidt**, Texas Intensive English Program, Austin, TX; **Mariah Schueman**, University of Miami, Coral Gables, FL; **Erika Shadburne**, Austin Community College, Austin, TX; **Mahdi Shamsi**, Houston Community College, Houston, TX; **Osha Sky**, Highline College, Des Moines, WA; **William Slade**, University of Texas, Austin, TX; **Takako Smith**, University of Nebraska – Lincoln, Lincoln, NE; **Barbara Smith-Palinkas**, Hillsborough Community College, Tampa, FL; **Paula Snyder**, University of Missouri, Columbia, MO; **Mary; Evelyn Sorrell**, Bilingual Education Institute, Houston TX; **Kristen Stauffer**, International English Center, Boulder, CO; **Christina Stefanik**, The Language Company, Toledo, OH; **Cory Stewart**, University of Houston, Houston, TX; **Laurie Stusser-McNeill**, Highline College, Des Moines, WA; **Tom Sugawara**, University of Washington, Seattle, WA; **Sara Sulko**, University of Missouri, Columbia, MO; **Mark Sullivan**, University of Colorado Boulder, Boulder, CO; **Olivia Szabo**, Boston University, Boston, MA; **Amber Tallent**, University of Nebraska Omaha, Omaha, NE; **Amy Tate**, Rice University, Houston, USA; **Aya C. Tiacoh**, Bilingual Education Institute, Houston, TX; **Troy Tucker**, Florida SouthWestern State College, Fort Myers, FL; **Anne Tyoan**, Savannah College of Art and Design, Savannah, GA; **Michael Vallee**, International English Center, Boulder, CO; **Andrea Vasquez**, University of Southern Maine, Portland, ME; **Jose Vasquez**, University of Texas Rio Grande Valley, Edinburg, TX; **Maureen Vendeville**, Savannah Technical College, Savannah, GA; **Melissa Vervinck**, Oakland University, Rochester, MI; **Adriana Villarreal**, Universided Nacional Autonoma de Mexico, San Antonio, TX; **Summer Webb**, International English Center, Boulder, CO; **Mercedes Wilson-Everett**, Houston Community College, Houston, TX; **Lora Yasen**, Tokyo International University of America, Salem, OR; **Dennis Yommer**, Youngstown State University, Youngstown, OH; **Melojeane (Jolene) Zawilinski**, University of Michigan – Flint, Flint, MI.

CREDITS

Photos

Cover Credit: Guang Niu/Getty Images
1 (t) 2009 TYRONE TURNER/National Geographic Image Collection, **2-3** (c) Kirklandphotos/Getty Images, (t) Cengage Learning, Inc., **5** (b) Alan Tan Photography/Shutterstock.com, **6** (c) ©National Geographic Maps, (bl) Franco Debernardi/Getty Images, **9** (br) Cengage Learning, Inc., (bl) USGS, 010-011 (b) mandritoiu/Shutterstock.com, **12** (t) VCG/Getty Images, **15** (t) DESIGN PICS INC/National Geographic Creative, **16** (cl) ©National Geographic Maps, (b) DESIGN PICS INC/National Geographic Creative, **19** (t) FRANCOIS GUILLOT/Getty Images, **21** (t) ©Brent Stirton/Reportage/Getty Images, **22** (l) AFP/Getty Images, **23** (r) ©Joel Sartore/National Geographic Photo Ark, **24** (b) Francois Gohier/VWPics/Alamy, **26** (tr) Science History Images/Alamy, **28** (b) PAUL NICKLEN/National Geographic Creative, **31** (c) Heather Lucia Snow/Shutterstock, **32** (t) ©Axel Gomille/NPL/Minden Pictures, **34** (b) ROBBIE GEORGE/National Geographic Creative, **36** (b) Edwin Remsberg/Alamy Stock Photo, **39** (b) Charles Mostoller/Reuters, **41** (t) Tristan Fewings/Getty Images, **42-43** (t) Anadolu Agency/Getty Images, **43** (r) Cengage Learning, Inc., **44** (tr) Tim Graham/Alamy Stock Photo, **46** (c) RightsLink, **49** (b) JODI COBB/National Geographic creative, **50** (t) ©Xavier Zimbardo/Getty Images, **52** (t) SARAH LEEN/National Geographic Creative, **53** (b) www.BibleLandPictures.com/Alamy Stock Photo, **54** (tr) Camila Turriani/Alamy Stock Photo, **56** (tl) ©Alex Soza, (cl) Tom Vickers/Newscom/Splash News/Ventura/CA/United States, (cl) Chung Sung-Jun/Getty Images, **60** (t) Alexey Kopytko/Getty Images, 61 (c) ©Marla Aufmuth/TED, **62-63** (c) © Matthew Mahon/Redux Pictures, (c) Daxiao Productions/Shutterstock.com, **66** (b) Grapheast/Alamy Stock Photo, **69** (c) ©National Geographic Maps, (b) ©National Geographic Maps, **71** (b) ©Mark Leong/Redux, 72 (t) ©Aaron Huey/National Geographic Creative, (tl) National Geographic, **74** (cr) Oliver Uberti/National Geographic Magazine, **75** (b) Meldmedia Inc., **76** (c) Oliver Uberti/National Geographic Creative, 81 (c) JOE RIIS/National Geographic Creative, **82-83** (c) Morris Ryan/National Geographic Creative, (c) John Stanmeyer LLC/National Geographic Creative, **84** (tl) Cengage Learning, Inc., **86** (t) MARK THIESSEN/National Geographic, **88** (b) Gregory Manchess/National Geographic Creative, **90** (b) ©Stephen Alvarez/National Geographic Creative, **92** (t) Frans Lanting/National Geographic Creative, (cr) Cengage Learning, Inc., **94** (cl) Martin Gamache/National Geographic Creative, **95** (b) Jonathan Eden/Alamy, **97** (b) MICHAEL NICHOLS/National Geographic Creative, **99** (b) JOEL SARTORE/National Geographic Creative, **101** (c) ERIKA LARSEN/National Geographic Creative, **102** (c) Marco Vernaschi/National Geographic Creative, **103** (c) MATTHIEU PALEY/National Geographic Creative, (t) Chris Minihane/Getty Images, **104** (cr) Martin Gamache/National Geographic, **106** (c) Atlaspix/Shutterstock.com, (cl) Cengage Learning, Inc., **109** (b) ©Jordan Banks/Robert Harding/Aurora Photos, **110** (t) Pete McBride/National Geographic Creative, **114** (tr) ©Catherine Jaffee, **116** (b) Carolyn Cole/Getty Images, **118** (t) John Warburton-Lee Photography/Alamy Stock Photo, **121** (c) MOHAMED EL-SHAHED/Getty Images, **122** (t) ©K. David Harrison, **122-123** (c) ©Christian Heeb/laif/Redux, **126** (b) Razvan Ionut Dragomirescu/Alamy Stock Photo, **132** (t) Bloomberg/Getty Images, 135 (b) Blend Images/Alamy Stock Photo, 136 (b) ©James Florio/Redux, **139** (t) David Litschel/Alamy Stock Photo, **141** (c) Steph Chambers/AP Images, **142-143** (c) KAZUHIRO NOGI/Getty Images, **146** (b) KONTROLAB/Getty Images., **149** (b) SEBASTIEN BOZON/Getty Images, **150** (b) Ashraf Jandali/Shutterstock.com, **152** (t) Petri Artturi Asikainen/Getty Images, **154** (bl) Boston Globe/Getty Images, **156** (b) Maridav/Shutterstock.com, **159** (c) Cengage Learning, Inc, **161** (c) Zephyr/Science Source, **162** (tr) Hero Images/Getty Images, (c) DAVID EVANS/National Geographic Creative, (b) NICK CALOYIANIS/National Geographic Creative, **162-163** (c) Digital Storm/Shutterstock.com, **163** (tl) DAVID EVANS/National Geographic Creative, (tr) BRUCE DALE/National Geographic Creative, (cr) Peter Cade/Getty Images, **166** (t) Peshkova/Shutterstock.com, **169** (t) Markus Mainka/Alamy Stock Photo, **171** (t) FatCamera/Getty Images, **172** (t) NORBERT MILLAUER/Getty Images, **175** (t) Joshua Davenport/Alamy Stock Photo, **176** (b) decade3d - anatomy online/Shutterstock.com, **181** (c) ©Craig Cutler/National Geographic Creative, **182-183** (c) JIM RICHARDSON/National Geographic Creative, **184** (tl) JIM RICHARDSON/National Geographic Creative, 186 (b) Jim Richardson/National Geographic Creative, **188-189** (b) Bloomberg/Getty Images, **190** (b) Getty Images/Getty Images, **192** (t) BRIAN J. SKERRY/National Geographic Creative, (cr) Cengage Learning, Inc., **194-195** (b) Richard Levine/Alamy Stock Photo, **198** (b) ©Robbie George/National Geographic Creative.

Maps

2–3 Created by MPS; **6** Mapping Specialists; **16** Mapping Specialists; **69** Adapted from "Interconnectivity," National Geographic Maps, 2014; **82–83** Adapted from "The Longest Walk," National Geographic, December 2013; **84** Adapted from "Early Americans," https://mrgrayhistory.wikispaces.com/UNIT+8+-+EARLY+AMERICAS; **92** Mapping Specialists; Map courtesy of Roy Safaris–Tanzania; **94** Adapted from "Who Owns This Land?" by Martin Gamache and Lauren C. Tierney, National Geographic, May 2016; **104** Adapted from "Extent of Hadza People," Martin Gamache and Lisa R. Ritter, National Geographic, December 2009; Mapping Specialists; **106** Mapping Specialists; **192** Mapping Specialists

Illustrations/Infographics

2–3 "The 10 Most Multicultural Cities In The World," https://theculturetrip.com/north-america/usa/california/articles/the-10-most-multicultural-cities-in-the-world/; "The 10 Most Visited Cities of 2017," http://www.cntraveler.com/galleries/2015-06-03/the-10-most-visited-cities-of-2015-london-bangkok-new-york/10 **9** Adapted from "Can Venice be Saved?" https://sites.google.com/site/unknownglobalhazards/subsidence-in-venice/why-is-subsidence-a-problem; **23** Adapted from "Meet Some of the Species Facing Extinction in the Wild," National Geographic/Joel Sartore, Photo Ark; **39** Adapted from "Saving Wildlife Through Licenses and Taxes," National Geographic, November 2007; **43** Adapted from "Top 3 Reasons for Trying to Look Good and Weekly Time Spent on Personal Grooming," https://blog.gfk.com/2016/01/what-makes-us-want-to-look-good/; **48** Adapted from "Countries with Top Number of Procedures, 2010," National Geographic, December 2012; **63** Adapted from "Future Work Skills 2020," http://www.iftf.org/futureworkskills/; **64** Adapted from "Net Employment Outlook by Job Family, 2015-2020," http://reports.weforum.org/future-of-jobs-2016/employment-trends/; **74** Adapted from "Revealed World," National Geographic, September 2010; **76** "Revealed World," National Geographic, September 2010; **79** Adapted from "Active Users of Key Global Social Platforms," https://wearesocial.com/special-reports/digital-in-2017-global-overview; **123** Adapted from "How Countries Spend Their Money," http://www.economist.com/blogs/graphicdetail/2015/09/daily-chart-9; **129** Adapted from "Top 3 Ways to Spend Spare Cash by Region," http://www.nielsen.com/be/en/insights/news/2015/saving-was-key-for-most-in-q1-but-millennials-outpaced-the-global-averages-for-spending-intentions.html; **130** Adapted from "Top 5 Savings Strategies by Region," http://www.nielsen.com/content/dam/corporate/us/en/images/news-trends/2015-newswire/9080-0729-cci-wire-image.jpg; **135** Adapted from "How Americans Spent Their Money in 2015," http://www.marketwatch.com/story/heres-how-americans-are-spending-their-money-2016-08-31; **159** Adapted from "How would you be interested in wearing/using a sensor device, assuming it was from a brand that you trust, offering a service that interests you?" https://www.mouser.com/images/microsites/wearable-consumer-survey.png; **189** Adapted from "Breeding Better Crops," National Geographic, October 2014; **196** Adatped from "These Countries Spend the Least on Food," and "These Countries Spend the Most on Food," https://www.weforum.org/agenda/2016/12/this-map-shows-how-much-each-country-spends-on-food/

Listening and Text Sources

6–8 "Vanishing Venice" by Cathy Newman, National Geographic, August 2009; "Venice Tourism Debate 2015: Residents Fear Visitors Are Destroying Their City, Demand Authorities Crack Down On Cruise Ships," http://www.ibtimes.com/venice-tourism-debate-2015-residents-fear-visitors-are-destroying-their-city-demand-2063682; "Venice

Matters to History – Ventians Matter to Me," http://news.nationalgeographic.com/news/2015/01/150129-venice-my-town-zwingle-grand-canal-motondoso-piazza-san-marco
-vaporetto/; **14** "10 Most Affluent Cities In The World: Macau and Hartford Top The List," http://www.newgeography.com/content/004853-10-most-affluent-cities-world-macau-
and-hartford-top-list; "List of countries and dependencies by area," https://en.wikipedia.org/wiki/List_of_countries_and_dependencies_by_area; "Singapore," http://www.
averagesalarysurvey.com/singapore; **16-17** "The Singapore Solution," by Mark Jacobson, National Geographic, January 2010; **17** "16 Odd Things that are Illegal in Singapore,"
http://www.businessinsider.com/things-that-are-illegal-in-singapore-2015-7; "$200 Fine for Anyone Caught Breeding Mozzies," http://www.straitstimes.com/singapore/
health/200-fine-for-anyone-caught-breeding-mozzies **24** "Species Guide," http://us.whales.org/species-guide?gclid=Cj0KCQjwn6DMBRC0ARIsAHZtCeON4EPNKq59YzOdMc1XIQ
0VABitwoyoKCAzJsrdXKxryetvrdqJvUYaAtpFEALw_wcB; "U.S. Leads New Bid to Phase Out Whale Hunting," http://www.nytimes.com/2010/04/15/science/earth/15whale.
html?_r=1&; **25** "International Convention for the Regulation of Whaling," https://en.wikipedia.org/wiki/International_Convention_for_the_Regulation_of_Whaling; "Which
Cetacean Species are Extinct?" http://baleinesendirect.org/en/which-cetacean-species-are-extinct/; "British Adventurer Builds Whale-shaped Boat to Sail to Canada," http://
www.cbc.ca/radio/asithappens/as-it-happens-wednesday-edition-1.3472671/british-adventurer-builds-whale-shaped-boat-to-sail-to-canada-1.3472704; **26–27** "Last One" by
Verlyn Klinkenborg, National Geographic, January 2009; "Listed Species Summary (Boxscore)," http://ecos.fws.gov/ecp0/reports/box-score-report; **34** "Wolf Wars" by Douglas
Chadwick, National Geographic, March 2010; **36–38** "Hunters: For the Love of the Land," by Robert M. Poole, National Geographic, November 2007; **46** "New 'Golden' Ratios for
Facial Beauty" by Pamela M. Pallett, Stephen Link, and Kang Lee, https://www.ncbi.nlm.nih.gov/pmc/articles/PMC2814183/; **46-47, 49** "The Enigma of Beauty" by Cathy
Newman, National Geographic, January 2000; **56–57** "Dreamweavers" by Cathy Newman, National Geographic, January 2003; "Artificial Spider Silk Could Be Used for Armor,
More" by Brian Handwerk, National Geographic Daily News, January 14, 2005; **67** "What Skills We Need to Succeed in the World," YouTube, posted by Globalization 101, August 23,
2010; WESO Trends 2017: The Disconnect Between Growth and Employment," http://www.ilo.org/global/about-the-ilo/multimedia/video/institutional-videos/WCMS_541539/
lang--en/index.htm; "Decision-making with Emotional Intelligence," https://www.ideasforleaders.com/ideas/decision-making-with-emotional-intelligence; **68** "Globalization
Terminology," https://en.wikipedia.org/wiki/Category:Globalization_terminology; **74** "Revealed World" by Tim Folger, National Geographic, September 2010; **76–77** "Is Pokémon
Go Taking Over the World?", https://kantanmtblog.com/2016/07/25/is-pokemon-go-taking-over-the-world/; "Pokémon Go Becomes Global Craze as Game Overtakes Twitter for
US Users," https://www.theguardian.com/technology/2016/jul/12/pokemon-go-becomes-global-phenomenon-as-number-of-us-users-overtakes-twitter; "Popular Augmented
Reality & Pokémon Go! Shows," https://www.mixcloud.com/discover/augmented-reality+pokemon-go/; "Virtual and Augmented Reality Could Take Online Meetings to the Next
Level," http://blog.clickmeeting.com/virtual-and-augmented-reality-could-take-online-meetings-to-the-next-level; "Deglobalization is Already Well Underway – Here are 4
Technologies that Will Speed it Up," http://www.mauldineconomics.com/editorial/deglobalization-is-already-well-underwayhere-are-4-technologies-that-will-s; **84** "Tracking
the First Americans" by Glenn Hodges, National Geographic, January 2015; **86–88** "The Greatest Journey: The Trail of Our DNA," by James Shreeve, National Geographic, March
2006; "From Africa to Astoria by Way of Everywhere" by James Shreeve, http://ngm.nationalgeographic.com/big-idea/02/queens-genes, August 17, 2009; **94** Adapted from "Who
Owns This Land?" by Martin Gamache and Lauren C. Tierney, National Geographic, May 2016; **96–97** "Heartbreak on the Serengeti" by Robert M. Poole, National Geographic,
February 2006; **99** "Animal Migration: Facts," idahoptv.org/sciencetrek/topics/animal_migration/facts.cfm; **104** "The Hadza: Tanzania's Hunter-Gatherers" by Michael Finkel;
Adapted from "Shifting Ground," National Geographic, December 2009; **106–107** "Bhutan's Enlightened Experiment" by Brook Larmer, National Geographic, March 2008; "The 4
Pillars of GNH," http://www.gnhcentrebhutan.org/what-is-gnh/the-4-pillars-of-gnh/; "The 9 Domains of GNH," http://www.gnhcentrebhutan.org/what-is-gnh/the-9-domains-
of-gnh/; "Bhutan to Become Self Sufficient in Vegetables," https://www.positive.news/2012/environment/agriculture/8644/bhutan-sufficient-vegetables/; **114** Adapted from
http://www.nationalgeographic.com/explorers/bios/catherine-jaffee/; **116–117** "Reviving Native Lands" by Charles Bowden, National Geographic, August 2010; **118** "New Year
Traditions from Around the World; How to Have a Happy New Year," http://www.almanac.com/content/new-year-traditions-around-world; "50 New Year Traditions from Around
the World," http://www.lifehack.org/articles/lifestyle/50-new-year-traditions-from-around-the-world.html; **126** "List of Circulating Currencies," https://en.wikipedia.org/wiki/
List_of_circulating_currencies; **126–127** "Can You Buy Happiness? Not How You Think . . . New Research," http://happinessbeyondthought.blogspot.com/2014/11/can-you-buy-
happiness-not-how-you.html; "So You Think Owning a Home Will Make You Happy? Don't Be Too Sure," http://knowledge.wharton.upenn.edu/article/so-you-think-owning-a-
home-will-make-you-happy-dont-be-too-sure/; "Homeownership, the Key to Happiness?" http://www.nytimes.com/2013/07/14/realestate/homeownership-the-key-to-
happiness.html; "Can Money Buy You Happiness?" http://www.wsj.com/articles/can-money-buy-happiness-heres-what-science-has-to-say-1415569538; **128** "Millennials and
Money," https://www.fasthorseinc.com/blog/2017/01/millennials-money-financial-literacy/; **146–147** "Big Data: A Game Changer in Healthcare," https://www.forbes.com/sites/
bernardmarr/2016/05/24/big-data-a-game-changer-in-healthcare/#760e3698525b; "Big Data Coming in Faster Than Biomedical Researchers Can Process It," http://www.npr.org/
sections/health-shots/2016/11/28/503035862/big-data-coming-in-faster-than-biomedical-researchers-can-process-it; **149** "The Top Six Challenges of Healthcare Data
Management," http://www.ingrammicroadvisor.com/data-center/the-top-six-challenges-of-healthcare-data-management; **154** "Health Technology in the Workplace:
Leveraging Technology to Protect and Improve Worker Health," http://healthyworkplaces.berkeley.edu/wellness/health-technology-in-the-workplace-leveraging-technology-to-
protect-and-improve-worker-health/; **162–163** "Anatomy of the Brain," https://www.mayfieldclinic.com/PE-AnatBrain.htm; "Human Brain Functions–Functioning of Human
Brain with Diagram," http://humanbrainfacts.org/human-brain-functions.php; **164** "Multiple Intelligences," http://www.tecweb.org/styles/gardner.html; "Multiple Intelligences:
Definitions & Examples," http://enhancinged.wgbh.org/research/multi/examples.html; **166–167** "Neuromyth 6: The Left Brain/Right Brain Myth," https://www.oecd.org/edu/
ceri/neuromyth6.htm; "The Truth about the Left Brain/Right Brain Relationship," http://www.npr.org/sections/13.7/2013/12/02/248089436/the-truth-about-the-left-brain-right-
brain-relationship; **169** "Fact or Fiction?: Babies Exposed to Classical Music End Up Smarter," https://www.scientificamerican.com/article/fact-or-fiction-babies-ex/; "Do People
Only Use 10 Percent of Their Brains?" https://www.scientificamerican.com/article/do-people-only-use-10-percent-of-their-brains/; "Do Opposites Really Attract? It's Complicated,"
https://www.psychologytoday.com/blog/head-games/201412/do-opposites-really-attract-its-complicated; "Lunacy and the Full Moon," https://www.scientificamerican.com/
article/lunacy-and-the-full-moon/; "A Review on the Current Research on Vocabulary Instruction," https://www2.ed.gov/programs/readingfirst/support/rmcfinal1.pdf; "Venting
Anger May do More Harm than Good," http://www.nytimes.com/1983/03/08/science/venting-anger-may-do-more-harm-than-good.html?pagewanted=all; **170** "The Invisible
Gorilla," http://theinvisiblegorilla.com/gorilla_experiment.html; "Pearls Before Breakfast: Can One of the Nation's Great Musicians Cut Through the Fog of a D.C. Rush Hour? Let's
Find Out," https://www.washingtonpost.com/lifestyle/magazine/pearls-before-breakfast-can-one-of-the-nations-great-musicians-cut-through-the-fog-of-a-dc-rush-hour-lets-
find-out/2014/09/23/8a6d46da-4331-11e4-b47c-f5889e061e5f_story.html?utm_term=.6b5690ff6e91; "Why Carlsberg's Toast to Courage Went Viral," http://mashable.
com/2012/05/10/carlsberg-viral-video/#8a3EkQ7umuqU; "Stereotypes: Why We Act Without Thinking," http://www.spring.org.uk/2010/01/stereotypes-why-we-act-without-
thinking.php; **174** "Animal Minds," http://www.economist.com/news/essays/21676961-inner-lives-animals-are-hard-study-there-evidence-they-may-be-lot-richer-science-once-
thought; "Animal Cognition," https://en.wikipedia.org/wiki/Animal_cognition; **176–177** "Remember This" by Joshua Foer, National Geographic, November 2007; **179** "How to
Pick the Fastest Line at the Supermarket," https://www.nytimes.com/2016/09/08/business/how-to-pick-the-fastest-line-at-the-supermarket.html; **182** "Arctic Stronghold of
World's Seeds Flooded After Permafrost Melts," https://www.theguardian.com/environment/2017/may/19/arctic-stronghold-of-worlds-seeds-flooded-after-permafrost-melts;
184 "Food Ark: How Heirloom Seeds Can Feed the World," by Charles Siebert, National Geographic, July 2011; **184, 186–187** "Food: How Altered?" by Jennifer Ackerman,
National Geographic, May 2002; **186–187** "Sen. Donna Nesselbush: Three Quarters of Processed Foods Have Genetically Modified Organisms," http://www.politifact.com/
rhode-island/statements/2015/mar/22/donna-nesselbush/sen-donna-nesselbush-three-quarters-processed-food/; "Genetically Modified Animals Will Be on Your Plate in No
Time," https://www.wired.com/2015/07/eating-genetically-modified-animals/; "GMO Safety Debate is Over," http://allianceforscience.cornell.edu/blog/mark-lynas/gmo-safety-
debate-over; **189** "Breeding Better Crops," National Geographic, October 2014; **190** "Tangelo," https://en.wikipedia.org/wiki/Tangelo; "GloFish," https://en.wikipedia.org/wiki/
GloFish; "Plant Breeding: A Success Story to be Continued Thanks to the Advances of Genomics," https://www.ncbi.nlm.nih.gov/pmc/articles/PMC3355770/; "Genetically Modified
Animals," http://www.enki-village.com/genetically-modified-animals.html; "The History of Wheat," http://prairiecalifornian.com/history-wheat/; "Pinebery & Pineberries," http://
strawberryplants.org/2010/09/pineberry-pineberries/; **194, 196–197** "The End of Plenty: The Global Food Crisis," by Joel K. Bourne, Jr., National Geographic, June 2009;
196–197 "The Global Staple," http://ricepedia.org/rice-as-food/the-global-staple-rice-consumers

INDEX OF EXAM SKILLS AND TASKS

Pathways Listening, Speaking, and Critical Thinking is designed to provide practice for standardized exams, such as IELTS and TOEFL. Many activities in this book practice or focus on the **key exam skills** needed for test success. In addition, a number of activities are designed to be the same as (or similar to) **common question types** found in these tests and to provide effective practice of these questions.

Listening

Key Exam Skills	IELTS	TOEFL	Page(s) / Exercise(s)
Distinguishing facts from theories	X	X	86 LS, 87 C, 99 D
Listening for advantages	X	X	66 LS, 67 C
Listening for clarifying answers	X	X	96 LS, 97 D
Listening for key details or specific information	X	X	56 LS, 56 C, 77 C, 96 C, 107 C, 127 C, 137 C, 167 C, 177 D, 197 D
Listening for main ideas	X	X	7 C, 46 B, 56 B, 76 B, 96 B, 106 B, 126 B, 136 B, 146 C, 156 B, 157 D, 166 B, 186 B, 196 B
Listening for positive or negative views	X	X	157 LS, 157 C
Listening for shifts in topic	X	X	137 LS
Taking notes: using abbreviations	X	X	7 NT, 7 D, 7 E
Taking notes: using a time line or idea map	X	X	87 NT, 87 D, 107 NT, 107 D, 117 D
Taking notes: using a T-chart	X	X	146 NT, 147 D
Understanding the introduction to a lecture	X	X	6 LS, 6 B
Using prior knowledge to listen effectively	X	X	36 LS, 36 A, 66 A, 96 A, 146 A, 156 A, 166 A, 196 A

Common Question Types	IELTS	TOEFL	Page(s) / Exercise(s)
Connecting content		X	146 C, 156 B, 166 B, 186 B
Matching	X		46 B, 137 D, 168 A
Multiple choice	X	X	6 B, 126 B
Multiple response		X	6 C, 76 B, 106 B, 136 B
Note completion	X		7 D, 27 D, 27 E, 47 C, 57 D, 67 C, 77 C, 87 D, 107 D, 117 D, 127 C, 147 D, 167 C, 177 E, 187 C, 187 D
Sentence completion	X		17 D
Short answer	X		177 D, 197 D

KEY

EL	Everyday Language
LS	Listening Skill
NT	Note-Taking Skill
PRON	Pronunciation
SS	Speaking Skill

INDEX OF EXAM SKILLS AND TASKS

Speaking

Key Exam Skills	IELTS	TOEFL	Page(s) / Exercise(s)
Approximating	X	X	88 SS, 89 B
Asking rhetorical questions	X	X	108 SS, 108 C
Brainstorming ideas	X	X	28 A, 59 A, 107 E, 119 B, 200 B
Citing research or knowledgeable groups	X		128 SS, 128 A, 128 B, 188 SS, 189 B, 191 B
Defining unfamiliar terms	X	X	68 SS, 68 A, 68 C
Discussing personal experiences or feelings	X	X	13 F, 71 C, 98 C, 165 D, 173 E, 195 F, 197 E
Discussing pros and cons	X	X	10 B, 10 C, 69 D
Emphasizing important information	X	X	148 SS, 148 A, 149 C
Expressing opinions and/or reasons	X	X	37 F, 38 B, 55 D, 78 B, 149 E
Expressing probability and possibility	X	X	89 C, 90 E
Linking	X	X	18 PRON, 18 A, 18 B, 18 C, 30 PRON, 30 E, 30 F, 30 G, 98 PRON, 98 A, 98 B, 98 C, 138 PRON, 138 A
Making suggestions or recommendations	X	X	171 EL, 171 C
Paraphrasing	X	X	49 SS, 53 E
Pronouncing reduced words	X	X	178 PRON, 178 A, 178 B, 199 PRON, 199 B, 199 C
Speaking about abstract concepts	X	X	5 D, 10 A, 15 E, 17 E, 19 D, 25 D, 26 A, 27 F, 28 B, 35 C, 45 E, 47 D, 49 C, 53 F, 57 E, 66 A, 77 D, 79 C, 85 E, 105 E, 113 F, 115 E, 117 E, 125 E, 133 F, 157 D, 175 D, 193 E
Speaking about causal relationships	X	X	168 SS, 169 D
Speaking about conditional situations	X	X	10 F, 13 F, 110 G, 127 D
Speaking about familiar, everyday topics	X	X	67 D, 78 B, 80 C, 89 B, 91 A, 91 B, 98 C, 118 A, 118 C, 120 F, 130 F, 131 B, 136 A, 151 B, 155 E, 165 C
Speaking about past actions or situations	X	X	71 B, 71 C
Speaking about problems and solutions	X	X	20 A, 20 D, 30 B, 30 C, 99 E, 180 E
Summarizing information you heard		X	87 E, 97 D, 177 F
Summarizing written or illustrated information	X	X	9 D, 38 C, 48 B, 189 C
Using correct stress	X	X	109 PRON, 109 D, 109 E
Using parentheticals to clarify ideas	X	X	78 PRON, 78 A, 78 B
Using signal phrases to introduce ideas	X	X	8 SS, 8 B

KEY

EL	Everyday Language
LS	Listening Skill
NT	Note-Taking Skill
PRON	Pronunciation
SS	Speaking Skill

Pathways	CEFR	IELTS Band	TOEFL Score
Level 4	**C1**	**6.5–7.0**	**81–100**
Level 3	B2	5.5–6.0	51–80
Level 2	B1–B2	4.5–5.0	31–50
Level 1	A2–B1	0–4.0	0–30
Foundations	A1–A2		

You do'not use name in thesis statment.
            really begins right here.
very daitl thesis — complex sentence   (grown as a writer).
                              you suppost to
  ↓   paraphrase or
 it is not a simple sentence
exalent   Quote — use anectode.
1) Topic sentence. — bravissimo
2.) Important invasion, ⇒   yet is conduction
        diffrant condiction.   but however.

do not be redantand.
3) _Good_   21